A Pra o
Benefi

Other titles in this series

A Practitioner's Guide to Advising Charities
A Practitioner's Guide to Charity Fundraising
A Practitioner's Guide to Contentious Trusts and Estates
A Practitioner's Guide to the Court of Protection
A Practitioner's Guide to Drafting Trusts
A Practitioner's Guide to Executorship and Administration
A Practitioner's Guide to Inheritance Claims
A Practitioner's Guide to Legacies
A Practitioner's Guide to Powers and Duties of Trustees
A Practitioner's Guide to Powers of Attorney
A Practitioner's Guide to Probate
A Practitioner's Guide to Trustee Investment
A Practitioner's Guide to Trusts

A Practitioner's Guide to Beneficiaries' Actions

Arabella Saker
Solicitor, Allen & Overy
with a contribution by
Richard Wilson LLB, LLM
of the Middle Temple, Barrister

LexisNexis™ UK

Members of the LexisNexis Group worldwide

United Kingdom	LexisNexis UK, a Division of Reed Elsevier (UK) Ltd, Halsbury House, 35 Chancery Lane, LONDON, WC2A 1EL, and 4 Hill Street, EDINBURGH EH2 3JZ
Argentina	LexisNexis Argentina, BUENOS AIRES
Australia	LexisNexis Butterworths, CHATSWOOD, New South Wales
Austria	LexisNexis VerlagARD Orac GmbH & Co KG, VIENNA
Canada	LexisNexis Butterworths, MARKHAM, Ontario
Chile	LexisNexis Chile Ltda, SANTIAGO DE CHILE
Czech Republic	Nakladatelství Orac sro, PRAGUE
France	Editions du Juris-Classeur SA, PARIS
Germany	LexisNexis Deutschland GmbH, FRANKFURT and MUNSTER
Hong Kong	LexisNexis Butterworths, HONG KONG
Hungary	HVG-Orac, BUDAPEST
India	LexisNexis Butterworths, NEW DELHI
Ireland	LexisNexis, DUBLIN
Italy	Giuffrè Editore, MILAN
Malaysia	Malayan Law Journal Sdn Bhd, KUALA LUMPUR
New Zealand	LexisNexis Butterworths, WELLINGTON
Poland	Wydawnictwo Prawnicze LexisNexis, WARSAW
Singapore	LexisNexis Butterworths, SINGAPORE
South Africa	LexisNexis Butterworths, Durban
Switzerland	Stämpfli Verlag AG, BERNE
USA	LexisNexis, DAYTON, Ohio

A CIP Catalogue record for this book is available from the British Library.

ISBN 0 754 519473

Typeset by Kerrypress Ltd, Luton, Beds

Printed and bound in Great Britain by The Cromwell Press Limited, Trowbridge, Wiltshire

Visit LexisNexis UK at www.lexisnexis.co.uk

Preface

'It's about a Will, and the trusts under a Will – or it was, once. It's about nothing but Costs, now. We are always appearing, and disappearing, and swearing, and interrogating, and filing and cross-filing, and arguing, and sealing, and motioning, and referring, and reporting, and revolving about the Lord Chancellor and all his satellites, and equitably waltzing ourselves off to dusty death, about Costs. That's the great question. All the rest, by some extraordinary means, has melted away'.

(Charles Dickens, *Bleak House*)

Any dispute relating to trusts has the potential, unless carefully managed, to become an expensive, complex matter, in which the parties adopt entrenched or unnecessarily combative positions. The aim of this book is to highlight the various possible grounds which can give rise to a dispute involving beneficiaries and trustees, and to set out the ways in which such disputes can be resolved or, if necessary, brought before the court for determination. I hope that it does this in three ways. Whilst it is written principally from the perspective of the beneficiary (what rights have they, and how can these be enforced?), it is also intended to guide trustees on how they can deal with their powers, duties and discretions so as to avoid the risk of a dispute, or so as to minimise the risk of any dispute escalating. Thirdly, it is meant to offer practical guidance for practitioners, since our role is in large part to reduce what Dickens called *Wiglomeration* – the well-meaning ability of lawyers to turn a relatively simple question into infinitely more convoluted proceedings.

In writing this book, I have been helped by the input and advice of a number of other members of Allen & Overy's Trust, Asset Tracing and Fraud Litigation Group (to which I belong), and especially by Richard Wilson of 9 Stone Buildings, whose chapter on Breach of Duty of Care appears at Chapter 6. I am also grateful for the help and encouragement of all the team at LexisNexis UK, particularly John Meredith, whose cheerful advice to me (when I fretted as to whether or not I could manage 100,000 words) was 'It's all right, you can use some of them twice'.

Arabella Saker
September 2003

Contents

Table of Cases

Table of Statutes

Paragraph numbers in **bold** type indicate where the Act is set out in part or in full

Table of Statutory Instruments

Chapter 1

Introduction

History of trust disputes

1.1 Popular legal history has it that trusts have their origins '*in days of old, when knights were bold*' and, on departing for the crusades, gave their estates to their trusted retainers to hold them for the maintenance of their wives and children. (Under laws in force in England and Wales until the enactment of the Married Women's Property Act 1907 and the Law Reform (Married Women and Tortfeasors) Act 1935, married women suffered considerable disability in owning or dealing with property independently, even as trustees, during their marriage.)

Disputes relating to trusts probably began shortly thereafter. Although history has no record of the first, there are fictional examples aplenty of what we might now know as breaches of fiduciary powers and duties. Is part of the tragedy of Webster's 17th-century *Duchess of Malfi* in the fact that the eponymous heroine is unable either to marry as she wishes or to control her fortune without the consent of her brothers? Her struggle to manage her own destiny results in five stabbings, four strangulations and a poisoning, although happily this is atypical of most trust disputes. In Mozart's *Magic Flute*, the husband of the Queen of the Night, on his deathbed, entrusted Sarastro with his most treasured possession, the 'sevenfold circle of the sun'. Sarastro makes use of it for his own purposes (in breach of trust) and the Queen's attempts to recover this powerful symbol result in the loss of her daughter, and her powers.

English literature's most tragic trust dispute is catalogued in Dickens' *Bleak House*, where the Jarndyce family have been locked in litigation for so long that, as Dickens puts it, '*this scarecrow of a suit has, in course of time, become so complicated, that no man alive knows what it means. The parties to it understand it least . . .*'. Plaintiffs, defendants and counsel have been born into the case, lived, died and been replaced, and the dispute is no nearer to its close for having ruined the family.

Perhaps the real tragedy of that tale is that it had its basis in truth. As Dickens explained in his preface, '*at the present moment there is a suit before the Court which was commenced nearly twenty years ago; in which from thirty to forty counsel have been known to appear at one time; in which costs have been incurred to the amount of seventy thousand pounds; which is a friendly suit; and which is (I am assured) no nearer to its termination now than when it was begun* (the editor of Oxford World's Classics 1996 edition of *Bleak House* believes this to refer to the case of *Day v Croft*, begun in 1838 and still being heard in 1854). '*There is another well-known suit in Chancery, not yet decided, which was commenced before the close of the last century, and in which more than double the amount of seventy thousand pounds has been swallowed up in costs*' (in the same edition, the editor attributes Dickens' reference to *Jennings' case*, which commenced in 1798 and was finally settled in 1878).

Some significant cases

1.2 Despite Dickens' despair over the ponderousness of the Chancery Division, many of the modern roots of trust litigation are found in Victorian times, when there began to be decided important cases such as *Speight v Gaunt (1884) 9 App Cas 1, HL*, which spelled out for the first time the legal principle that trustees must exercise the same prudence and care which a reasonably prudent and careful man would exercise in the management of his own affairs. That principle was developed in *Learoyd v Whiteley (1887) 12 App Cas 727, HL*, where it was established that trustees must, in selecting investments, exercise that degree of care which a prudent man would use in making an investment for the benefit, not of himself, but of other persons for whom he felt morally bound to provide. (The modern duty of care is discussed in CHAPTER 6.) The case of *Re Beddoe [1893] 1 Ch 547, CA*, followed, upon which trustees have ever since relied, by applying to the Court for leave to bring or defend a claim, in order to protect their entitlement to take their costs of that litigation out of the trust fund (see CHAPTER 11).

The next wave of key cases in trust litigation began in the 1960s, with cases such as *Re Londonderry's Settlement [1965] Ch 918, CA*, which sought to establish the classification of 'trust documents' which beneficiaries are generally entitled to inspect. The exercise of this right – or the trustees' failure to give effect to it – is frequently the subject matter of litigation, or substantiates an otherwise suspected breach (see CHAPTER 4). *Bartlett v Barclays Bank Trust Company [1980] Ch 515* sets out the duty of professional trustees, and emphasises the need for trustees to be actively involved in the management and supervision of companies in which the trust has a substantial stake.

In the 1990s, *Nestle v National Westminster Bank plc [1994] 1 All ER 118, CA*, established, among other things, the need for the beneficiaries to prove their loss by reference to what a prudent trustee would have done in the same circumstances (see CHAPTERS 5 AND 6). *Armitage v Nurse [1998] Ch 241, CA*, gave us Lord Millett's famous judgment that '*there is an irreducible core of obligations owed by the trustees to the beneficiaries*' but that these do not include '*the duties of skill and care, prudence and diligence*', such that a trustee may be protected by a suitably worded exculpation clause, '*no matter how indolent, imprudent, lacking in diligence, negligent or wilful he may have been, so long as he has not acted dishonestly*' (CHAPTER 12 discusses exculpation clauses).

Classification of trust disputes

1.3 In another highly significant case, *Alsop Wilkinson v Neary [1995] 1 All ER 431*, Lightman J found that trust-related litigation fell into three broad categories:

- *'Trust disputes'*, which are disputes relating to the trusts on which the trustees are holding the assets. Claims under this heading include 'friendly' claims for construction of the trust instrument, and 'hostile' claims by creditors, victims of fraud or family members that, in truth, the assets of the trust belong to them and are not held on the (purported) express trusts at all;
- *'Beneficiaries' disputes'*, which are 'internal' claims by the beneficiaries relating to the propriety of actions taken (or omitted to be taken) by the trustees, or which they may take in future, including questions over the management or administration of the trust, or the exercise of the powers, duties and discretions of the trustees. Claims under this category may be breach of trust claims, or claims for the removal of trustees; and
- *'Third party disputes'*, that is, claims by or against the trustees involving only third parties, such as contractual disputes.

The classification of the dispute is necessary because of the differing ways that costs are dealt with in each kind of dispute, and the procedures and attitudes that trustees must adopt in dealing with them —

- With trust disputes, such as that in *Alsop Wilkinson v Neary* itself, the trustees' duty is to stay neutral, and to provide the court with any factual information which might assist in determining the claim. This is because the case goes to the question of who are the true beneficiaries (or beneficial owners) of the trust funds. If the trustees were to expend trust monies in arguing one side or other of the case, they might in effect be favouring one class of possible beneficiaries over another, or even expending the true beneficiaries' own funds in an attempt to defeat their claim. The court may, of course, make costs orders against any party or order that the costs be paid out of the trust funds if that is appropriate.
- In third party disputes, in contrast, the trustees have a duty to protect the trust assets, and so are usually entitled to an indemnity for their costs in bringing or defending a claim of this kind. It is prudent for trustees to seek the leave of the court under the procedure in *Re Beddoe* (above) in order to avoid any later accusation from the beneficiaries that they brought or defended the claim wrongly and should not be entitled to take their costs out of the trust fund.

Overview of this book

1.4 This book addresses the claims which are available to beneficiaries under each of the three *Alsop Wilkinson* categories of trust-related disputes, either in their capacity as beneficiaries or (as in CHAPTER 11) to give effect to some right that they possess independently of the trust.

Reasons for disputes

1.5 The past decade or so has seen a substantial increase in the number of beneficiaries' disputes. The reasons for this increase remain unclear, but it may arise from simple factors of scale – due to the tax advantages, in particular, of creating offshore trusts from the 1960s up to the early 1990s (and even now, for non-UK domiciled families), larger numbers of trusts were created than ever before. This has created many problems, including the following:

- In many cases, the settlor of the trust has now died, leaving a family of beneficiaries who may not understand the reasons for his having created the trust, and who may wish to have more control over the assets, be independent of one another, or have the trust dissolved entirely.
- In other cases, with hindsight, the settlor's investment and other wishes may be perceived as too controlling – extreme examples of this behaviour may give rise to allegations of sham, while other instances may simply fuel claims that the trustees' own conduct fell below the standard expected of them.
- The large number of trusts created, the large numbers of professional trust companies established to administer them, and the increasing sophistication of many private investors has meant that the industry expanded for many years without (in many jurisdictions) changes in the legal and regulatory frameworks keeping pace. (Consider, for example, how until the Trustee Act 2000, many English law trustees had only those powers of investment contained in the Trustee Investments Act 1961.)

Whatever the reason for the dispute, practitioners will recognise that disputes within families, or involving family money, can be particularly bitter, with parties often taking entrenched positions. It is essential for practitioners to encourage the parties to conduct proceedings reasonably and within practical and proportionate limits, as required by the Civil Procedure Rules (discussed in CHAPTER 2), and to give appropriate consideration to the use of alternative methods of dispute resolution (discussed in CHAPTER 15).

Chapter 2

Overview of litigation procedure

Rules for conduct of trust proceedings

> 'There never was such an infernal cauldron as that Chancery . . . Nothing but a mine below it on a busy day in term time, with all its records, rules, and precedents collected in it, and every functionary belonging to it . . . and the whole blown to atoms with ten thousand hundred-weight of gunpowder, would reform it in the least!'
>
> (Charles Dickens, *Bleak House*)

2.1 Dickens' criticism in *Bleak House* of the slowness of trust-related proceedings was (as mentioned earlier in CHAPTER 1) founded in truth. Under the former Rules of the Supreme Court, in force until 1999, the court had little power to hasten proceedings, which were largely application-driven. Substantial delays could therefore occur between the issue of proceedings and their ultimate conclusion. This has now been entirely reformed (without the need for gunpowder).

The new Civil Procedure Rules for England and Wales ('CPR') apply to trust-related proceedings with effect from 2 December 2002. The CPR had come into effect for most types of case on 26 April, 1999, following a complete overhaul of the court rules over several years under the supervision of Lord Woolf, but the old RSC continued to apply to certain classes of proceedings (including trust cases) for some time. Trust proceedings are now governed by the new CPR Part 64.

Procedure for commencing proceedings

2.2 Claims are now begun by the issue of a claim form (formerly a writ or summons). Generally, there are two separate procedures for bringing a claim:

- *Part 7 Claims*, which are claims that formerly would have been commenced by a writ; and
- *Part 8 Claims*, which would, before the introduction of the CPR, have been commenced by originating summons.

Many claims available to beneficiaries would appear to have the possibility of being brought under either CPR Part 7 or CPR Part 8. By way of general guidance, it is suggested that the appropriate choice may depend on the following factors:

- if the beneficiaries have a specific action (or omission) in mind about which they wish to complain, or there is likely to be substantial dispute as to fact, CPR Part 7 is more appropriate;
- if the beneficiaries do not have an identified defalcation that they wish to address, but have a more general, open-ended concern as to which the court's guidance or directions are required, the CPR Part 8 procedure is more appropriate; but
- in both cases, these guidelines are subject to the specific provisions of CPR Part 64 (and its two Practice Directions) as to the matters which *must* be brought under CPR Part 8 (see below in paragraph 2.3).

Part 8 claims

2.3 Because of the nature of most trust-related proceedings, Part 8 would appear to be the most appropriate procedure to use for many types of claim. CPR Part 64 puts this beyond doubt by providing expressly that certain trust-related claims *must* be commenced using the Part 8 procedure if they are claims for the court to determine any question relating to the execution of a trust. This is clarified in the two Practice Directions which accompany that Part (CPR 64 PD and CPR 64B PD), where it is explained that such claims may include:

- claims relating to a beneficial interest in any property subject to a trust;
- claims regarding the rights or interest of any person claiming to be beneficially entitled under a trust;
- claims for any of the following remedies:
  - (i) an order requiring a trustee to provide and/or verify accounts;
  - (ii) an order requiring a trustee to pay trust money into court;
  - (iii) an order requiring a trustee to do, or not to do, any act;
  - (iv) an order approving any transaction (eg sale, purchase, or compromise); or
  - (v) an order directing any act to be done which the court could order to be done if the trust were being administered or executed under the direction of the court;
- applications for directions by the trustees.

A claim form under CPR Part 8 must contain the following matters:

- a statement that Part 8 applies to the claim;

- a statement as to the remedy sought, or the questions the court is asked to determine;
- a summary of the legal basis on which that remedy is sought, which should always include reference to the fact that the claimant is a beneficiary and the defendant is a trustee (or as the case may be);
- a declaration as to whether the issues arising contain any matter to which the Human Rights Act 1998 would apply; and
- a statement of truth.

The claimant must file and serve the evidence on which he wishes to rely in the form of a witness statement at the same time as the claim form.

The trustees have 14 days in which to acknowledge service of the claim form. If they wish to rely on any evidence other than that submitted by the claimant, they must file and serve their evidence in the form of a witness statement at the same time as they acknowledge service, unless the time for service of the witness statement is extended (see APPENDIX 1), in which case the agreement for the time extension must be filed at the same time as the acknowledgment of service. The claimant may, if he wishes to do so, file and serve further evidence in reply within 14 days of service of the defendant's evidence (which may also be extended, see APPENDIX 1).

The matter will then proceed in accordance with the procedure and timetable set out in the remainder of this chapter and appendix until trial. (APPENDIX 1 contains a sample time-line which is intended to give an overview of the likely timetable for claims under CPR Part 8.)

Consistently with the fact that most claims under CPR Part 8 are to seek the court's guidance or determination of a particular matter, the procedure under CPR Part 8 does not usually permit expert evidence or oral witness evidence at trial. Similarly, the defendants are not required to defend any allegations made by the claimants, but need only (if at all) provide an alternative explanation. Disclosure of documents is rarely ordered, and summary judgment is not a remedy which would usually be relevant.

Part 7 claims

2.4 The alternative procedure in CPR Part 7 must be used wherever there are substantial disputes as to fact, as will be the case for many claims for breach of trust. Under the former Rules of the Supreme Court, it was held to be inappropriate to bring claims alleging breach of trust otherwise than by way of writ, and this practice is also likely to be followed under the new CPR (*Dowse v Gorton [1891] AC 190, HL)*.

A claim form under CPR Part 7 must contain the following:

- a statement that Part 7 applies to the claim;

- a statement as to the remedy sought;
- if possible, a full explanation of the facts of the claim (or if not, a summary of the legal basis on which that remedy is sought, which should always, as with CPR Part 8, include reference to the fact that the claimant is a beneficiary and the defendant is a trustee (or as the case may be));
- if the claim is for money, details of the amount claimed;
- a declaration as to whether the issues arising contain any matter to which the Human Rights Act 1998 would apply; and
- a statement of truth.

The claimant must, usually at the same time as the claim form is filed and served, file and serve full details of the claim he is making, in the form of particulars of claim. These must contain a statement of the facts upon which he relies, and details of any documents and witnesses relevant to his claim. If interest is claimed (which is often the case for breach of trust) then he must explain the basis on which it is sought. The claimant may elect to serve the particulars separately, within 14 days of the service of the claim form; however, the claim form must always be accompanied by forms for acknowledgment of service, for notice of intention to defend, and for notice of admission of the claim.

The defendants then have 14 days after service of the particulars of claim (not the claim form) in which to serve one or more of the forms supplied with the claim form:

- he need only file an acknowledgment of service of the claim form if either he wishes to have a further 14 days for service of a defence, or if he intends to dispute the jurisdiction of the court from which the claim form was issued;
- he may file and serve his defence within that 14 days; or
- he may file and serve a notice of admission if he intends to admit part or all of the claim. This may be done at any time, provided that the claimant has not yet obtained judgment in default.

The defence, when served, must specifically address each of the claims made by the claimant. If the defendant refutes a claim, it must be specifically denied, supported by the alternative facts and evidence upon which he relies. He may elect to put the claimant to proof on certain claims, by not admitting them (but must make this clear). He may admit certain facts and claims. Any allegations not expressly denied or not admitted will be deemed to be admitted, unless it is clear on the face of his defence (for example, by the inclusion of a contrary explanation) that the defendant intends to put the claimant to proof on them. In the context of claims under CPR Part 7, counterclaims or third party claims may be appropriate, if the defendant trustees wish to obtain contribution from one of their number, or from a third party. Such claims (made under CPR Part 20) can be made as of right if notice of the Part 20 claim is served with the defence and the claim is against the claimant, but otherwise, the leave of the court is required.

The matter will then proceed in accordance with the procedure and timetable set out in the remainder of this chapter and APPENDIX 2 (which contains an overview of the likely timetable for claims under CPR Part 7) until trial or, in appropriate cases, judgment in default. Significantly, however, witness evidence in Part 7 claims is unlikely to be required to be served until after service of claim form and defence, track allocation, and disclosure of documents. It is, therefore, a longer and more complex process than the Part 8 claim, which may take several months before even the witness statements are served.

The overriding objective

2.5 Following the introduction of the new Rules, all proceedings in the courts of England and Wales are to be conducted in accordance with the 'overriding objective' of enabling the court to deal with cases justly. This Rule is set out in detail in CPR Part 1, which explains that 'justly' means:

- ensuring that the parties are on an equal footing;
- saving expense;
- dealing with the case in ways which are proportionate to the amount of money involved, to the importance of the case, to the complexity of the issues, and to the financial position of each party;
- ensuring that the case is dealt with expeditiously and fairly; and
- allotting to the case an appropriate share of the court's resources.

The furtherance of the overriding objective is required both of the parties themselves, and of the court when exercising its powers or interpreting the Rules. For the parties, one important factor which the court will take into account is whether they have complied with any relevant pre-action protocol (PAP). There are specific PAPs for a number of different types of case, governing the standards of conduct which parties ought appropriately to follow when considering whether or not to issue proceedings, and in their dealings with one another. As yet, there is no agreed PAP for trust-related disputes, (but a draft PAP prepared by the Association of Contentious Trust and Probate Specialists (ACTAPS) is available on their website at www.actaps.com. APPENDIX 4 contains some general guidance on the conduct of the pre-action stages of a trust-related dispute. Generally, the conduct of the parties will be considered throughout the proceedings (and before they begin) and may be taken into account by the court when determining key issues such as the question of costs.

Active case management

2.6 In line with the overriding objective, the court's new case management powers require the court to undertake active management of cases, which includes:

- encouraging the parties to co-operate in the conduct of proceedings;
- identifying the issues at an early stage;
- deciding which issues need full investigation, and disposing summarily of others;
- deciding the order in which issues are to be resolved;
- encouraging the parties to use alternative methods of dispute resolution;
- helping the parties to settle all or part of the case;
- fixing timetables and controlling the progress of the case;
- considering whether the likely costs of taking a particular step are justified;
- dealing with as many aspects of the case as possible on the same occasion;
- dealing with the case without the parties needing to attend at court;
- making appropriate use of technology; and
- giving directions to ensure that the trial of a case proceeds quickly and efficiently.

Track allocation

2.7 Consistently with the court's powers of active case management, the Rules require that, following service of the claim form and any defence, each party to a claim under CPR Part 7 is required to complete an allocation questionnaire in order to assist the court in fulfilling one of the terms of the overriding objective, namely the allocation of the court's resources. Proceedings under CPR Part 8 do not usually require an allocation questionnaire to be completed, as they are automatically allocated to the multi-track (see below) although a court may require the parties to provide information about the conduct of the case from time to time, especially at the Case Management Conference (see paragraph 2.8 below), which may cover similar ground.

In the allocation questionnaire, the parties provide the following information:

- details of compliance with any relevant PAPs;
- details of what (if any) attempts at settlement have been made, including the use of alternative dispute resolution – the parties may request a stay of up to one month to conduct settlement negotiations;
- which 'track' the parties consider most suitable to the case (see below);
- identification of factual witnesses whose evidence is likely to be required;
- details of whether (and why) any expert witnesses are required;

- an estimate of the amount of time needed for trial;
- details of any other applications likely to be made, such as the joining of other parties, or application for summary judgment – such applications must usually be made before, or at the time of, filing the questionnaire;
- details of costs incurred to date, and an estimate of costs up to the date of trial; and
- any other information the court may require to assist it in managing the case and/or giving directions (see CPR 26 PD).

When the last allocation questionnaire has been filed, or the time to do so has expired, the court will then consider:

- the financial value of the claim (if any);
- the nature of the remedy sought;
- the likely complexity of the facts, law or evidence;
- the number of parties;
- the value and complexity of any counterclaim or third party claim;
- the amount of oral evidence which may be required;
- the importance of the claim to persons who are not parties;
- the views expressed by the parties; and
- the circumstances of the parties.

Based on these factors, the court allocates the case to a 'track' (usually without the need for a hearing). There are three such tracks:

(a) *small claims track* (CPR Part 27), which is broadly intended for claims with a financial value of not more than £5,000;

(b) *fast track* (CPR Part 28), which governs cases where the financial value exceeds the small-track limit but is below £15,000, and where the issues are not so complex as to require detailed procedures; and

(c) *multi-track* (CPR Part 29), for cases which have a financial value exceeding £15,000 or where the issues are sufficiently complex that a trial would last more than one day.

Owing to the complex nature of most trust proceedings, they are likely to be allocated to the multi-track. All CPR Part 8 proceedings are allocated to the multi-track.

Case management conference (CMC)

2.8 For multi-track cases, the court will give directions as to how they are to proceed, setting out a strict timetable and detailing the steps which are necessary before trial. These may include directions as to what expert and witness evidence will be needed, and which (if any) issues could be disposed of summarily, with or without a hearing. It may in many cases be possible to give such directions without the need for a hearing. However, in many multi-track cases, in order to set a timetable and give these directions, the court will hold a CMC hearing, which must be attended by a representative of each party who has authority to deal with any issues likely to arise at the hearing.

Before the hearing (or where one is not held) each party may be required to agree a 500-word summary of the case (including a chronology of relevant events), and costs estimates for the case. Additionally, throughout the case, the parties are expected to co-operate with one another, so as to assist the court in giving directions and generally in the conduct of the proceedings.

Other CMCs, or a pre-trial review, may be held from time to time during very complex cases where more directions are required or the nature of the issues necessitate timetable changes.

Specific procedures

2.9 In addition to the general details of claims under CPR Part 7 and Part 8 in paragraphs 2.4 and 2.5 above, specific details of the types of beneficiaries' actions, and the appropriate procedures for each claim, are set out in each of CHAPTERS 3 TO 11, 14 AND 16 below. An example time-line for the issue and conduct of proceedings under Part 8 is set out in APPENDIX 1. A similar time-line for Part 7 proceedings is set out in APPENDIX 2.

Representation of parties

2.10 In the context of litigation procedure, it is perhaps helpful to consider the parties and their representation. Whether the Part 7 or Part 8 procedure is used, all the trustees must be parties to the claim. However, there is considerable latitude as to which other persons should be joined, which will depend upon the nature of the claim and who has an interest in its determination, or needs to be bound by the order ultimately made.

In many cases, it is suggested, all the beneficiaries will need to be joined. Adult beneficiaries who have the same views and interests should, wherever possible, be jointly advised, so as to reduce the overall costs (or a representative can be appointed under CPR Part 19).

Minor beneficiaries, and unborn and unascertained beneficiaries, will need to be represented and advised in groups according to their interests:

- for minor beneficiaries, CPR Part 21 provides that a litigation friend (formerly a guardian ad litem) should be appointed – again, in the interests of saving costs – this should ideally be a relative or other unpaid person, and it does not need to be a professional person. The litigation friend is not permitted to give instructions based solely on his or her own views. The legal interests of the children must be considered, and an opinion of counsel is usually required as to what those interests require in the particular circumstances of the case, taking into account the financial interests of the children, as well as the need for familial harmony and stability, and other relevant factors making up their broader interests. The litigation friend's decisions are then based upon the opinion of counsel;

- CPR Part 19 provides that unborn and unascertained beneficiaries (and beneficiaries who cannot be found) are, wherever possible, to be represented by a living beneficiary with similar interests to their own, and a representation order is made so that (for example) a child represents his or her unborn siblings. In some cases, this may prove impossible (such as where no remaindermen have yet been born). In such cases, counsel is appointed by the court to speak for the interests of those classes of beneficiary.

Trustees should strive to be jointly represented wherever possible, so as to reduce the overall costs. In *Gaunt v Taylor (1840) 2 Beav 346*, Lord Langdale MR said (at page 347): '*Where several persons are made defendants in respect of a joint fiduciary character only, or if the beneficial interest which any of them may have . . . is in no way conflicting with their duty, they ought . . . to defend together; if they do not, and there are no special circumstances, then, according to the settled rule of the court, they will be allowed one set of costs only.*' He went on to acknowledge that there will be exceptions to that general rule, such as:

- where one trustee has a personal interest which conflicts with his fiduciary duty; or
- if one of several trustees can admit facts which the others believe not to be true.

Clearly, in such cases the trustees cannot be jointly represented, but the question of whether they are entitled to two sets of costs depends on the circumstances of the case. The question will be whether there were reasonable grounds for them to sever their defences. If so, more than one set of costs may be allowed (or part of the costs). If they have acted unreasonably in being separately advised, then some or all of their costs may be disallowed.

In hostile litigation, the successful trustee(s) will always have a lien over the trust fund as security for their costs to be paid by the unsuccessful claimant beneficiary (*Re Spurling's Will Trusts, Philpot v Philpot [1966] 1 All ER 745*) but are not entitled to sell the assets to reimburse themselves, only to refuse to release trust monies until they are paid (*Darke v Williamson (1858) 25 Beav 622*). Trustees whose defence to hostile litigation is unsuccessful are never entitled to recoup their costs out of the trust fund (confirmed in *Armitage v Nurse [1998] Ch 241, CA*).

Chapter 3

Actions for account

The trustees' duty to account

3.1 In the well-known case of *Armitage v Nurse [1998] Ch 241, CA*, Lord Millett said (at pages 253–4): '. . . *there is an irreducible core of obligations owed by the trustees to the beneficiaries and enforceable by them which is fundamental to the concept of a trust. If the beneficiaries have no rights enforceable against the trustees there are no trusts*'.

Chief amongst this 'irreducible core of obligations' is one of the most basic of fiduciary duties, the duty of trustees to account to their beneficiaries for their dealings with the trust assets. It has been said that '*it has always been the law that persons in a fiduciary position are bound to account to those for whom they are fiduciary, and that extends beyond pure trust claims to such matters as agents who hold property . . . the basis of the duty to account is the fiduciary relationship*' (*A-G v Cocke [1988] Ch 414*, per Harman J at pages 420–1).

The duty to account encompasses three important inter-linked obligations on the part of the trustees:

- the trustees are obliged to keep accurate records of all transactions involving trust monies, together with the receipts and other documentation which substantiate those transactions;
- the trustees have a duty to provide information to the beneficiaries on request (*In Re, Londonderry's Settlement, Peat v Walsh [1965] Ch 918, CA*); and
- the trustees must, if called upon to do so, explain and, if necessary, justify their dealings with the trust assets.

As Lord Millett's judgment in *Armitage v Nurse* explained, the fundamental duties of trustees are those without which no trust would exist, and which must be capable of enforcement by the beneficiaries. It follows that the beneficiaries' rights of enforcement in relation to the 'core obligation' of the duty to account entitle them, at any time, to call upon the trustees:

- to provide information about the trust fund and its assets, and to allow the beneficiaries to inspect and (at their own expense) take copies of documents and records (*In re Londonderry's Settlement, Peat and others v Walsh [1965] 1 Ch 918, CA*); and

- to provide a full and detailed account of their dealings with the trust assets and to make good any sums which are due after deduction from the account of losses resulting from breaches of trust and other wrongful dealings.

The duty to provide information is discussed in CHAPTER 4; this chapter concerns the right to obtain an explanation of the trustees' dealings with the trust assets, which is enforceable through an application to the court if not otherwise forthcoming. This process is known as an action for account, and there are three different bases on which an account may be required:

- common account, the purpose of which is to compel the trustees to fulfil their accounting obligation and, if appropriate, to obtain compensation for loss;
- account on the basis of wilful default, to obtain compensation for loss resulting from breaches of trust; and
- account of profits, whereby the beneficiaries seek restitution of gains or profits made by the trustees themselves in breach of trust.

The nature of each of these claims is set out in detail later in this chapter.

Purpose of claim

3.2 As can be seen from the preceding paragraphs, an action for account usually has as its aim the enforcement of the rights of the beneficiaries, coupled with either compensation for loss, or restitution of any assets lost to the trust or profits improperly made or retained by the trustees. In *Bartlett v Barclays Bank Trust Co Ltd (No 2)* Brightman J said (at page 543): '*the obligation of a defaulting trustee is essentially that of effecting restitution to the trust estate'*. He continued (at page 545): '*the obligation of a trustee who is held liable for breach of trust is fundamentally different from the obligation of a contractual or tortious wrongdoer. The trustee's obligation is to restore to the trust estate the assets of which he has deprived it.*' Any departure from the terms of the trust, therefore, is sufficient to create a liability on the part of the trustee (absent any proper defence or excuse, as discussed in CHAPTER 12) to make good the whole of the loss that has resulted to the trust fund, together with interest.

Restitution or damages?

3.3 In considering Brightman J's use (in *Bartlett* above) of the words 'restore' and 'restitution', it is important to distinguish between:

- compensation (damages) for loss to the trust fund, which is intended to restore the trust fund in the position it would have been in, but for the breach giving rise to the loss; and

- restitution to the trust fund of assets which properly belong to it, including assets paid to strangers in breach of trust, or profits made by the trustees in breach of trust (which therefore ought to belong to the trust). Restitution is based on the trustees' duty to return to the trust in specie every trust asset or its proceeds of sale.

As noted in paragraph 3.1 above, claims for a common account or for an account on the basis of wilful default usually have as their aim the payment of compensation, but may incidentally include a claim for restitution of trust assets paid away in breach of trust; claims for an account of profits are purely restitutionary in nature.

It may alternatively (rarely) be the case that compensation is payable, or restitution is due, to the beneficiaries themselves, and not to the trust fund. The trustees' usual obligation is to make reparation or restitution to the trust fund which has been deprived of assets. In some instances, however, this would be an insufficient or unfair remedy. It may sometimes be the case that certain beneficiaries should in all the circumstances receive compensation or restitution personally. In *Target Holdings Limited v Redferns [1996] AC 421, HL*, it was said that '*liability is fault-based – the defendant is only liable for the consequences of the legal wrong he has done to the [Claimants] and to make good the damage caused by such wrong*'. If the damage has been suffered by certain beneficiaries only, or by some of them in different proportions to others, then it is equitable that the compensation should be paid, or restitution made, to those beneficiaries who have suffered loss, and not to the trust fund. This may be the case where, for example, the trust is a life interest trust, or the trust has come to an end, or some of the beneficiaries have already released the trustees from liability (as in *Re Salmon (1889) 42 Ch D 351*).

Interest

3.4 In relation to both compensatory and restitutionary awards, interest is relevant. Quite unlike claims for breach of contract and other non-equitable claims, interest is not calculated by reference to fixed rates. The court will, in all cases (and not only where wrongdoing is alleged) select a rate of interest appropriate to the claim, and will take into account the fact that the trust (or its beneficiaries) have been deprived of the use of the money (*Re Barclay [1899] 1 Ch 674*). The calculation differs depending on the nature of the remedy sought:

- for compensatory awards of damages (whether to the beneficiaries or the trust fund), interest is calculated by reference to what the money or assets would have earned, had they remained part of the trust fund and not been lost at the time when they were lost. The court considers what use the trustees might most likely have made of the funds, had they not been lost. Compound interest may be available if the trustees had a duty to invest at compound interest (*Jones v Foxall (1852) 15 Beav 388*);

- for restitutionary claims, the interest is calculated by reference to what the trustees *actually* earned on the misused or misappropriated funds. Again, compound interest is available if that is what they themselves received, or if the assets were misused by them for the purposes of a business owned by them personally (*Wallersteiner v Moir (No 2) [1975] QB 373, CA*).

No time limit

3.5 Given the fundamental nature of the duty to account, it is unsurprising that it should be seen as a continuing obligation on the part of the trustees. In fact, it persists without limit of time, even after the trusts have come to an end. In the case of *A-G v Cocke [1988] Ch 414*, Harman J said (at page 421), approving Sir Robert Megarry VC's judgment in *Tito v Waddell (No 2) [1977] Ch 106*, '*I think [his conclusion] is the same as the conclusion I have come to, that a claim to an account simpliciter based upon a fiduciary relationship and nothing more is not barred by any period of limitation*'.

However, in the case of *Nelson v Rye [1996] 2 All ER 186*, Laddie J said (at page 198): '(*1*) *An action for breach of fiduciary duty simpliciter is outside the provisions of the Limitation Act 1980 and therefore is not subject to a period of limitation.* (2) *Where a breach of fiduciary duty gives rise to a constructive trust, the provisions of section 21 of the 1980 Act determine whether there is a limitation period.* (3) *An action for breach of an express trust is . . . subject to the provisions of section 21*'.

In other words, the obligation to account is one which can always be enforced by the beneficiaries; the right of recovery of any trust assets which have been lost (whether by way of recovery of the assets in specie from the trustee or a third party, or by way of action for damages for breach of trust) is, however, governed by the Limitation Act 1980. Section 21(3) of the Limitation Act 1980 provides that, '*Subject to the preceding provisions of this section, an action by a beneficiary to recover trust property or in respect of any breach of trust . . . shall not be brought after the expiration of six years from the date on which the right of action accrued . . .*'. Unless the facts giving rise to the claim have been known to the beneficiaries for less than the relevant limitation period, or there is a claim for fraud or dishonest concealment of the breach, the action for account may not provide restoration of any loss discovered to have occurred, therefore. (For more detailed discussion of breach of trust, see CHAPTER 5; limitation periods are covered in detail in CHAPTER 13.)

Account as both remedy and relief

3.6 An action for account may be brought in two ways:

- It may be brought as a standalone claim on its own merits, by way of pure enforcement of the duty to account (ie when it is the only relief sought). This may be a useful tool where, as may be the case, the beneficiaries lack the information necessary to identify whether or not any breaches of trust have occurred for which they could pursue the trustee. When the account is delivered, it may reveal breaches for which a claim can then be made; or

- An account may be requested following, or as part of, a broader claim for breach of trust or fiduciary duty (see CHAPTERS 5 AND 6), when it can be used as the basis for calculating compensation due to the trust fund. In such cases, the account constitutes the remedy, or means of calculating the remedy, for another claim.

Types of account

Common account

3.7 As noted in paragraph 3.1 above, the purpose of a common account is simply to compel the trustees to fulfil their duty to account. No allegation of breach of trust or impropriety is required, since the right to an 'account simpliciter' is an absolute right of the beneficiaries, arising out of the mere existence of a fiduciary relationship. The basic nature of the right to a common account is best explained by Harman J in *A-G v Cocke [1988] 1 Ch 414* (at pages 420–1): '*It is important to notice that the court, in a case where there is no allegation of any impropriety but merely an allegation of a relationship of a fiduciary and an object of the fiduciary duty, will frequently make a common form order for an account.*'

If the court orders an account, the trustees must provide an account in the specified form, which lists all credits and debits to the trust fund, including additions to the trust fund, investments made and realised, payments to beneficiaries, costs and expenses, and their own fees. They must, if ordered, permit inspection of the documents supporting the account, and the beneficiaries can object to entries in the account, and demand a fuller explanation or justification.

The account, once completed, may reveal losses which cannot be explained or justified, and entries which represent breaches of trust. If so:

- entries which represent matters beyond the powers of the trustees are deleted entirely from the account, as if they had never occurred at the expense of the trust fund; and

- transactions which have given rise to a loss resulting from a breach of trust are 'surcharged', that is, the amount of the loss is chargeable to the trustees,

and in either case, this gives rise to a duty on the part of the trustees to provide compensation to the trust fund for such losses as are caused by their breach of trust. To recover these sums, the beneficiaries must either amend their existing proceedings with the leave of the court (*Gordon v Gonda [1955] 2 All ER 762, CA*) or issue a new claim which uses the account as the basis of calculating the compensation due (*Re Wrightson [1908] 1 Ch 789*).

It is important to appreciate that not every loss shown on the account is a loss which must be made good by the trustees, since, as Staughton LJ said in *Nestle v National Westminster Bank plc [1994] 1 All ER 118, CA* (at page 132): '*Of course it is not a breach of trust to invest the trust fund in such a manner that its real value is not maintained*', and therefore (at page 135) '*The trustees' performance must not be judged with hindsight: after the event, even a fool is wise, as a poet said nearly 3000 years ago*'. Lindley LJ put it even more clearly in *Re Chapman [1896] 2 Ch 763, CA*, when he said that '*a trustee is not a surety, nor is he an insurer; he is only liable for some wrong done by himself, and loss of trust money is not per se proof of such wrong . . . Trustees acting honestly, with ordinary prudence and within the limits of their trust, are not liable for mere errors of judgment*'.

An order for a common account is not, therefore, one which imposes strict liability on the trustees to make good all losses. The losses for which the trust fund must be compensated are those losses (if any) arising from breaches of trust. Breach of trust is discussed more fully in CHAPTER 5 (and the important question of what constitutes a 'loss' for these purposes is discussed in CHAPTERS 5 AND 6) but such losses may include, for example:

- the making of unauthorised investments, or losses on investments which have been made or retained in breach of trust;
- transactions at an undervalue, or payments out of the trust fund to strangers in breach of trust;
- costs and expenses wrongly deducted from the trust fund (including, for example, trustees' fees deducted in excess of the charging provisions); and
- transactions which cannot be accounted for because the trustees are in breach of their duty to keep accounting records.

Account on the basis of wilful default

3.8 An account on the basis of wilful default is available to beneficiaries to enable them to obtain compensation for loss to the trust fund. 'Wilful default' for the purposes of a claim for account on this footing was defined by Brightman J in *Bartlett v Barclays Bank Trust Co Ltd (No 2) [1980] 1 Ch 515* (at page 546) as follows: '*Wilful default by a trustee in this context means a passive breach of trust, an omission by a trustee to do something which, as a prudent trustee, he ought to have done – as distinct from an active breach of trust, that is to say, doing something which the trustee ought not to have done. If an instance of wilful default is pleaded and proved . . . the court is entitled to order an account on the footing of wilful default*'. Examples may include:

- failing to collect in or receive all the assets that they should have held as trustees (*Armitage v Nurse [1998] Ch 241, at 252*);
- neglecting to take legal proceedings, as in *In re Forest of Dean Coal Mining Company (1878) 10 Ch D 450*, where the trustees, by so doing,

> could have recovered damages which would have constituted a trust asset. The trustees' failure to sue would render them liable for 'want of due diligence' (per Jessel MR at page 451).

Significantly, therefore, mere neglect or omission is sufficient to constitute wilful default for the purposes of an action for account on that footing. 'Wilful default' for these purposes does not require any intentional wrongdoing to be pleaded, nor even necessarily a breach of trust. It therefore does not have the same meaning as 'wilful default' for other purposes (such as exculpation clauses, or section 30 of theTrustee Act 1925, as to both of which see CHAPTER 13 below). In such other cases, that expression connotes a degree of deliberate or reckless wrongdoing.

Wilful default must be specifically pleaded in order to obtain an account on that footing (*Gordon v Gonda [1955] 2 All ER 762, CA*). Should facts emerge after proceedings have been issued for a common account, which would indicate that a pleading of wilful default would be appropriate, the existing action for a common account cannot be converted to an action for an account on the footing of wilful default without the leave of the court (*Partington v Reynolds (1858) 4 Drew 253, Job v Job (1877) 6 Ch D 562, HL*).

An account ordered on this footing is wider in nature than a common account, as it also requires details of the assets that the trustees should or could have received or recovered, had they not failed in their duty. This clearly carries a greater onus on the defendant to prove the propriety of its dealings. Because of this, such an account will usually not be ordered unless the beneficiaries are able to demonstrate at least one instance where wilful default can be shown to have occurred, and is unlikely to be ordered unless there is a good prima facie case for believing that it has occurred in other instances (*Re Tebbs [1976] 2 All ER 858*).

Account of profits

3.9 The third type of account, an account for profits, is made in order to obtain restitution of gains or profits improperly made or retained by the trustees. This kind of account is based on the fundamental obligation of trustees not to profit from their office as trustees. If they do so in a way which is not permitted either by the general law or by the trust deed, then they are obliged to return to the trust fund the profits and gains that they have made. Examples of this may include:

- profits made through a conflict of interest between the trustee's personal interests and those of the trust;
- overcharging of trustee fees; or
- straightforward misappropriation of trust assets.

Whereas a common account requires the trustees to disclose all dealings with trust assets, and an account on the footing of wilful default requires them also to disclose what *ought* to have been received by the trust, an account of profits obliges them to go further, by disclosing their own private dealings outside the trust. Clear allegations of wrongdoing are therefore required and there must be a strong prima facie case for believing that the trustees have misappropriated trust assets, or made private profits, before such an account will be ordered. If ordered, it is coupled with an order to repay the misappropriated assets and/or to pay over to the trust a sum equal to the profits made.

An important difference between a claim for an account on this footing, and the claims for a common account or account on the footing of wilful default, is that the trustees' liability here is strict – that is, the breach of duty itself is sufficient to make the trustees liable, and no loss need be proved to have flowed from the breach. There may be an obvious loss in the context of misappropriated assets, and it is clear that every trust asset (or its proceeds of sale) ought to be returned to the trust from which they have wrongfully been derived. However, in cases where the trustees are alleged to have made private profits, even if the trust has suffered no loss, the trustees must restore to the trust all the profits they have made in breach of their fiduciary duties (*Boardman v Phipps [1967] 2 AC 46, HL*).

Recovery of assets or compensation for loss

3.10 In cases where a trustee has diverted trust assets for his own use, the calculation of what is due to the trust will largely go to the question of whether his misuse was profitable or not. Lord Millett explained this in *Foskett v McKeown [2001] 1 AC 102*, HL, when he said: '*the beneficiary is entitled* at his option *either to assert his beneficial ownership of the proceeds or to bring a personal claim against the trustee for breach of trust and enforce an equitable lien or charge on the proceeds to secure restoration of the trust fund. He will normally exercise the option in the way most advantageous to himself. If the traceable proceeds have increased in value and are worth more than the original asset, he will assert his beneficial ownership and obtain the profit for himself. There is nothing unfair in this. The trustee cannot be permitted to keep any profit resulting from his misappropriation for himself . . . If the traceable proceeds are worth less than the original asset, it does not usually matter how the beneficiary exercises his option. He will take the whole of the proceeds on either basis . . . Both remedies are proprietary and depend on successfully tracing the trust property into its proceeds*' (emphasis added).

So –

(a) If the trustee made a gain, and if the whole of the profit he made resulted from the use of trust assets, then the beneficiaries are likely to elect to take the assets and their profits. If so, the whole of the profit must be returned, although the court may make an allowance for any special efforts or skills he used in making the profits (as in *Boardman v Phipps [1967] 2 AC 46, HL*). If he mingled them with other assets of his own, and the profits were not wholly attributable to the trust assets, then a proportionate allowance is made (*Vyse v Foster (1874) LR 7 HL 318*). However, the court has a broad discretion, and may refuse the claim entirely if the beneficiaries (knowing of the misuse) have, in effect, waited to see whether the venture was a successful one or not before bringing their claim (*Re Jarvis [1958] 2 All ER 336*). In quantifying the profits to be returned to the trust, as explained in *A-G v Alford (1855) 43 ER 737* (per Lord Cranworth at page 741): '*What the court ought to do, I think, is to charge [the trustee] only with the interest which he received, or which it is justly entitled to say he ought to have received, or which it is so fairly to be presumed that he did receive that he is estopped from saying that he did not receive it.*' In the case of *Wallersteiner v Moir (No 2) [1975] QB 373, CA*, interest was awarded at a rate which the court considered fairly represented the profit that the defendant could be presumed to have made.

(b) If he made a loss, the beneficiaries will choose between having the assets returned to the trust (and suffering any loss that is carried with them) or rejecting the assets but retaining a lien over them as security for the trustee's liability to make good the loss suffered by the trust at the time of its removal, plus interest. In so choosing, the beneficiaries are likely to consider first, what use he made of the assets, and secondly, to what use they might have been put if they had remained in the trust. Factors to consider include the following:

(i) In cases involving trust funds mixed with the trustee's own funds, the trustee is always deemed to spend his own money first (*Re Hallett's Estate (1879) 13 Ch D 696, CA*). Accordingly, while the whole venture or transaction may be loss-making, the beneficiaries may still be able to claim the return of the whole sum wrongly diverted from the trust fund, albeit without profit (for example, where the funds were diverted to purchase a house, which has fallen in total value);

(ii) If the trustee is insolvent, it may be preferable to take the assets back (loss-making or not) rather than to seek to enforce a personal claim against him, which will rank with the claims of his other creditors;

(iii) the assets may have made a loss, but carry the hope of future profits;

(iv) if the asset has been profitable in the past, the beneficiaries cannot 'have it both ways' by taking the profits, plus interest from the date when it ceased to be profitable (*Heathcote v Hulme (1819) 37 ER 322*);

(v) the beneficiaries' lien over the loss-making assets (if rejected) does not entitle them to take the assets immediately in part-payment of the debt arising on the personal claim against the trustee. It is a security interest over assets which belong personally to the trustee, and does not give the beneficiaries an immediate right to take those specific assets in part-payment (which would also be a case of 'having it both ways'). If the trustee fails to pay the personal claim, they may take the charged assets first, ahead of his other creditors.

Claim for pure personal profit

3.11 In other cases, as noted in paragraph 3.9 above, no loss may have occurred to the trust and no trust assets may have been diverted to the trustees' own use. Nonetheless, they remain liable to account to the trust for profits made by actions undertaken by them privately in conflict with, or in breach of, their duties to the trust. For example, the trustees may honestly decide not to make an investment using trust monies, or may lack the powers or the necessary funds to do so. In such a situation, if they may make the investment for themselves, using their own money, they do so in breach of their duty to the trust and are liable to account for the profits (as in *Keech v Sandford (1726) 25 ER 223*, and *Boardman v Phipps [1967] 2 AC 46, HL*).

Again, the judgment of Lord Cranworth in *A-G v Alford (1855) 43 ER 737* is relevant to the calculation of the sum due to the trust, so that the court will order the trustee to repay the pure profit that he made, or (if that cannot be ascertained) a sum representing the profits which the court can fairly assume he ought to have received, or actually did receive.

Procedure

3.12 As discussed in CHAPTER 2, CPR 64.3 provides that a Part 8 claim form must always be used for trust-related claims within 64.2. In the Practice Direction appended to CPR Part 64, CPR 64 PD.1(2)(a) deals expressly with claims for account, where it states that a claim '*for an order requiring a trustee to provide and, if necessary, verify accounts*' is one within 64.2. Were it not for that express requirement for actions for account to be made under CPR Part 8, it might be difficult to reconcile the use of the Part 8 procedure for an account on the footing of wilful default, or an account for profits, with the general practice that it is inappropriate to bring claims alleging breach of trust otherwise than by way of claim under CPR Part 7 (derived from the previous rule that it was improper to do so otherwise than by writ – *Dowse v Gorton [1891] AC 190*).

The CPR Part 8 claim form must contain:

- a statement that Part 8 applies to the claim;
- a statement that the remedy sought is an account (and in which of the three forms);
- a summary of the legal basis on which that remedy is sought, which will always be on the footing that the claimant is a beneficiary and the defendant is a trustee, but the details of the basis on which that particular account is sought will differ depending on which type of account is sought (eg where an account on the footing of wilful default is sought, wilful default must be specifically pleaded); and
- a statement of truth.

The claimant must file and serve the evidence on which he wishes to rely in the form of a witness statement at the same time as the claim form. In the case of a common account, it may be that very little needs to be said in the witness statement at all, if the existence of the fiduciary relationship is made clear on the face of the claim form (see *A-G v Cocke [1988] Ch 414*). Seemingly, the witness statement for a claim for a common account need not necessarily contain anything further than an explanation of how the fiduciary relationship arises (or is alleged to arise) and does not need to allege wrongdoing or breach of trust by the defendant trustees (*A-G v Cocke*). For either of the other two forms of account, the circumstances and facts upon which the claimant relies must be specifically detailed in the witness statement.

The trustees have 14 days in which to acknowledge service of the claim form, and (unless the time is extended – see APPENDIX A) must file and serve their evidence in the form of a witness statement at the same time as they acknowledge service.

The matter will then proceed in accordance with the procedure and timetable set out in CHAPTER 2 and APPENDIX A until trial. The order then made will require the trustees within a specified time limit to produce an account in the specified form of all their dealings with the trust moneys (and any other dealings relevant to an account on the footing of wilful default or an account of profits) since the date specified in the order, or since the inception of the fiduciary relationship. As explained in paragraph 3.14 below, the order made at trial will not usually include provision for costs, which will be dealt with after the account has been settled.

Once the account has been settled, separate proceedings will usually follow for the repayment of any sums due from the trustees, or the claim for account may be amended with the leave of the court so that it continues in the form of an action for recovery of the sums due.

It is not usually possible to re-open a settled account, unless the beneficiaries can show clear evidence of why it should be amended (*Pit v Cholmondeley (1754) 2 Ves Sen 565, HC*).

Parties

3.13 CPR Part 64.4(1) provides that '*In a claim to which this Section applies . . . (a) all the trustees must be parties; . . . (c) the claimant may make parties to the claim any persons . . . with an interest under the trust, who it is appropriate to make parties having regard to the nature of the order sought*'. The claimant beneficiary/ies will therefore issue the claim form naming all the trustees as defendants, but the circumstances will dictate whether or not they need to join any other beneficiaries as defendants.

Interestingly, Harman J's judgment in *A-G v Cocke [1988] Ch 414* suggests that a mere allegation of a fiduciary relationship may, in some cases, suffice to justify an order to be made for an account. Harman J explained the simple nature of the claim for account at pages 420–1 (quoted above, but worth repeating): '*It is important to notice that the court, in a case where there is no allegation of any impropriety but merely an allegation of a relationship of a fiduciary and an object of the fiduciary duty, will frequently make a common form order for an account.*' This may be of assistance in situations where the claimant does not even know whether he is a beneficiary of the trust at all. There is some doubt as to the extent to which (if at all) the trustees have a duty to inform the object of the trust that they are beneficiaries. Cases such as *Chaine-Nickson v Bank of Ireland [1976] IR 393*, and *Spellson v George [1987] 11 NSWLR 300* indicate that they should do so, whereas *Re Manisty's Settlement [1973] 2 All ER 1203* suggests that there is no duty to inform discretionary objects of their potential interest, so long as nothing is due to be paid to them and no request for information has been received (see further in CHAPTER 10 at 10.2). It is clear that, in some situations, such as the recent case of *Schmidt v Rosewood Trust Limited [2003] UKPC 26*, the claimant may not know where he stands and the defendant may not be prepared to tell him. A claim for a common account might, therefore, disclose whether the claimant is a beneficiary. It appears that it could be used to disclose whether the claimant is a beneficiary because, presumably, if the defendant could show that he did not stand in a fiduciary relationship as regards the claimant, no account would be ordered, as the claimant would have no interest capable of enforcement through an account. (In *A-G v Cocke*, the Attorney-General had an interest in enforcing trusts which were for the public benefit.) Recalling that no allegation of impropriety or breach is necessary for a common account to be ordered, an order for an account will nonetheless inform the claimant (if he is indeed a beneficiary) about any breaches that have occurred, and generally about the affairs of the trust of which he is a beneficiary.

Costs

3.14 The costs of an application for an account are likely to follow the event, that is to say, that they may be payable:

- by the claimant beneficiaries if no loss is shown and not all the beneficiaries are claimants, and those who are not claimants successfully argue that the trust fund should not be charged with the cost of an unsuccessful action;
- by the defendant trustee(s) if a loss is shown to have occurred for which they are liable; or
- out of the trust fund if no loss is shown and either all the beneficiaries are claimants, or if the court thinks fit.

The order for costs is therefore not usually made until the end of the process of accounting. In *A-G v Cocke [1988] Ch 414*, Harman J said (at pages 420–1): '*[the court] will not make any order in respect of the costs of [the] application, reserving those costs until the account has been taken. That is because the duty to account arises, but if the accounting party is innocent and produces a true and good account, it would be quite wrong that the act of carrying out that duty should be thrown upon the innocent accounting party.*'

The trustees are not, by the same logic, entitled to use their ordinary right of reimbursement to take their costs of the accounting process out of the trust fund, pending the outcome of the proceedings, which will disclose whether they are innocent (and entitled to be paid either by the claimants or out of the trust fund) or not (in which case they may be liable to bear all the costs themselves). In *Armitage v Nurse [1998] Ch 241*, CA, Millett LJ said (at page 262): '*Trustees are entitled to a lien on the trust fund for the costs of successfully defending themselves against an action for breach of trust . . . But on what principle can one justify their right to recoup themselves out of the trust fund for the costs of unsuccessfully defending themselves against such an action? It offends all sense of justice.*' For this reason, it will usually be inappropriate for the trustees to exercise their ordinary right of reimbursement pre-emptively so as to meet their costs of complying with an order to account. If they do so, and are later found liable to repay any sum to the trust fund, they must also repay the costs they have wrongly deducted.

The beneficiaries are likely to incur professional fees in bringing the proceedings and in inspecting records and questioning the account before it is finalised and a costs order is ultimately made. In some cases, this may cause hardship or may mean that (in practice) the claim for account could not be brought. The Practice Direction, CPR 64 PD, provides (at paragraph 6) that if the trustees have power to agree to pay the costs of the beneficiaries, they may exercise that power at any time without the leave of the court. If they choose not to exercise the power, or do not have such power, the beneficiaries may apply to the court for a prospective costs order. The court may (if the beneficiaries would otherwise be unable to fund the proceedings) make a prospective costs order in relation to the costs of any of the beneficiaries.

The trustees may also apply for a prospective costs order, but the court is unlikely (for the reasons given above) to make such an order in favour of the trustees themselves pending the outcome of the account, for the reasons given above.

Other steps

3.15 If the account, when finalised, results in the trustees being found liable to pay or repay sums to the trust, the beneficiaries may wish to consider taking steps for the removal of the trustee (considered in CHAPTER 8), or taking steps to safeguard the assets in future, such as an injunction, or the appointment of a receiver (discussed in CHAPTER 9).

Chapter 4

Claims for inspection of documents

Introduction to the claim

4.1 It is clear that, in order to enforce his rights under the trust, a beneficiary may require access to documents and information in the possession of the trustees in that capacity. He may know or suspect that a breach of trust has occurred, and wish to inform himself about it; or he may simply wish to have a better understanding of how the trust is managed and administered.

However, the basis upon which he is entitled to such access has been the subject of much debate for more than a century, centring on whether he has a 'proprietary' right to the documents, and if so, what 'proprietary' means. The competing views in the most prominent judgments on the subject were set out in full in the recent important case of *Schmidt v Rosewood Trust Limited [2003] UKPC 26* (discussed at paragraph 4.2 below).

The modern explanation of the term 'proprietary' in this context was neatly summarised by an Australian judge, Doyle CJ, in the case of *Rouse v IOOF Australia Trustees Limited [2000] WTLR 111* (at page 126): *'I consider that the true position [on the beneficiary's right to inspection] is as stated . . . in Breen v Williams (1996) 186 CLR 71 HC of A at page 89:* "But the right of access of a beneficiary to trust documents arises because of the beneficial interest of the beneficiary in the trust property and it is in that sense that the right may be described as proprietary" . . . *The other approach is that the right of a beneficiary to inspect trust documents is founded not upon any equitable proprietary right but upon the fiduciary duty of a trustee to keep the beneficiary informed and to render accounts. On this approach the existence of a proprietary right may be sufficient to grant a right of access, but it is not necessary.'* It can therefore be seen that a beneficiary's interest in acquiring information about the trust and the trustees' dealings with trust property arises out of:

- the mere fact of his having an interest in the trust (whether fixed or discretionary); and/or
- the duty of the trustees to account to their beneficiaries for their dealings with the trust assets (discussed in CHAPTER 3).

The beneficiary's interest in seeking documents is 'proprietary' in the broadest sense of the word. The beneficiary has an identifiable interest in knowing what is happening, and has happened, in the trust of which he is a beneficiary.

However, the beneficiary's having an interest in seeing documents, or even an entitlement to ask, is not the same as saying he has a *right* to inspect all the documents in the trustees' possession as trustees. Earlier cases, such as *Re Londonderry's Settlement [1965] Ch 918, CA*, concentrated on the narrow task of identifying categories of documents, called 'trust documents', which a beneficiary was said to have a right to inspect. That term was defined in *Londonderry* by Salmon LJ (at page 940): '*The category of trust documents has never been comprehensively* defined . . . *[they] do, however, have these characteristics in common: (1) they are documents in the possession of the trustees as trustees;* (2) *they contain information about the trust which the beneficiaries are entitled to know;* (3) *the beneficiaries have a proprietary interest in the documents and, accordingly, are entitled to see them. If any parts of a document contain information which the beneficiaries are not entitled to know, I doubt whether such parts can truly be said to be integral parts of a trust document.*' The documents which their Lordships concluded were trust documents included the trust deed, any supplementary deeds and trust accounts. Documents excluded from the category of trust documents included minutes of trustees' meetings and agendas/documents prepared for those meetings; correspondence between the trustees and appointors and beneficiaries; and correspondence between the trust's solicitors and the trustees and among the trustees.

The most recent cases have concentrated on the broader question of whether or not the beneficiary has a right to inspect *any* documents – and if so, which ones. In considering that question, they have tended to consider the following distinct issues:

- Is a beneficiary entitled to seek documents?
- Does the beneficiary have a right to see those documents he seeks to see?
- Is there a discretion on the part of the trustee to refuse to permit inspection?

In this chapter, those issues are considered in detail, together with the following related issues:

- How does the general position contrast with the right to discovery in litigation?
- Can the beneficiaries obtain information from any other person?

Appendix 5 contains guidance for trustees and beneficiaries in relation to requests for information.

The 'right' to request information

4.2 The starting point for the debate as to the nature of a beneficiary's right to receive information is the judgment of Lord Wrenbury in *O'Rourke v Darbishire [1920] AC 581, HL*, where he said (at pages 626–7):

> '*[A beneficiary] has a right to access to the documents which he desires to inspect upon . . . a proprietary right. The beneficiary is entitled to see all*

> *trust documents because they are trust documents and because he is a beneficiary. They are in a sense his own. Action or no action, he is entitled to access to them. This has nothing to do with discovery. The right to discovery is a right to see someone else's documents. The proprietary right is a right to access to documents which are your own. No question of professional privilege arises in such a case. Documents containing professional advice taken by [the trustees] contain advice taken for their [beneficiaries] and the beneficiaries are entitled to see them because they are beneficiaries.*'

This explanation has, it is now recognised, been much misunderstood. In *Rouse v IOOF Australia Trustees Limited [2000] WTLR 111*, mentioned above, the judge believed that Lord Wrenbury had intended the words 'proprietary right' to have the broader meaning referred to in paragraph 4.1 above. The argument that a beneficiary is only entitled to see trust documents if he has a fixed and transmissible interest in the trust assets, is too narrow, as is the other interpretation of the words 'proprietary right' as meaning that a beneficiary must – by virtue of that status – be absolutely entitled, without right of refusal by the trustees, to see every document capable of categorisation as a trust document.

In another well-known Australian case, *Hartigan Nominees Pty Ltd v Rydge (1992) 29 NSWLR 405*, Kirby P said: '*I do not think it is imperative to determine whether [a] document is a "trust document" . . . or whether the [beneficiary] has a proprietary interest in it . . . Much of the law on the subject of access to documents has conventionally been expressed in terms of the "proprietary interest" in the document of the party seeking access to it. Thus it has been held that a [beneficiary] has a "proprietary right" to seek all documents relating to the trust . . . This approach is unsatisfactory. Access should not be limited to documents in which a proprietary right may be established. Such rights may be* sufficient; *but they are not* necessary *to a right of access which the courts will enforce to uphold the [beneficiary's] entitlement to a reasonable assurance of the manifest integrity of the administration of the trust by the trustees*' (existing emphasis).

This approach was expressly approved by the Privy Council in the recent case of *Schmidt v Rosewood Trust Limited [2003] UKPC 26*, where Lord Walker said, at paragraph 50 of his judgment: '*The Board does not find it surprising that Lord Wrenbury's observations [in O'Rourke v Darbishire] have been so often cited, since they are a vivid expression of the basic distinction between the right of a beneficiary arising under the law of trusts . . . and the right of a litigant to disclosure of his opponent's documents . . . But the Board cannot regard it as a reasoned or binding decision that a beneficiary's right or claim to disclosure of trust documents or information must always have the proprietary basis of a transmissible interest in trust property.*'

It follows, therefore, that any beneficiary – no matter how small his interest, or whether he is a discretionary beneficiary – has a right to *request* information. An object of a power probably does not have such a right, unless and until such power is exercised in his favour, as he has no interest in the trust property. The question of whether the beneficiary has a right to *receive* all or any of the information he requests is separate, and in that sense the right to ask is not proprietary in the narrow sense that if he asks, he must be entitled as of right to receive.

The 'right' to receive information

4.3 It was said as long ago as 1886 that the right of a beneficiary to receive the information he had requested was subject to a discretion on the part of the trustees – and the court – to refuse his request. In *In Re Cowin (1886) 33 Ch D 179*, North J said (at pages 186–7): '*[A beneficiary is] entitled to see the deeds, subject to this, that there might be circumstances which would justify the trustees in withholding them from him . . . I do not say that he is entitled as of right, but only that he is entitled under the circumstances, because there might be a state of circumstances under which the right to production would not exist.*'

This was echoed by Doyle CJ in *Rouse,* where he said (at page 127): '*Describing the right as a proprietary right does not do away with the issue of whether there are circumstances under which a trustee can refuse to permit inspection of trust documents.*'

Other courts around the world have looked at the issue in similar ways in recent years. In *In the matter of the Rabaiotti 1989 Settlement (Royal Court of Jersey, 30th May 2000)* the court considered whether the right to see trust documents is an absolute right or whether the court has a discretion to refuse a beneficiary permission to inspect trust documents in some circumstances. It was concluded that: '*One starts with a strong presumption that a beneficiary is entitled to see trust documents of the nature described. There would have to be a good reason to refuse disclosure of such documents. But . . . the court has an overriding discretion to withhold documents where it is satisfied that this is in the best interests of the beneficiaries as a whole.*'

In *Rosewood,* however, the position was stated more clearly by Walker LJ at paragraph 51 of his judgment, where he rejected the 'absolute proprietary right' approach, and described what he called 'the more principled and correct approach' as being that the right to seek disclosure of trust documents is '*one aspect of the court's inherent jurisdiction to supervise, and if necessary to intervene in, the administration of trusts. The right to seek the court's intervention does not depend on entitlement to a fixed and transmissible beneficial interest. The object of a discretion (including a mere power) may also be entitled to protection from a court of equity, although the circumstances in which he may seek protection, and the nature of the protection he may expect to obtain, will depend on the court's discretion*'. He went on to say (at paragraph 67): '*no beneficiary (and least of all a discretionary object) has any entitlement as of right to disclosure of anything which can plausibly be described as a trust document.*'

Under the law as it now stands, therefore, the position of the beneficiary is as follows:

- by virtue of his status as beneficiary and/or by virtue of the trustees' duty to account, he is entitled to ask for information relating to the trust;
- if the trustees refuse his request, he has a right to apply to the court for assistance under the inherent jurisdiction of the court to supervise trusts and intervene as necessary; and
- the court will determine whether the circumstances are such that the trustees do have a discretion to refuse his request, or whether they have none.

The trustees' discretion to refuse production

4.4 In no sense do the recent cases (including *Rosewood)* give the trustees *carte blanche* to refuse all requests for documents out of hand. They must consider whether there is a proper reason for refusing the disclosure of each document (or category of document) requested. In many cases, it is anticipated, there will be no proper reason for trustees to refuse to disclose the information requested. Appendix 5 contains a flowchart summarising the proper considerations which ought to be applied by trustees in receipt of a request for information.

A 'proper' reason would not, for example, include the trustees' fear of being exposed to personal liability by producing documents which would disclose a breach of trust they had committed. In deciding whether there is a 'proper' reason, the trustees must (as with every other duty they have as trustees) consider the interests of the beneficial class as a whole, and never their own interests. In *Rouse*, Doyle CJ explained it thus, at page 128: '*the law [needs] to recognise some scope for a trustee to refuse to disclose information on the grounds that it is confidential and on the further ground that the disclosure is not in the interests of the beneficiaries as a whole.*' He continued by saying, at pages 128–9: '*I wish to make it clear that the discretion that I envisage is a limited one, and must always be limited by the general duty of disclosure by a trustee . . . The existence of the discretion cannot be used as an excuse for paternalism or to disregard the interests of beneficiaries. Its existence depends upon the need to protect the trustee's ability to discharge its obligations.*'

Grouped together, 'proper' reasons are likely to be identified as reasons which have in common the question of confidentiality, as explained by Walker LJ in *Rosewood* (at paragraph 67 of his judgment): '*Especially when there are issues as to personal or commercial confidentiality, the court may have to balance the competing interests of different beneficiaries, the trustees themselves, and third parties. Disclosure may have to be limited and safeguards may have to be put in place. Evaluation of the claims of a beneficiary (and especially of a discretionary object) may be an important part of the balancing exercise which the court has to perform on the materials placed before it. In many cases the court may have no difficulty in concluding that an applicant with no more than a theoretical possibility of benefit ought not to be granted any relief.*'

Mere 'family confidentiality' is probably not enough. Every family may wish to avoid having its linen aired in public, but that is unlikely (save in exceptional circumstances) to be a sufficient excuse for the trustees in considering whether or not to refuse a request for the disclosure of information by a beneficiary. This was the view of Doyle CJ in *Rouse*, at pages 127–8: '*I consider that the trustee must be entitled to refuse access to trust documents, and not only when that is done to maintain the confidentiality of the reasons for the exercise of a discretion . . . there may be cases in which an obligation of confidentiality attaches to documents in possession of the trustee by virtue of the circumstances in which those documents were received. The fact that a person is a beneficiary may mean that the obligation of confidentiality is not an objection to the person inspecting the documents, but . . . it is conceivable that there will be cases where a trustee receives a document under circumstances such that, to allow inspection by a beneficiary, would give rise to a breach of obligations of confidentiality imposed upon the trustee.*'

'Proper' reasons for claiming confidentiality, and for refusing the disclosure of documents, can therefore be divided into two categories:

- legal reasons; and
- commercial reasons,

in both cases being reasons where it can reasonably be said that disclosure would adversely affect the interests of the beneficiaries as a whole, or the ability of the trustees to continue to administer the trust effectively.

Legal reasons

4.5 There may be many legal reasons why a trustee should not be obliged to disclose information to a beneficiary. Principal among them, however, are two main areas of legal confidentiality:

- legal professional privilege; and
- the confidentiality attaching to the matters surrounding an exercise of the trustees' discretion.

Legal professional privilege

4.6 Trustees are under an obligation to seek appropriate legal (and other professional) advice when required in relation to the management and administration of the trust. In some cases, there may be no proper objection to releasing the advice, such as in situations where the advice related to long-past appointments, or advice concerning the tax effects on the beneficiaries of a particular course of action. However, it is clearly not desirable that that advice should always be available to the beneficiaries as of right, even if paid for out of the trust fund. In *O'Rourke v Darbishire [1920] AC 581, HL*, it was said (by Viscount Finlay at page 602) that: '*Trustees are entitled to consult a solicitor with reference to the affairs of the trust, and the communications between them and their legal adviser are privileged if for the purpose of obtaining legal advice . . . the privilege is confined to communications genuinely for the purpose of getting legal advice. It would not extend to mere business communications with reference to the trust . . ..*'

This privilege does not extend to all communications with the trustees' solicitors, however. In *Re Londonderry's Settlement [1965] Ch 918, CA*, Harman LJ said (at page 933): '*On the other hand, if the solicitor advising the trustees commits to paper an aide-memoire summarising the state of the fund or of the family and reminding the trustees of past distributions and future possibilities, I think that must be a document which any beneficiary must be at liberty to inspect.*' In some cases, therefore, the trustees may not be able to claim legal professional privilege in respect of correspondence with, or documents prepared by, their solicitors.

In cases where legal professional privilege does apply, the documents may nonetheless be disclosable if a prima facie case of fraud can be made out. Privilege will not be lifted on the strength of a mere allegation of fraud or wrongdoing.

Documents relating to the exercise of the trustees' discretion

4.7 Until *Rosewood*, one of the most authoritative judgments on the question of disclosure of trust documents was that in *In re Londonderry's Settlement, Peat v Walsh [1965] Ch 918, CA*. Whilst the idea that a beneficiary must have a proprietary right in the trust in order to obtain documents (espoused in *Londonderry* just as much as in *O'Rourke v Darbishire [1920] AC 581, HL*) has been consigned to history by *Rosewood*, many of the principles in *Londonderry* remain good.

Whilst, as noted in paragraph 4.1 above, *Londonderry* concentrated on the (perhaps too narrow) question of what was a 'trust document', the thinking behind that categorisation is likely to prove still to be sufficient grounds for refusal by the trustees to disclose information. Harman LJ's comments on the non-disclosable documents were as follows:

(a) Minutes of trustees' meetings and agendas/documents prepared for meetings: '*In my judgment [these] are, in the absence of an action impugning the trustees' good faith, documents which a beneficiary cannot claim the right to inspect. If [a beneficiary] is allowed to examine these, [she] will know at once the very matters which the trustees are not bound to disclose to her, namely, their motives and reasons*' (at page 933);

(b) Correspondence between the trustees and appointors and beneficiaries: '*I cannot think that communications passing between individual trustees and appointors are documents in which beneficiaries have a proprietary right.' 'I do not think letters to or from an individual beneficiary ought to be open to inspection by another beneficiary.'* (at page 934); and

(c) Correspondence between the trust's solicitors and the trustees and among the trustees: '*if one of the trustees commits to paper his suggestions and circulates them among his co-trustees; or if inquiries are made in writing as to the circumstances of a member of the class; I decline to hold that such documents are trust documents the property of the beneficiaries*' (at page 933) (but see his proviso for aides-memoire prepared by solicitors, at paragraph 4.6 above).

These categories of documents have in common the fact that they are ones which would, or might, disclose the reasons surrounding an exercise of the trustees' discretion. (As Harman LJ said in *Londonderry* at pages 928–9: '*trustees exercising a discretionary power are not bound to disclose to their beneficiaries the reasons actuating them in coming to a decision. This is a long-standing principle and rests largely I think on the view that nobody could be called upon to accept a trusteeship involving the exercise of a discretion unless, in the absence of bad faith, he were not liable to have his motives or his reasons called in question either by the beneficiaries or by the court.*') As such, it must be the case, even following *Rosewood*, that these are categories of documents which are not ordinarily disclosable – not because, under the old categorisation, they are not 'trust documents', but because, on their individual merits, they are confidential.

It remains the position that, to the extent that the documents requested do not relate to the exercise of the trustees' discretion, they are unlikely to be protected by 'legal' confidentiality. This might be the case, for example, in relation to minutes of trustees' meetings discussing ordinary trust business not related to distributions. Such documents may, however, be protected by virtue of being 'commercially' confidential (see paragraph 4.10 below).

Letters of wishes

4.8 Letters of wishes are a category of document not expressly considered in *Londonderry*, but worth considering separately for a moment. It follows from the judgment in *Londonderry* that, if a document discloses the reasons surrounding the exercise of trustees' discretion, it need not ordinarily be disclosed. This conclusion has been applied on many occasions to withhold letters of wishes from beneficiaries (see, for example, the Australian case of *Hartigan Nominees v Rydge (1992) 29 NSWLR 405*).

Interestingly, the minority view in *Hartigan* was that, since the trustees had regard to the content of the letter of wishes in determining the interests of the beneficiaries, it should be regarded as a document supplemental to the trust deed, and should be disclosed unless marked 'confidential' by the settlor. In *In the matter of the Rabaiotti 1989 Settlement (Royal Court of Jersey, 30th May 2000)*, at paragraph 53 of its judgment, the court approved *Hartigan,* holding that a letter of wishes is generally intended to be confidential, and in any event is likely to disclose the reasons for the exercise of the trustees' discretions. However, it was found that the court's general supervisory jurisdiction over trusts (the overarching aim of which is to ensure that the trustees are accountable to the beneficiaries) means that it must have the power to order disclosure of a letter of wishes if it is satisfied that it is necessary, and in the interests of the beneficiaries as a whole, to do so. The case of *Re Manisty's Settlement [1974] Ch 17* suggests that the trustees must not act capriciously, perversely or in a manner irrelevant to the sensible expectations of the settlor. In a situation where the beneficiaries believed a decision of the trustees to be impeachable on these grounds, it might be necessary, and in the interests of the trust, to grant them sight of the letter of wishes in order to know what the settlor's intentions were.

However, *Rabaiotti* confirmed that the presumption lies firmly against disclosure of confidential documents, and the burden lies on the beneficiary who requests the order to order the disclosure to show why it should be ordered. The judgment in *Rabaiotti* therefore provides an interesting, but logical, counterbalance to the finding in *Rosewood* that there is a rebuttable presumption in favour of disclosing other trust-related documents to beneficiaries, with the onus being on the trustees to show why disclosure should not be ordered.

Other legal reasons

4.9 There are, as noted above, many conceivable legal reasons why a trustee should not give disclosure of trust documents. For example, they may be subject to an earlier order of an English court that they should not do so, or an undertaking by them to some other person that they would not do so. The provisions of the Data Protection Act 1998 (which would apply, for example, to some UK-based trustees) may place restrictions on the kinds of information that they can properly disclose about other persons, but conversely may also be used (for example, under sections 7 and 8 of that Act) so as to require them to produce, on receipt of a written request made in accordance with the 1998 Act, information that they hold about a specified beneficiary.

The criminal law might also prove an obstacle to disclosure. It is established law that '*a court cannot compel a man to commit a criminal offence*' (*Rowell v Pratt [1937] 3 All ER 660, BCCI v Price Waterhouse [1997] 4 All ER 781*). However, there is an element of debate about what a 'criminal offence' for these purposes is. In *Morris v Banque Arabe et Internationale d'Investissement SA [2000] 2 ITELR 492*, Neuberger J identified different areas of possible objection to the production of documents:

- where the very act of permitting inspection causes the person to commit a crime in England, disclosure will not be required in any circumstances (*Rowell v Pratt [1937] 3 All ER 660, BCCI v Price Waterhouse [1997] 4 All ER 781*);
- where, as a result of permitting inspection, a person would reveal that he has or may have committed an act which would be a crime in England, inspection probably would not be ordered (s 14(1)(a) Civil Evidence Act 1968);

- where the very act of permitting inspection might cause a person to commit a crime abroad, it is not accepted that the court cannot order inspection, as different national interests do conflict and countries have their own interests to pursue (*Brannigan v Davison [1997] AC 238, PC*); and
- where, as a result of permitting inspection, a person would reveal that he has or may have committed an act which is a crime abroad, similarly it is not automatically the case that the court would not order disclosure.

Commercial reasons

4.10 In *Schmidt v Rosewood Trust Limited [2003] UKPC 26*, it was acknowledged that there may be good commercial reasons why trustees should not disclose information to beneficiaries. In *Rouse v IOOF Australia Trustees Limited [2000] WTLR 111*, it was also said that the position of a trustee conducting a business might be made impossible if the beneficiary of the trust had an absolute right to inspect documents concerning the conduct of the business. It might be, for example, that a trustee had documents which would disclose price-sensitive information (in the context of a listed company), or documents relating to commercially sensitive negotiations.

Not all information in the possession of the trustees and relating to companies or businesses will be regarded as commercially sensitive, of course. Even if a document contains commercially sensitive information, if the reason for that sensitivity lapses (for example, at the end of a 'closed period' when those closely involved with the management of a company are prohibited from trading publicly-listed shares prior to important announcements), the documents may become disclosable. A more significant exception, perhaps, relates to the disclosure of information in the hands of trustees as shareholders, rather than as managers or directors.

The case of *Butt v Kelson [1952] Ch 197, CA* (approved in *Walker v Cherry (1994) unreported*) established that beneficiaries are generally entitled to see information concerning underlying companies in which the trust has an interest. They cannot (consistently with *Rosewood*) have access to all the information that the trustees possess, which may come into their possession as directors or managers of the business. Romer LJ explained it thus (at page 205): '*where a business is carried on by a limited company and the beneficiaries are interested not in the business itself but as [beneficiaries] of shares held by the trustees, then the only rights that the beneficiaries have are rights to see that the trustees use their voting power attaching to the trust holding in the best interests of the beneficiaries themselves . . .*' The beneficiaries are therefore entitled to be treated as though they were the registered shareholders of the shares, and to obtain such information as the articles of association (and the general law) usually allow shareholders to see. However, this does not entitle them to see management documents and other information not usually available to shareholders, and Romer LJ's further pronouncement that the beneficiaries were, in effect, entitled to compel the trustees to exercise their voting rights over the shares has been doubted (not least for its inconsistency with the contrary finding in *Re Whichelow [1954] 1 WLR 5*).

However, Romer LJ foresaw (again consistently with the approach in *Rosewood*) that there might be some valid objection raised by the directors of the company, so there remains an element of discretion as to commercially or legally sensitive matters.

The role of the court

4.11 As noted in paragraph 4.3 above, if the trustees refuse a beneficiary's request for information, he has a right to apply to the court. But to what end? As discussed in CHAPTER 7, a court cannot generally interfere in the exercise of a trustee's discretion; even if the trustee gives reasons for the exercise of his discretion, the court's role is only to determine whether those reasons are valid ones or not, but the court cannot usually exercise the trustees' discretion on their behalf.

Lord Walker, in *Rosewood,* saw the role of the court as:

- to decide whether a beneficiary should be granted any relief at all;
- if so, what classes of documents should be disclosed;
- whether those documents should be disclosed completely or with redactions; and
- whether any safeguards should be imposed on the form of disclosure offered.

The first question, as to whether any relief should be granted, goes to the question of whether the trustees actually have a discretion, in all the circumstances, to refuse disclosure. In other words, the court examines whether there is a valid legal or commercial reason to withhold the documents sought. In *Rouse v IOOF Australia Trustees Limited [2000] WTLR 111* it was held that the function of the court is to decide *whether* the trustee has a discretion to refuse to permit inspection, and not (as noted above) to exercise that discretion. In considering whether there is a discretion, the court will balance the competing interests of different beneficiaries, the trustees themselves (eg where disclosure might put them in an onerous or difficult position), and third parties (eg where there are commercial reasons to refuse disclosure) (*Rosewood*). The purposes of the applicant in seeking information may be relevant – where the applicant (guardian ad litem for her children, the beneficiaries) wished to use the documents to attack the trust and it was held that she could not, on the one hand, attack the trust, and on the other hand, claim documents by virtue of her children's rights as beneficiaries under it. If the trust was invalid, as she claimed, the children had no such rights. Disclosure was refused in any event as not being in the interests of the beneficiaries as a whole (*In the matter of the M and L Trusts (Royal Court of Jersey, 7th January 2003*), approving *Lemos v Coutts & Co (Cayman) Ltd (1992–3) CILR 5* and *Rabaiotti).*

Establishing whether or not there is a discretion will then resolve the question of which classes of document can properly be withheld, and which ought to be disclosed (there being no operative discretion).

In cases where there is some doubt as to whether a particular document (or class of document) ought to be subject to the discretion to withhold, the court may consider whether the objection to disclosure would be removed if safeguards were put in place. The sorts of safeguards which might be of assistance are:

- redaction of sensitive parts of a document;
- disclosure being made by way of inspection by the beneficiary's professional advisers; or
- disclosure being made subject to undertakings by the beneficiary and his professional advisers as to the use to which the information will be put (as was the case, for example, in the Cayman case of *Lemos v Coutts & Co (Cayman) Ltd (1992–3) CILR 5*).

As noted in paragraph 4.4 above, it is important to note that the recent developments in case law do not mean that trustees should (or could) refuse requests for disclosure with impunity. Trustees who are found not to have any reasonable grounds for believing that there is a valid objection to disclosure may be at risk as to the costs of the beneficiary's application to the court (see paragraph 4.16 below).

Disclosure in the context of litigation

4.12 As Lord Wrenbury famously put it in *O'Rourke v Darbishire [1920] AC 581, HL 'The right to discovery is a right to see someone else's documents. The proprietary right is a right to access to documents which are your own.'* For Part 8 claims (the procedure used for many trust-related claims), 'discovery', that is, disclosure of documents in the context of litigation, is not usually relevant. However, the court has a discretion to make orders for the disclosure of documents by the parties if it thinks it appropriate to do so. In the alternative procedure under CPR Part 7 (used for many breach of trust claims), disclosure of documents is available.

Orders for disclosure of documents are to be contrasted with the beneficiaries' ordinary right to ask for documentation relating to the trust, because:

- the order will only be made in the context of extant litigation (or occasionally, pre-emptively when proceedings are contemplated, but not for a mere 'fishing expedition');

- the documents to be disclosed will be those relating to the issues the subject matter of the proceedings, which may be broader than, or narrower than, the beneficiaries' ordinary entitlement to request information. For example, if the nature of the claim is that bad faith or wrongdoing on the part of the trustees is alleged, then the beneficiaries may be able to obtain documents not otherwise available to them; and
- In line with the overriding objective of the CPR (discussed in CHAPTER 2), disclosure orders are made under the CPR on a much narrower basis than the swingeing rules which applied under the former Rules of the Supreme Court. The principal aim is proportionality. Therefore, parties are not usually required to disclose every item of relevance (no matter how remote) to the case; rather, an order for 'standard disclosure' under CPR 31 will usually require a party to disclose:
  - the documents on which he relies;
  - documents which adversely affect his claim or defence;
  - documents which support the claim or defence of another party; and
  - documents which adversely affect another party's claim or defence.

The number of documents, the complexity of the proceedings, the difficulty or expense of locating documents, and the relative importance of any documents likely to be found are all relevant considerations in determining what level of disclosure (if any) is appropriate to the case.

Disclosure to third parties

4.13 A person who is not a beneficiary, or even a mere object of a power, may lack the standing for there to be a presumption in favour of disclosing documents to them; indeed, there may be an initial presumption against disclosure of documents which relate to a private trust to a person who is not among the beneficiaries. However, following Lord Walker's judgment in *Rosewood*, it is clear that the disclosure of documents is always within the court's jurisdiction relating to the administration of trusts – seemingly, the identity of the applicant is not relevant to the existence of the jurisdiction, but only to the question of how likely it is that the balance of interests will be weighted against disclosure. This point was made in the Jersey case of *In the matter of the C A Settlement and the representation of AA (Royal Court of Jersey, 2nd May 2002)*, where a non-beneficiary applied for the disclosure of documents which might reveal whether or not the trust was capable of attack by her. On the facts, disclosure was refused, because (as under English law) a potential claimant is not entitled to an order requiring the potential defendant to produce documents which will show the potential claimant whether or not he has a cause of action. Whilst 'fishing expeditions' of this kind will always be refused, it remains the case that the court may order disclosure of trust documents to non-parties if it is in the interests of the trust to do so.

Disclosure from third parties

4.14 It is possible that a beneficiary may be able to obtain information from persons other than the trustees. For example, either the settlor or the protector may have information which would assist the beneficiary, or even another beneficiary. The relevant procedure is that in CPR Part 31, and the person seeking information from the non-party must show that the documents sought are likely to assist or adversely affect either case, and that disclosure is necessary in order fairly to dispose of the claim, or to save costs.

However, the court also has a more general equitable jurisdiction to order disclosure by anyone who may have information relevant to the claimant's case. *Murphy v Murphy [1998] 3 All ER 1* was just such a case. The claimant beneficiary believed that he was a beneficiary of a trust created by his father, but did not know the identity of the trustees. It was held that the court had power to compel the father to identify the trustees, as the claimant had an identifiable interest in knowing who were the trustees in whom the trust property was vested.

Procedure

4.15 It follows from all the recent decisions that the right place to start is still for the beneficiary (or his solicitors) to make his first requests through correspondence with the trustees (or their solicitors). This obvious point is worth emphasising simply because of the existence of some debate over the extent to which *Rosewood* entitles trustees to refuse all requests, or even requires all requests to be made through the medium of a court application. Such views seem inconsistent with the reasoning of the *Rosewood* judgment, however, and if the trustees adopted such an approach, it might be criticised for unreasonableness and inconsistency both with their fiduciary duties and with the overriding objective in CPR Part 1.

It also remains the case that the enquiring beneficiary must give an undertaking to pay the trustees' reasonable costs of providing the information he has requested. This has always been the position, as a beneficiary who wishes to receive information can only have it (if at all) at his own expense (*Re Londonderry's Settlement [1965] Ch 918, CA*).

On receipt of a written request for information, trustees need to consider (with appropriate advice) whether they have reasonable grounds for refusing disclosure in relation to *each* document or class of document sought (grounds for refusing disclosure of one not necessarily being sufficient to refuse all). If they do refuse, the beneficiary may bring a claim, requesting the court to give directions as to whether disclosure is to be made. It is suggested that, in many cases, the CPR Part 8 procedure will be the more appropriate, as the court is being invited to consider, as discussed throughout this chapter, whether there is an operative discretion on the part of the trustees to refuse, and/or to give directions as to which documents can properly be disclosed. The CPR Part 7 procedure is less likely to be relevant unless the order for disclosure of documents is made in the context of an allegation of breach of trust.

The beneficiary's claim form should contain the following matters:

- a statement that Part 8 applies to the claim;
- a statement that the remedy sought is the disclosure of documents (the specific documents, or classes of document, sought should be identified);
- a summary of the legal basis on which that remedy is sought – a statement that the claimant is a beneficiary and the defendant is a trustee should suffice in most cases. (NB if the beneficiary is seeking documents to which confidentiality may be asserted to attach, it may be helpful to give (in the evidence accompanying the claim form) a summarised explanation of the circumstances and why any claimed confidentiality should be overridden); and
- a statement of truth.

If the claim is brought under CPR Part 8, the trustees' role is not to defend the claim, as they are not being accused of anything. They must simply provide the court with all the facts and circumstances which may be relevant to the question to be determined. They may actively argue against disclosure if they believe that to be in the interests of the trust (and its beneficiaries) but they are at risk of costs being ordered against them if they argue strongly against disclosure, and it is later ordered (see paragraph 4.17 below).

The matter will then follow the procedure and timetable set out in CHAPTER 2 and APPENDIX 1 until trial.

Parties

4.16 As well as the claimant beneficiary, and defendant trustees, it is necessary to consider whether any other persons should be parties to the proceedings:

- it may be that other beneficiaries have views on the question of whether or not the documents sought should be disclosed; and
- it may be appropriate to join as defendants the directors of an underlying company in respect of which disclosure is sought, if they are opposed to disclosure being made (*Butt v Kelson [1951] Ch 197, CA*).

Costs

4.17 It should be noted that the beneficiary's costs undertaking (discussed in paragraph 4.15 above) applies only to the ordinary production of documents, and covers only costs such as photocopying and perhaps any time spent by the trustees in extracting the documents. It does not cover the costs of the trustees obtaining advice as to whether or not they should disclose the documents; and it does not apply to the costs of any court proceedings which become necessary following a refusal by the trustees. Those costs are within the discretion of the court, and a number of different possible orders may be made.

The costs order is likely in most cases to reflect the outcome of the application, so that they may be payable:

- by the claimant beneficiaries if their application is unsuccessful and the court thinks fit. This may happen where those beneficiaries (if any) who are not claimants successfully argue that the trust fund should not be charged with the cost of an unsuccessful action;
- by the defendant trustee(s) if they are held to have acted unreasonably in refusing the beneficiary's initial request; or
- out of the trust fund, if the court thinks it appropriate.

A recent example of a case in which costs were ordered against the trustees personally was *Hogg v Williamson (Royal Court of Jersey, 7 August 2003)*. The Deputy Bailiff confirmed the general rule under Jersey law (which reflects the English legal position) that where a trustee acts reasonably in seeking directions concerning the disclosure of trust documents, the court will not order the trustee to pay the costs of the application. On the facts of that case, the trustee had denied the existence of the trust, and that the applicant was a beneficiary, both of which statements were untrue, in an effort to prevent her obtaining trust documents. It was therefore just to order the trustee to pay all the costs personally.

Although an application for disclosure is unlikely to be (in most cases) particularly complex or expensive, it may sometimes be the case that a beneficiary may lack the necessary means even to bring the proceedings. If a beneficiary has not received any distributions, and lacks independent means, he may wish to seek ways of funding the application. Under CPR Part 64, as discussed in CHAPTER 3, the court has power to make a costs order at any time in relation to trust-related proceedings, where the trustees either do not have power under the trust deed to pay the costs of the parties, or have such power but choose not to use it. A pre-emptive costs order can be made if the court believes that the application is in the interests of the trust itself, and/or those of a wide class of beneficiaries, when it may order that the costs of funding the application should be paid pre-emptively out of the trust fund. This might be the case where, for example, the beneficiaries are seeking information about what has happened to certain trust assets, and the result of the disclosure will benefit the trust (*Wallersteiner v Moir (No 2) [1975] QB 373, CA*). Many of the cases reported to date have involved litigation at the expense of the funds of a company (*Wallersteiner,* and *Re Biddencare Limited [1994] 2 BCLC 160*) or even pension funds (*McDonald and others v Horn and others [1995] 1 All ER 961, CA*). They have in common the court's desire to render the trustees (or directors) accountable to those to whom they have fiduciary duties. A similar approach may be followed for private trusts in appropriate cases.

Chapter 5

Breach of trust

Introduction

5.1 Trustees are obliged to act in accordance with the terms of the trust deed, as supplemented by any duties or powers conferred on them by the general law, and '*any act or neglect on the part of a trustee which is not authorised or excused by the terms of the trust instrument, or by law, is called a breach of trust*' (Underhill and Hayton's *Law of Trusts and Trustees*, approved specifically in *Green v Russell [1959] 2 QB 226, CA*). In the case of *Tito v Waddell (No 2) [1977] Ch 106*, Megarry V-C expanded the Underhill analysis when he gave the following explanations of the meaning of 'breach of trust':

> 'The expression "breach of trust" has never been defined in English law. The wider view is that every omission or violation is a breach of trust; the narrower view is that only the breach of duties imposed on the trustees as trustees are breaches of trust, so any duty to which a non-trustee is subject is not a breach of trust if breached.'

So, on the narrower analysis, which Megarry V-C preferred, a breach of fiduciary duty, such as a breach of the self-dealing rule (as in *Tito* itself), is not a breach of trust since fiduciary duties can be imposed on persons other than trustees.

In this book, for convenience:

- this chapter deals with mechanical breaches of trust, where the trustees have done something which they had no power to do, or have failed to do something in contravention of the terms of the trust instrument or the duties and powers conferred on them by the general law. Included in this chapter are breaches of fiduciary duty, therefore; and

- those breaches which result from a breach of the trustees' duty to exercise reasonable care and skill are considered in CHAPTER 6 (Breach of duty of care).

It is notable, however, that Megarry V-C's judgment in *Tito* goes to the important question of whether claims are time-barred by the Limitation Act 1980. Megarry V-C concluded that claims for breach of fiduciary duty are outside the scope of the claims for 'breach of trust' which (save in special circumstances) become time-barred after six years by virtue of section 21 of that Act. (Limitation periods are discussed more fully in CHAPTER 12.)

The determination of whether trustees are liable for breach of trust depends on the answer to the question, did the trustees' conduct differ from what they ought to have done, bearing in mind the duties and powers available to them? If the answer is yes, then in principle they are liable for breach of trust, subject to the following additional factors:

- What was the effect of that difference?
- How is it possible and appropriate to make good the damage caused?
- Do the trustees have any defences? (See CHAPTER 12.)

Identifying the breach

5.2 Proof of a loss to the trust fund is not the same as proof of a breach of trust. A trustee has no duty to act as insurer to the trust fund, to guard against all possible loss or harm (*Re Chapman [1896] 2 Ch 763, CA*). In particular, investment losses may happen to any person, and the trustees are not to be held liable for ordinary investment losses merely because the money invested and lost is not their own (see, for example, *Nestle v National Westminster Bank plc [1994] 1 All ER 118, CA*, per Staughton LJ at page 132: '*Of course it is not a breach of trust to invest the trust fund in such a manner that its real value is not maintained.*')

The trustees, therefore, are only liable for breach of trust if there is some act or omission on their part which can be shown to be 'wrong'. For the purposes of the mechanical breaches covered by this chapter, this may take the form of:

- failing to do something expressly required of them; or
- doing something which they had no power to do.

Failure to comply with obligations

5.3 If a trust deed gives power to the trustees to do something (for example, to permit a beneficiary to reside in a property owned by the trust) then, so long as the trustees act honestly in deciding whether or not to exercise the power, they cannot be held liable for failing to exercise it. That is not to say that the reasonableness of their decision cannot be challenged (as to which, see CHAPTER 7).

However, where the trust deed (or the general law) requires the trustees to do something, and they fail to do it, or requires them not to do something which they later do, they are guilty of breach of trust. Examples may include any of the matters set out in the following paragraphs 5.4 to 5.10.

Failing to identify and, if necessary, collect in the assets of the trust

5.4 The initial obligation of the trustees, on taking on their trusteeship, is to identify and, if necessary, take steps to obtain control of, the trust assets. (This is subject to the proviso that, if the costs of collecting in an asset are likely to outweigh its value to the trust, they need not do so.) This duty includes:

- a duty to collect in any debts which are due to the estate, which will include consideration of whether there are any rights to issue proceedings against other (or former) trustees, any beneficiaries, or third parties which ought to be pursued;
- a duty to convert assets of a wasting or reversionary nature, and unauthorised investments, into assets of a more conventional nature (*Howe v Lord Dartmouth (1802) 7 Ves 137*, but often excluded by trust deeds); and
- an ongoing duty to safeguard the assets, although it is doubtful whether this would amount to a duty to insure them (the exercise or non-exercise of the power of insurance being, seemingly, a matter to which the duty of care applies – see CHAPTER 6).

Trustees who fail in any of these duties are liable to make good the loss which results to the trust fund.

Failure to maintain accounts and records

5.5 As discussed in CHAPTER 3, trustees must keep proper accounts and records. If they fail to do so, in breach of trust, it is a matter which will be relevant to any order for account later made. So, for example, if a trustee cannot provide records of one or more transactions involving trust property, it may be presumed that those transactions were made in breach of trust, and they may be deleted from the account as if the transaction had never occurred at the expense of the trust.

Failure to take advice

5.6 Trustees have a duty to take appropriate advice before exercising their powers and discretions (and, in relation to investment powers, this duty is statutory – see Section 5 Trustee Act 2000). It is arguable that a failure to take advice, of itself, is a breach of trust which wholly impeaches the action which followed (so that, for example, an investment is *per se* improper and unauthorised, and should be deleted from the account later taken – see paragraph 5.12 below).

The contrary view (discussed in CHAPTER 6) is that an exercise of a power without advice is a breach of the duty of care. The latter view may be supported by *Nestle v National Westminster Bank plc [1994] 1 All ER 118, CA*, where Staughton LJ said (at pages 132–3): '*The misunderstanding of the investment clause and the failure to conduct periodic reviews do not by themselves . . . afford [the beneficiary] a remedy. They were symptoms of incompetence or idleness . . . [but she] must show that, through one or other or both of those causes, the trustees made decisions which they should not have made or failed to make decisions which they should have made.*'

One decisive factor would certainly be if the trust deed contained a direction to the trustees to take, and act upon, the advice of a specified person or type of person. A breach of the direction in such a case would clearly lead to an unauthorised investment (but conversely, fulfilment of it would relieve the trustees from liability, even if loss resulted from the directions given).

The difference between an unauthorised act and breach of duty of care goes to the quantum of damages which the trustee is liable to pay. In the former case, the entire transaction is struck from the account, so that he is strictly liable for the whole sum invested, plus interest. In the latter case, the account is simply 'surcharged' with the amount of the loss made. (See further below at paragraph 5.16 and CHAPTER 6).

Failure to comply with directions regarding investment

5.7 Occasionally, the trust instrument may contain mandatory directions to the trustees, such as, for example:

- a direction not to sell particular investments, but to retain them (particularly, it is suggested, in the case of shares in family businesses, or homes – see *Hayim v Citibank [1987] AC 730, PC*);
- a direction (rare nowadays) to invest at compound interest (*Jones v Foxall (1852) 15 Beav 388*); or
- a duty to obtain a valuation under particular conditions. In one case concerning wills, the executors were directed to obtain a valuation of the assets at the date of the testator's death, and it was improper for them to allow the valuer to take into account the possibility of future events which might affect the value of the assets (*In Re Bliss [2001] 1 WLR 1973).*

If they fail, in breach of trust, to comply with those directions, they are liable to restore the trust (or the affected beneficiaries) to the position it ought to have been in, had they complied with the directions. (Conversely, if they comply with the directions, they are not liable to the beneficiaries for any loss that thereby results, as in *Hayim v Citibank [1987] AC 730, PC.*)

Failure to pay funds to the right beneficiaries

5.8 If the trustees are required to pay income and/or capital to certain persons, and they fail to do so, it is a clear breach of trust. The beneficiaries to whom payment ought to have been made are entitled to recover the sums which ought to have been paid to them (see CHAPTER 10). Similarly, if, in breach of an express provision of the trust deed, the trustees pay money to a person who is not entitled to benefit (who is not a beneficiary, or *a fortiori* is an Excluded Person) they are personally liable to make good the consequences of that breach.

Failure to take action against defaulting co-trustee

5.9 If a trustee becomes aware of an actual or threatened breach of trust by his co-trustee, he commits a breach of trust of his own if he does not take action to prevent it (if possible) or to oblige the defaulter to make good his breach (*Gough v Smith [1872] WN 18*). The quantum of his liability depends upon whether, and to what extent, it is possible later to recover the sums due from the first wrongdoer.

Ultra vires and excessive exercises of a power

5.10 Trustees must act within the limits of the powers conferred on them by the trust instrument and the general law. Accordingly, if they act in a way which is beyond the scope of their powers, or act notwithstanding the fact that they have no power to do the thing in question, the act of doing the unauthorised thing is a breach of trust. This is subject to the court's power, under section 57 of the Trustee Act 1925, to confer upon trustees any necessary additional powers to do a particular act where they lack the necessary powers to effect the disposition or transaction in question, and it is one which is found by the court to be expedient. Some of the ways in which trustees may act excessively or *ultra vires* are considered in the following paragraphs 5.11 to 5.15.

Failure to act unanimously

5.11 As discussed in CHAPTER 7, the trustees must act unanimously unless expressly authorised to act by majority. If they purport to act without the necessary unanimity (in form and substance), this is clearly beyond the scope of their powers, and their actions are a breach of trust and void. The resolution may, however, be properly ratified by the trustee who has not taken part in the relevant decision.

Investment powers

5.12 As noted in paragraph 5.5 above, a failure to take advice relating to investments may itself be a breach of trust, such that the investment then made may be unauthorised, as being one which the trustees had no power to make in the absence of appropriate advice. It might (on the facts) be construed as an excessive exercise of their powers, rather than an act contrary to a direction (as in paragraph 5.5 above). As noted, CHAPTER 6 discusses the alternative view that the exercise of a power without advice is a breach of the duty of care. A decision not to follow the advice given would (if it proved loss-making) be a breach of the duty of care, however.

However, there are other ways in which investment powers may be exceeded. Commonly, modern trust deeds contain very broad powers of investment (now also found in the Trustee Act 2000). However, some financial arrangements are not, in fact, investments at all, such as derivatives. Derivatives are inherently speculative (since they generally consist, in effect, of a bet on the future), and are not even 'non-income-producing' as they are not designed to produce income. Many of the broad general investment clauses in trust deeds would therefore not appear sufficient to authorise the trustees to purchase derivatives (see, for example, *Westdeutsche Landesbank Girozentrale v Islington London Borough Council [1996] AC 669, HL*).

Failure to consult beneficiaries or other persons

5.13 Generally, trustees are not obliged to consult beneficiaries before an exercise of a power or discretion, although they should give proper consideration to any views or wishes actually expressed by the beneficiaries (*X v A and others [2000] 1 All ER 490*). However:

- the trust deed may require the trustees to consult the beneficiaries and/or some other person (such as a protector) before exercising particular powers; and
- section 11 of the Trusts of Land and Appointment of Trustees Act 1996 requires them to consult beneficiaries of full age and capacity who have an interest in possession in land before exercising any function in relation to that land,

so, if they do not consult in either of these cases, it is a prima facie breach of trust. It is likely that, in many cases, a failure to consult would mean that a mandatory condition precedent for the exercise had not been fulfilled, such that the purported exercise was excessive and void (as in *Waller v Waller [1967] 1 WLR 451*).

Failure to obtain consent

5.14 By extension, if the trustees are required to obtain the consent of any person, under the terms of the trust deed (such as, for example, the protector, or a spouse), a failure to do so would clearly mean that a necessary precondition for a valid exercise of the power was not present, making the exercise *ultra vires* and void (*Bateman v Davis (1818) 3 Madd 98*, but cf. *Stevens v Robertson (1868) 37 LJ Ch 499* where the required consent after the fact was held sufficient).

Personal benefit in breach of trust

5.15 A trust deed may frequently contain express terms which relax the usual absolute rule that a trustee must not profit from his trust. Remuneration clauses are one example, and indeed, the Trustee Act 2000 now also includes general provisions for the remuneration of trustees in certain circumstances.

However, if the trustees' actions benefit themselves, to a greater extent (if any) than is expressly permitted by the trust deed or the general law, then those actions are a breach of trust.

The interpretation in *Tito v Waddell (No 2) [1977] Ch 106* was that the self-dealing rules place the trustee under a disability or limitation in dealing with the assets to which the duties attach. On this analysis, any transaction or dealing in breach of the rule is *ultra vires*. The dealing is voidable at the instance of the beneficiaries (within a reasonable time) and, if they choose to assert their rights, the trustee is liable to make good the consequences of his improper dealings. In *Holder v Holder [1968] Ch 353*, this was held to mean that the item wrongly sold to the trustee should be resold, but, if it could not realise a price as high as that paid by the trustee, he should be obliged to purchase it at the original price. As a postscript, it was also noted that, if all the beneficiaries agreed (but not otherwise), the item should be restored to the trust.

Measure of liability

5.16 Although, as noted in paragraph 5.2 above, proof of a loss is not the same as proof of a breach of trust, where a breach of trust has been shown, proof of loss (including loss of opportunity, or a gain made by another person) is essential in order to render the trustees liable. Whilst a breach that resulted in no loss to the trust and no gain to any other person could nonetheless be impeached (and the trustees, for example, could be ordered to sell an unauthorised investment), there might be little practical point in pursuing it.

Broadly, a claim for breach of trust against the trustees is one:

- to have the loss to the trust fund made good, in relation to discretionary trusts;
- to restore to any income beneficiary sums which he ought to have received, had the breach not been committed (for example, by following a policy of investing for capital growth to the exclusion of the income beneficiary's interest); or
- to restore to the capital of the trust fund *and* the income beneficiaries the sums which have been lost by the breach (where the breach was a loss to capital which consequentially led to loss to the income beneficiary).

Whilst the question of *whether* a trustee is liable for breach of trust is not one which is judged with hindsight (in *Nestle v National Westminster Bank plc [1994] 1 All ER 118, CA*, Staughton LJ commented at page 133: '*The trustees' performance must not be judged with hindsight: after the event, even a fool is wise, as a poet said nearly 3000 years ago.*'), once found liable, the measure of his liability is assessed as at the date of judgment, with the full benefit of hindsight (*Target Holdings v Redferns [1996] AC 421, HL*).

More difficult is the situation where a loss, though apparent, cannot easily be quantified. This is perhaps more often the case in connection with breach of duty of care (see CHAPTER 6), where it may be impossible to say what the trustee *should* have done if he had fulfilled his duty. It may, on the facts, be possible to show that the trustees should not have sold a particular investment in breach of a direction not to do so, in which case they may be ordered to repurchase the investment in question.

However, where a trustee has invested in unauthorised investments, it might appear difficult – despite being able to show the precise act which he ought *not* to have done – to show what he should have done. See, for example, *Nestle v National Westminster Bank plc [1994] 1 All ER 118, CA* (per Dillon LJ at page 126): '*The starting point must, in my judgment, be that, as [the beneficiary] is claiming compensation, the onus is on her to prove that she has suffered loss. In some cases, it is sufficient to prove loss of a chance because in such cases . . . the outcome, if the plaintiff had not lost the chance, can never be proved . . ..*' This problem is dealt with by ordering an account to be drawn up (see CHAPTER 3). On the preparation of the account, every transaction in breach of trust is deleted (and every transaction in breach of fiduciary duty is surcharged for the amount of the loss – see CHAPTER 6). So, for example, the purchase of unauthorised derivatives at £100,000 is simply deleted from the account, leaving the trustee to make good that £100,000. To reflect the loss to the trust fund in not having the use of those funds since the date of the breach, interest is applied (see paragraph 5.18 below). In calculating what interest is appropriate to reflect the use that might have been made of the funds, had they not been applied in breach of trust, some assistance may be derived from the use of indices showing what other trustees and private investment managers had achieved over the same period (such as the APCIMS index, prepared by the Association of Private Client Investment Managers), and by the further pronouncement in *Nestle* (at page 140) that, in calculating loss, the court is entitled to presume that a prudent trustee would have made the most profitable use of the trust fund (approving *Guerin v The Queen [1984] 2 SCR 335 (can SC)*).

The quantum of the trustees' liability for breach of trust is not reduced by the concepts of causation, foreseeability or remoteness (see, for example, *Bartlett* and *Nestle*). They are strictly liable for the whole loss, no matter how unexpectedly or unforeseeably it has arisen, or how lacking in bad faith the trustee was (*Clough v Bond (1838) 3 Myl & Cr 490, HC*). In *Royal Brunei Airlines Sdn Bhd v Philip Tan Kok Ming [1995] 2 AC 378, PC*, Lord Nicholls said (at page 390): '*So far as the trustee himself is concerned the legal analysis is straightforward. Honesty or lack of honesty is not the test for his liability. He is obliged to comply with the terms of the trust. His liability is strict. If he departs from the trust terms he is liable unless excused by a provision in the trust instrument or relieved by the court.*'

The concept of 'strict liability' was explained in *Target Holdings v Redferns*, where it was held that the duty of the trustees is to restore the trust fund to the position it would have been in, but for the breach of trust. This was also the approach in *Bartlett and others v Barclays Bank Trust Co Ltd (no 2) [1980] 1 Ch*

515, where it was said that: '*the obligation of a trustee who is held liable for breach of trust is fundamentally different from the obligation of a contractual or tortious wrongdoer. The trustee's obligation is to restore to the trust estate the assets of which he has deprived it.*'

As noted above, the most usual way of arriving at a figure for the trustees' liability is for the court to order an account (see CHAPTER 3). After deducting from the account all those transactions which constituted breaches of trust, the overall quantum of the loss is made clear. This figure is repayable to the trust fund by the trustees, with interest.

No set-off

5.17 In calculating the total loss repayable, trustees are not usually permitted to set off a gain made on one breach of trust against a loss made on another. A limited exception to this is found in the circumstances of *Bartlett v Barclays Bank Trust Co Ltd [1980] 1 Ch 515*, where Brightman J held (at page 538): '*The general rule . . . is that where a trustee is liable in respect of distinct breaches of trust, one of which has resulted in a loss and the other in a gain, he is not entitled to set off the gain against the loss, unless they arise in the same transaction . . . [But] the Guildford development stemmed from exactly the same policy and . . . exemplified the same folly as the Old Bailey project . . . I think it would be unjust to deprive the bank of this element of salvage in the course of assessing the cost of the shipwreck.*' Set-off is therefore permitted only if the profitable and loss-making breaches arose from the same event, or the same policy.

Interest

5.18 Interest is chargeable on the damages payable to the trust fund by trustees in breach of trust. When calculating the interest due, the court's aim is to restore the trust fund to the position it should have been in, but for the breach, and to compensate it for not having had the use of those funds during the period in which they were lost to the trust.

Interest used to be charged at the fixed rate of 4%, but, as Brightman J said in *Bartlett v Barclays Bank Trust Co Ltd (Numbers 1 and 2) [1980] 1 Ch 515 (at page 546–7)*: '*In former days a trustee was as a rule charged only with interest of 4 per cent. unless there were special circumstances . . . I think it would be unrealistic for a court of equity to abide by the modest rate of interest which was current in the stable times of our forefathers*'. The court therefore has a broad discretion when determining a rate of interest to be applied, and:

- the court looks at the use that *would* have been made of the funds if the breach had not occurred (*Re Barclay [1899] 1 Ch 674*), if there is clear evidence of the likely alternative use;

- failing specific evidence as to likely use, the court is entitled to presume that a prudent trustee would have made the most profitable use of the trust fund (*Guerin v The Queen [1984] 2 SCR 335, (Can SC)*, and *Nestle*);

- as noted above, the court may refer to indices showing what other trustees and private investment managers had achieved over the same period (eg the APCIMS index); and

- the court may order interest at compound rates, particularly if the trustees had a duty to invest at compound rates and failed (*Jones v Foxall (1852) 15 Beav 388*).

It is questionable whether the trustees' motive or blameworthiness (if any) in committing the breach of trust is relevant to the calculation of interest. Under English law, interest is not imposed by way of punishment, but the cases tend to show that a higher rate of interest is imposed to reflect factors such as the use that could have been made of the funds, or (if they have been applied for the trustee's own benefit) the use that he in fact derived from them. In the Australian case of *Re Dawson [1966] 2 NSWLR 211*, for example, the judge imposed a high rate of interest precisely to reflect the fact that the breach was deliberate.

However, in *Armitage v Nurse [1998] Ch 241, CA*, Millett LJ acknowledged that some deliberate breaches of trust are nonetheless well-intentioned (at page 251): '*By consciously acting beyond their powers* (*as, for example, by making an investment which they know to be unauthorised*) *the trustees may deliberately commit a breach of trust; but if they do so in good faith and in the honest belief that they are acting in the interest of the beneficiaries their conduct is not fraudulent. Hence the remark famously attributed to Selwyn LJ by Sir Nathaniel Lindley MR in the course of argument in Perrins v Bellamy [1899] 1 Ch 797, 798: "My old master, the late Selwyn LJ, used to say, 'the main duty of a trustee is to commit judicious breaches of trust"*'. If the risk they take goes wrong, the trustees are of course liable to make good the loss, and if their honesty does not relieve them from liability (see CHAPTER 12), then at least the interest rate chosen may reflect their good intentions.

Remedies/relief available

5.19 As well as the payment of damages and interest, it may be appropriate to consider whether other remedies are available to the beneficiaries. Notably:

- breach of trust may be grounds for removal of one or more of the trustees (see CHAPTER 8);

- imposition of a receiver may be of assistance if the breaches have resulted in wide-scale disorder of the trust's affairs (see CHAPTER 9);

- injunctive relief may be available to prevent an anticipated breach, or to prevent further dealings in breach of trust; and

- either or both of the beneficiaries and the trustees may seek directions as to the future conduct of the administration of the trust (see CHAPTER 11).

Procedure

5.20 If the beneficiaries know of the particular breach or breaches that they wish to attack, then the appropriate procedure is that in CPR Part 7, the details of which are discussed in CHAPTER 2 and APPENDIX 2.

In some cases, it may be that the beneficiaries do not know of a specific breach, or are uncertain whether the circumstances indicate a breach or not – such as, for example, where they are aware of losses but without being aware of their cause – and in such cases, it may be appropriate to start by bringing a claim for account under CPR Part 8, as discussed in CHAPTER 3. The account, once completed, may reveal losses which have resulted from breaches of trust, and the beneficiaries can then apply for leave to amend their claim for account to one for repayment of the sums due, or may commence a separate claim to recover the sums shown on the account as lost. The CPR Part 8 procedure is discussed more fully in CHAPTERS 2 and 3 and APPENDIX 1.

Parties

5.21 All the trustees should be made defendants to the claim, which may be brought by any beneficiary (no matter how remote his interest). Not all the beneficiaries need be parties, however, and the court can give guidance as to which beneficiaries should be joined to the proceedings if it is not apparent from the circumstances (see generally in CHAPTER 2). Those beneficiaries who are not claimants should be joined as defendants.

Costs

5.22 The costs of an action for breach of trust will, as is normal for hostile litigation, almost invariably follow the event:

- a trustee found liable for breach of trust will therefore most likely be ordered to pay the costs of all parties from his own pocket;
- where a trustee has been successful in defending a claim for breach of trust, costs will normally be ordered against the claimant beneficiaries personally, and not out of the trust fund;
- however, where a trustee is party to any proceedings, to the extent he cannot recover his costs from any other party, he is usually entitled to take his costs on an indemnity basis out of the trust fund (CPR 48.4). If the trustee is successful in his defence, but is unable to recover his costs from the unsuccessful claimant, therefore, he may be able to take them from the trust fund in any event.

A difficulty may arise where the trustees have incurred more than one set of costs, as may be the necessary case, for example, where one trustee had a conflict of interests or was able to admit facts that the others were unable to admit, such that they were unable to mount a joint defence. In *Gaunt v Taylor (1840) 2 Beav 346*, Lord Langdale MR said (at page 347): '*Whether they are entitled to two sets of costs depends on the circumstances of each particular case. If a party creates unnecessary expense it is just that he should be deprived of his costs; and if several trustees unnecessarily sever their defences, it is right that one set of costs only should be allowed: the question always is, whether there was reasonable ground for them to sever.*' (See also *Re Spurling's Will Trusts, Philpot v Philpot and others [1966] 1 All ER 745*).

It may, as considered in previous chapters (see particularly CHAPTERS 2 and 3) be desirable or appropriate for the beneficiaries to apply for a pre-emptive costs order, if the trustees lack (or are unwilling to exercise) a power to pay their costs out of the trust fund. It is perhaps less likely, in the ordinary course, that the beneficiaries should be permitted to take their costs out of the trust fund when trustees are not (pending the outcome of the case) but the court has a broad discretion. If there is clear *prima facie* evidence of a breach of trust, it may be just to allow the beneficiaries their costs in pursuing it, since:

- in cases where the breach is alleged against some only of the trustees, and not others, the 'innocent' trustees ought themselves to take action to pursue the wrongdoers;
- in other cases, the right to pursue all the trustees for breach of trust can be regarded as an asset of the trust;

and in either case, it may be open to the beneficiaries to apply for a *Beddoe* order (see CHAPTER 11) for leave to pursue the wrongdoers (ie to recover an asset of the trust) on behalf of, and at the expense of, the trust fund.

Other effects of breach of trust

5.23 Where the trustees are liable for breach of trust which they are liable to make good, the right of reimbursement is lost to the extent of that loss (*Re Knott (1887), Re Evans (1887)*). The trustees may not, until they have made good that loss, exercise their right of reimbursement in respect of any outgoings, including their own trustee fees. But seemingly, therefore, set-off does apply here – in other words, the sums which would otherwise be properly due to the trustees are deducted from their overall indebtedness to the trust.

Chapter 6

Claims for breaches of duties of care

Introduction

6.1 In addition to the duties referred to elsewhere in this book, trustees are required to act with reasonable care and skill in administering their trusts. This chapter considers the nature and scope of such duties, and the way in which beneficiaries may bring claims against trustees for breach of those duties.

The statutory duty of care

6.2 Section 1(1) of the Trustee Act 2000 imposes upon trustees (a term which is not defined in the Act, leaving open the question of whether it includes all trustees, including bare trustees, and constructive or resulting trustees) a duty to exercise such care and skill as is reasonable in the circumstances.

Prior to the Trustee Act 2000, trustees were subject to an equitable duty of care which required them to act with the care and skill to be expected from the 'ordinary prudent man of business' (as to which see below, at 6.10–6.11). There was certainly no evident intention on the part of Parliament to exclude or restrict that pre-existing equitable duty when enacting the newer statutory duty, as the Trustee Act 2000 makes no reference whatsoever to that pre-existing duty. In the Law Commission report which preceded the Trustee Act 2000 (and which included as an appendix the draft bill that was to become the Trustee Act 2000) it is stated that the newer statutory duty of care is not intended to '*detract in any way from the fundamental common law duties*' of the trustee. Therefore, it would seem that the equitable duty of care and skill which existed prior to the Trustee Act 2000 continues to exist, and the interaction (and potential overlap) between the two duties of care is an issue that must be considered when bringing a claim against a trustee who has acted without the requisite degree of care, and is discussed below at 6.12 *et seq*.

The standard of care

6.3 The statutory duty of care requires trustees to exercise such care and skill as is reasonable in the circumstances (section 1(1)), and therefore the question of whether a trustee has acted with the requisite degree of care and skill will be one of fact and degree in each case. However, section 1(1) provides that it is necessary in all cases to have particular regard to the factors set out in sections 1(1)(a) and (b). Section 1(1)(a) refers to '. . . *any special knowledge or experience that [the trustee] has or holds himself out as having*'. Therefore when determining what standard of performance it is 'reasonable' to expect from any given trustee, the court must judge the trustee in light of:

(a) any 'special knowledge' or expertise the trustee does in fact have (whether he has claimed to have it or not); and

(b) any 'special knowledge or experience' that he claims to have (whether or not he actually has that special knowledge or experience).

Furthermore, where the trustee acts in the course of a business or profession (for example, a trust company, or a solicitor who ordinarily acts as trustee), section 1(1)(b) is relevant to the standard of care expected from that trustee. Section 1(1)(b) refers to '. . . *any special knowledge or experience that it is reasonable to expect of a person acting in the course of that kind of business or profession*'. Therefore the duty of care of a professional trustee is ascertained by reference to both the factors relating to that particular trustee (under section 1(1)(a)) and factors relating to other professional trustees (section 1(1)(b)). The intended effect of this distinction is presumably to require a higher standard of care from a professional trustee than from other trustees.

Trustees' conduct is to be judged on the basis of the facts that exist at the time the conduct took place, and also on the basis of the facts and circumstances which the trustees knew about (or ought to have known about) at that time (see *Nestlé v National Westminster Bank plc (No.2) [1994] 1 All ER 118, CA per Staughton LJ*). This case was, of course, decided in relation to the equitable duty of care and prior to the introduction of the statutory duty of care. However, it is considered that the principle enunciated therein is of equal application to the statutory duty.

Application of the duty

6.4 The statutory duty of care does not automatically apply to every act (or omission) of trustees in that capacity. It applies subject to the following limitations:

(a) Trustees are subject to the duty only in the instances listed in Schedule 1 to the Trustee Act 2000, namely:

- investment matters (see 6.5);
- acquisition of land (see 6.6);
- dealing with agents, nominees and custodians (see 6.7)
- compounding liabilities (see 6.9)
- insuring trust assets (see 6.8); and

- dealing with reversionary interests, valuation and audit (see 6.9)

(b) as the Act came into force on 1 February 2001 (SI 2001/49 Trustee Act 2000, (Commencement) Order 2001), the duty of care applies from that date, but to all trusts whether created before or after that date; and

(c) the application of the duty is subject to the possibility of exclusion by the trust instrument. Paragraph 7 of Schedule 1 to the Act states that the duty does not apply if or in so far as it appears from the trust instrument that it is not meant to apply. In post-February 2001 trust deeds, the relevant exclusion will usually take the form of a clause stating 'the statutory duty of care imposed by section 1 of the Trustee Act 2000 shall not apply to this trust'. However, there is nothing in the wording of paragraph 7 which suggests that the statutory duty of care has to be referred to explicitly in order to be excluded, therefore wider exclusion clauses (and perhaps most importantly for trustees of pre-February 2000 trusts) clauses in trust deeds pre-dating commencement of the Trustee Act may be worded in such a way that the Court will hold that there has been a valid exclusion of the statutory duty of care.

It is, however, notable that paragraph 7 Schedule 1 refers only to the exclusion of the *duty* and not *liability* for breach of the duty. However, given that as a matter of general law it is permissible for the settlor to seek to limit the liability of the trustees by the inclusion in a trust deed of a clause which excludes all liability for breach of trust, except where the breach has been committed dishonestly (see *Armitage v Nurse [1998] Ch. 241 CA per Millett LJ*) it is possible for the liability for breach of the statutory duty of care to be excluded, rather than the duty itself. (See CHAPTER 12 for exclusion clauses generally). Whilst the practical consequence for beneficiaries of either form of exclusion is usually likely to be the same (in that a claim by the beneficiary will be precluded), in cases where the liability for breach has been excluded, but the duty remains, it may be possible to obtain a remedy which does not seek to compensate the beneficiaries for loss, but which compels the trustees to carry out their duty (for example, an injunction to stop the trustees acting in a way which constitutes a breach of the duty of care).

Investment

6.5 Paragraph 1 of Schedule 1 to the Act applies the duty of care to the exercise by trustees of the 'general power of investment' (conferred by section 3 of the Trustee Act 2000) or of any other power of investment. In addition, the duty applies in relation to the duties relating to the exercise of investment powers imposed by sections 4 and 5 of the Trustee Act 2000, namely;

- the duty to consider the standard investment criteria (section 4); and
- the duty to take proper investment advice (section 5).

A common situation in which beneficiaries may seek to pursue a claim for breach of the statutory duty of care is where the trust investments have performed badly, perhaps falling substantially in value. It may be argued that the trustees have failed to act with the requisite degree of care and skill in:

- choosing the trust investments (ie choosing ones which perform badly); or
- failing to sell the investments at the appropriate time before their value fell,

or perhaps both. It should be noted that the fact that investments fall in value does not necessarily mean that the trustees have acted in breach of their duty of care (as noted in CHAPTER 3 for example). Therefore, in order for a beneficiary to succeed in establishing a breach of duty of care it must be shown not simply that the trustees have obtained a poor return on investment, but that the poor return is a result of a failure on their part to take reasonable care in managing the investments.

Further, trustees are entitled to be judged on the basis of the performance of the entirety of the portfolio of investments (*Nestlé v National Westminster Bank plc (No.2) [2000] WTLR 795 per Hoffman J*). It is not therefore open to a beneficiary to take the benefit of investments that perform well and seek to pursue a claim in respect of those which do not, unless it can be shown that the investments which have performed badly are unauthorised, for example, by being outside the scope of the trustees' investment powers. In practice, this is unlikely to be possible in many cases, given the width of the investment power conferred by section 3 of the Trustee Act 2000. Therefore, where trustees

- ensure that they seek proper advice in relation to the trust investments (in accordance with their duty under section 5),
- have due regard to the standard investment criteria of suitability and diversification (section 4); and
- review the investment portfolio regularly (taking action when the review process causes them to consider it necessary to do so),

they are unlikely to be found liable for breach of the statutory duty of care.

It should be noted that the statutory duty of care does not apply to a failure by the trustees to invest the trust fund, but only to the care and skill they employ '*. . . when exercising. . .*' their investment powers (paragraph 1, Schedule 1). A failure to invest the trust fund is ordinarily a breach of trust, and a trustee will be called to account for his failure to invest accordingly (*Stafford v Fiddon (1857) 23 Beav 386*) (and see generally CHAPTER 5 on breaches of trust).

It is not clear whether a failure by trustees to take advice in relation to the investment of the trust fund (as they are ordinarily required to do by section 5 of the Trustee Act 2000) constitutes a breach of the statutory duty of care, or whether it renders the investment made in the absence of advice unauthorised (see also CHAPTER 5). The significance of the distinction is that if it is the former, the investment in question must be considered as part of the entire portfolio of investments as mentioned above, but if the investment is an unauthorised investment the beneficiaries may have the account falsified so as to treat the investment as never having been made (see CHAPTER 5 as to breach of trust, and CHAPTER 3 as to claims for account). There is no direct authority on this point, although the Scottish case of *Martin v City of Edinburgh District Council 1988 SCLR 90* suggests that the correct analysis is that the investment is rendered unauthorised.

Powers in relation to land

6.6 By virtue of the Trustee Act 2000, Schedule 1, paragraph 2 the statutory duty of care applies to trustees when:

- exercising the power to acquire land conferred by section 8 of the Trustee Act 2000;
- exercising any other power to acquire land; and
- when exercising any other power in relation to land acquired in exercise of a power to acquire land.

In many cases, land will have been purchased as an investment by trustees, but the separate application of the duty of care to the acquisition and management of land mirrors the way in which the substantive powers to acquire and manage land are conferred by the Act. Further, land may not only have been purchased by trustees for the purposes of investment. It may be purchased for the purposes of providing a home for a beneficiary, for any other purpose (section 8(1)(b) and (c)).

The fact that a separate power to acquire land as an investment is conferred means that trustees are not subject to the general investment duties imposed by sections 4 and 5 of the Trustee Act 2000. However, in order to discharge their duty of care, trustees should take similar steps to diversify any portfolio of investment land, and to take appropriate advice in relation to the appropriateness of purchasing any particular land and its value. A failure to do so is likely to be considered by the Court to be a breach of the statutory duty of care. Similarly, where trustees purchase land for purposes other than investment (such as occupation by a beneficiary) they should again ensure that they obtain professional advice as to the state and value of the property from a suitably qualified surveyor.

Agents, nominees and custodians

6.7 By virtue of paragraph 3 of Schedule 2 of the Trustee Act 2000, trustees are subject to the statutory duty of care when:

- entering into arrangements under which a person is to act as their agent under section 11 of the Trustee Act 2000;
- entering into arrangements under which a person is appointed as their nominee under section 16 of the Trustee Act 2000;

- entering into arrangements under which a person is appointed as a custodian of trust assets under section 17 or section 18 of the Trustee Act 2000;
- entering into arrangements under which a person is appointed to act as their agent, nominee or custodian under any power, however conferred; and
- carrying out their duty to review the activities of their agent, nominee or custodian under section 22 of the Trustee Act 2000.

'Entering into arrangements' is defined by paragraph 3(2) which provides that the term includes, in particular:

(a) selecting the person who is to act;

(b) determining the terms on which he is to act, and

(c) if the appointment involves the delegation of asset management functions (as defined by section 15(5)), the preparation of a policy statement.

As regards the selection of agents, nominees and custodians, trustees must ensure that they take reasonable steps to make the best choice in the interests of the trust. This will inevitably involve the trustees considering the available candidates in terms of their expertise, suitability, and the terms of business on which they are prepared to be engaged (including their proposed fees), and making the decision that they consider to be the best for the beneficiaries. A failure to do so may be a breach of the statutory duty of care.

It should be noted that, where trustees seek to use the statutory power conferred by section 11 of the Trustee Act 2000 to appoint an agent, they are specifically prohibited from appointing a beneficiary as their agent (section 12). Similarly, when appointing a nominee or custodian, trustees are required to appoint a person within the categories set out in section 19. If the trustees appoint a person whom they are not authorised to appoint, they are likely to commit a breach of the statutory duty of care. It does not render the appointment void, due to section 24, which provides that if the trustees exceed their delegation powers under the Act, the appointment is not invalidated.

When agreeing the terms upon which an agent, nominee or custodian is to act, trustees are constrained by the terms of section 14 (in relation to agents) and section 20 (in relation to nominees and custodians), which provide that certain terms may not be included unless it is 'reasonably necessary' for the trustees to agree to them. The terms are:

- a term permitting the agent custodian or nominee to appoint a substitute;
- a term restricting the liability of the agent, nominee or custodian (or nay substitute) to the trustees or any beneficiary;
- a term permitting the agent, nominee or custodian to act in circumstances capable of giving rise to a conflict of interest.

If a trustee consents to the inclusion of any of the above terms without it being 'reasonably necessary' to do so, it would again seem to follow that a breach of the duty of care will have been committed. Whether the inclusion of a term in the agreement between the trustees is reasonably necessary or not is a question of fact and degree to be determined in each case. Relevant factors are the standard terms and conditions offered by the various agents, nominees and custodians who are suitable for appointment (for example, if all of the relevant candidates for appointment would insist on such terms, they are likely to be 'reasonably necessary') and the levels of fees to be charged (it may be justifiable to accept restrictions of liability where the fees charged for services are lower). Provided the trustees consider issues such as this, they are in a position to make a decision as to the need to agree to the inclusion of such types of term.

There is an element of uncertainty over whether the requirements imposed by section 14 of the Trustee Act 2000 apply in relation to the appointment of agents, nominees and custodians under an express power as opposed to the powers conferred by the Trustee Act 2000. It is the writer's view that these restrictions apply in relation to *all* delegation on the basis that the restrictions are wide in scope and are not restricted to the exercise of the statutory powers. This must be contrasted from the restriction on the appointment of a beneficiary under section 12, which expressly relates only to the use of the power conferred by section 11.

Where asset management functions (as defined by section 15(5)) are delegated by trustees, they are required to produce a written policy statement which provides guidance to the agent, and which is formulated with a view to ensuring that the delegated functions will be exercised in the best interests of the trust (section 15(3)). In addition, trustees must ensure that the agreement under which the agent is appointed is either evidenced or made in writing, and contains a term securing compliance with the policy statement prepared by the trustees. Clearly, failure to do these things may be argued by a beneficiary to constitute breaches of the statutory duty of care.

The duty of care applies in relation to trustees' duties to review the activities of their agents, nominees and custodians (imposed by section 22 of the Trustee Act 2000). Whilst the wording of paragraph 3(1)(e) of Schedule 1 of the Trustee Act 2000 (which applies the duty of care to review activities) is expressed in the present continuous tense ('*. . . when carrying out his duties under section 22. . .*'), it would seem absurd if trustees were to be liable for a breach of the statutory duty of care if they carry out their review duties negligently, but not if they fail to carry them out at all. Therefore, it is considered that a failure to carry out the review duties constitutes a breach of the duty of care. When trustees do carry out a review process, it must deal with the arrangements under which the agent, nominee or custodian is appointed. The trustees must also consider whether, in light of the actions of the agent, nominee or custodian, there is any need for them to use any power of intervention they may have retained. If they do consider that there is such a need, they must use the power. Again, failure to do any of these things is likely to constitute a breach of the statutory duty of care.

Where asset management functions have been delegated by the trustees, the review process includes the additional aspect of consideration of matters relating to the policy statement prepared in compliance with section 15. Trustees are required to assess whether the policy statement is being complied with, to consider whether it is necessary to amend or replace the policy statement, and if they consider that there is such a need, to do so. Where trustees fail to do these things, it is possible for the beneficiaries to argue that they have committed a breach of the duty of care.

Insurance

6.8 Trustees are subject to the statutory duty of care '. . . *when insuring* . . .' trust property (paragraph 5, Schedule 1). However, having suggested in its consultation paper that trustees should be subject to a duty to insure trust property, the Law Commission did not include such a duty in the Trustee Act 2000, due to the responses to the consultation proposal. Therefore, a trustee is not liable for breach of the statutory duty of care if he fails to insure trust property. Even if there is no breach of the statutory duty of care by failing to insure trust property, however, it may well be that such a failure constitutes a breach of the equitable duty of care and skill (see below, at 6.10–6.11). The trustee may, of course, be liable for breach of the statutory duty of care if, having taken the decision to insure trust property, he does so without proper care and skill (for example, by failing to take out adequate cover, or neglecting to pay a premium, thereby causing the insurance policy to lapse).

Compounding of liabilities, reversionary interests, valuations and audit

6.9 In addition to the circumstances set out above, the statutory duty of care applies in relation to the following:

- the exercise of powers under section 15 of the Trustee Act 1925 (power to compound liabilities), or any corresponding power, however conferred (Trustee Act 2000, Sch 1, para 4);
- the exercise of powers under section 22(1) or (3) of the Trustee Act 1925 (valuations) or any corresponding power, however conferred.

The equitable duty of care

The standard of care

6.10 Prior to the introduction of the statutory duty of care, the only duty of care owed by a trustee to the beneficiaries was the equitable duty to '. . . *take such care as an ordinary prudent man would take if he were minded to make an* *investment for the benefit of other people for whom he felt morally bound to provide. . .* ' (see *Learoyd v Whiteley (1886) 33 Ch D 347*). However, while the general standard of care is as stated in the previous sentence, higher standards of care are expected from those trustees who are remunerated for their services (see *Re Waterman's Will Trusts [1952] 2 All ER 1054 per Harman J*), and trust corporations (see *Bartlett v Barclays Bank Trust Co. Ltd [1980] Ch 515 per Brightman J*). The basis for a higher standard of care being expected from a paid trustee would appear to be that it is the natural *quid pro quo* of receiving remuneration: a person who is paid for a service is to be expected to perform it to a higher standard than one who acts gratuitously. The justification for the higher standard required of a trust corporation is that provided by Brightman J in *Bartlett*, namely '. . . *a higher duty of care is plainly due from someone like a trust corporation which carries on a specialised business of trust management. A trust corporation holds itself out in its advertising literature as being above ordinary mortals*'.

Whilst the higher standards of care owed by paid or corporate trustees appears to resemble the standard of care under section 1(1) of the Trustee Act 2000, in ascertaining the precise standard of care owed by particular classes of trustee by reference to the knowledge and experience that a member of a particular class of trustee is to be expected to have (indeed the Law Commission described the statutory duty as '*no more than a codification*' of the equitable duty of care) there is a fundamental distinction that must be drawn. In none of the cases by which the equitable duty has been developed has the Court made reference to the actual or professed knowledge and expertise of the particular trustee. Rather, as can be seen from the *dicta* of Brightman J in *Bartlett* trustees are subject to higher standard of care by reason of the type of trustee they are (ie a trust corporation). Whether this distinction will prove to be material in any case remains to be seen.

Trustees are not insurers (see *Bartlett v Barclays Bank Trust Co Ltd [1980] Ch 515 per Brightman J* and *In re Godfrey (1883) 23 Ch D 483 per Bacon V-C*) and are not liable for mere 'errors of judgement' (*Re: Chapman [1896] 2 Ch 763 per Lindley LJ*) and that is reflected to some degree in the formulation of the test set out above, which requires the trustee merely to act with the care and skill of the ordinary prudent man, rather than to achieve excellence.

As noted above at 6.3, trustees' conduct is to be judged in light of the facts that they knew (or ought to have known) at the time of the conduct in question, rather than by using hindsight.

The application of the duty

6.11 Unlike the statutory duty of care, the equitable duty is of general application and therefore has a wider application than the prescribed situations in which the statutory duty is relevant. Whereas the wording of Schedule 1 to the Trustee Act 2000 (in the present continuous tense) gives rise to the question of whether the statutory duty of care can apply to omissions as well as acts, there is no doubt in the case of the equitable duty, which does apply to omissions. It is perhaps because of the recognition of the width of the scope of application of the equitable duty that the statutory duty does not purport to amend, alter or replace the equitable duty in any way. Indeed the Trustee Act 2000 itself makes no reference to the equitable duty of care whatsoever. The Law Commission Report which contained the Bill that ultimately became the Trustee Act 2000 did state that the intention behind the introduction of the statutory duty of care was to codify the equitable duty (*Law Com number 260, paragraph 2.35*). However, as can be seen from the foregoing paragraphs, that end was not achieved.

Even where the statutory duty of care applies, it is not stated to override or replace the equitable duty. Therefore, it is arguable that the two duties now co-exist, and that a beneficiary aggrieved with a trustee's actions can (where the alleged conduct is within the scope of Schedule 1 to the Trustee Act 2000) bring a claim for breach of either (or both) of the duties of care. However, it is considered that, if presented with such a dual claim, the Courts would, in all likelihood, find that where the statutory duty applies, it replaces the equitable duty. Until such a decision has been made (and the precise scope of the statutory duty has been defined), it would seem wise for aggrieved beneficiaries to bring their claims in the alternative, and allege breaches of both duties.

One situation in which the equitable duty of care and skill is the clear basis for a claim is where loss is suffered by reason of a trustee's failure to insure trust assets. As discussed above (at 6.8) the statutory duty of care does not apply to a failure to insure, as the Law Commission was clear that it was not their intention that the Trustee Act 2000 should impose a duty to insure trust property, as no such duty existed in equity. Whilst there is old authority which supports that proposition (see *Bailey v Gould (1840) 4 Y & C Ex 221; Fry v Fry (1859) 28 LJ Ch 593* and *Re McEachern (1911) 103 LT 900*) it does seem questionable whether, in modern times, it can be said that a trustee who fails to insure trust property has acted with the care and skill to be expected of the prudent man. Therefore, it is certainly arguable that, in such circumstances, a beneficiary has the ability to pursue a claim for breach of the equitable duty of care, and that the older authorities should not be followed.

Bringing claims for breaches of duties of care

Form of claim

6.12 Where the trust is continuing, it seems clear that it is appropriate for a beneficiary to bring a claim for an account on the footing of wilful default, in which the default alleged is that of a breach of the relevant duty of care (see *Target Holdings Ltd v Redferns [1996] AC 421 HL at 434 per Lord Browne-Wilkinson* for a discussion of the appropriate remedy for breach of trust). For commentary concerning the procedural aspects of a claim for an account on the footing of wilful default see generally in CHAPTER 3. If the beneficiary succeeds in his claim, the account will be surcharged with the amount that the trustee has lost through his breach of duty and the trustee will be required to account on the basis that the losses caused by his breach of duty had not been sustained.

It is conceivable that a beneficiary may wish to bring a claim for breach of duty of care at some point after the trust has been distributed and terminated. As the limitation period for a claim to be brought by a beneficiary in respect of an innocent breach of trust is six years (Limitation Act 1980, section 21(3)). In such circumstances, the appropriate claim will not be for an account, but for a payment of equitable compensation (again, see *Target Holdings Ltd v Redferns [1996] AC 421 HL at 434 per Lord Browne-Wilkinson*), which in certain respects resembles (but is by no means the same thing as) an award of common law damages.

The introduction of the statutory duty of care has brought a degree of uncertainty in relation to the form of claim that should be brought. The statutory duty of care may be categorised as an equitable duty which forms part of the trustee's normal duties to his beneficiaries, in a similar way to the equitable duty which preceded it (and still survives, see 6.11 ANTE). The normal remedy for breach of such a duty is, as discussed above, an account or alternatively equitable compensation. However, nowhere in the Trustee Act 2000 does it say that the statutory duty of care is such a duty and that breach of it is to be remedied in that way. The absence of any provision setting out the nature of the duty, or giving any indication as to the way in which a claim in respect of breach is to be brought, means that it remains arguable (but perhaps no better than arguable) that a breach of the statutory duty of care gives rise to a cause of action in tort for breach of statutory duty. In order for a statutory duty to be actionable in tort, it is necessary to show that:

(a) the statutory duty was intended to give rise to a private law right (see: *X v Bedfordshire County Council [1995] 3 All ER 353, HL*) and

(b) a breach of the duty gives rise to damage generally remediable in tort.

The first of those two conditions is clearly satisfied. Whilst the Trustee Act 2000 does not state explicitly that the duty is owed by a trustee to a beneficiary, and is intended to provide the beneficiary with a means of obtaining redress against the trustee if the trustee fails to act with the requisite degree of care and skill, that is clearly the purpose of the duty. There is no criminal sanction for breach of the duty, nor does the Act provide for any regulatory structure. The presence of either of these factors might indicate that it was not intended to confer any private law rights. Their absence lends support to the contrary view.

The more difficult question to answer is that of whether the damage sustained by a beneficiary when a trustee commits a breach of the statutory duty of care is of a type generally remediable in tort. The loss sustained by a beneficiary where a trustee breaches the statutory duty of care will almost invariably be pure economic loss. The courts have developed strict rules concerning the recoverability of pure economic loss, and the position is that such loss is irrecoverable unless it arises out of certain specific circumstances. It is not clear whether the courts will view the breach of a statutory duty of care by a trustee as being such a set of circumstances, and when claims for breach of the statutory duty of care come before the courts in due course, it is one of the questions that will have to be answered.

The writer's view is that the statutory duty of care is not actionable in tort, but rather as an equitable duty. However, until guidance is provided by the courts on this issue, it may be prudent to plead such claims on both alternative bases.

Procedure

6.13 A claim for breach of duty of care is most appropriately brought in the form of a Part 7 claim as, in most cases, it will involve substantial disputes of fact. This is consistent with the pre-CPR position, whereby claims for breach of trust were required to be brought by writ (see 3.13). However, the wording of the CPR gives rise to a degree of ambiguity in this regard. CPR Part 64.2 provides that the provisions in relation to the administration of estates and trusts applies to claims '*for the court to determine . . . any question arising in . . . the execution of a trust*' and it is arguable that where a beneficiary asserts that the trustee has failed to act with the requisite degree of care and skill, the claim is for the determination of the issue of whether the trustee has executed the trust properly (ie in accordance with his duties) and therefore a claim within the scope of Part 64.2. The practical consequence of a claim being within the scope of Part 64.2 is that it must be commenced by way of a Part 8 claim form (CPR Part 64.3). The Part 8 procedure is, it is submitted, wholly unsuitable for a matter which is factually contentious, as such matters require particularised factual allegations to be made by the claimant and responded to by the defendant. The Part 7 procedure is the appropriate way for this to be done. Therefore if the claimant were to commence a claim using the Part 8 procedure, the court would use its power (under CPR Part 8 Practice Direction, paragraph 1.6) to direct that the claim proceed as if the Part 8 procedure had not been used.

It would therefore seem sensible for a beneficiary bringing proceedings that are likely to give rise to substantial dispute of fact to commence his claim using Part 7. Even if it is successfully argued by the defendant trustee that the wording of Part 64 requires the use of a Part 8 claim form (which must be doubted) the court is unlikely to penalise a claimant for commencing under Part 7 in circumstances where the court itself would have ordered that the matter proceed as if commenced as a Part 7 claim.

It may, however, be the case that a claim for breach of duty of care will arise in a Part 8 claim. For example, trustees may apply to the court for an order approving their accounts, and discharging them as trustees upon distribution in accordance with the accounts produced. Such a claim is clearly one that has to be brought by way of the Part 8 procedure. In opposition to the claim, a beneficiary may take issue with the accounts on the basis that the amounts contained within them would be greater had it not been for breach of duty of care by the trustees. In such circumstances the matters will be raised by the beneficiary in his evidence in response to the Part 8 claim. However, where the issues give rise to substantial disputes of fact the court is likely to direct the matter to proceed as a Part 7 claim. For further discussion of CPR, see CHAPTER 2, and also APPENDICES 1 and 2.

Quantum

6.14 In awarding compensation for breach of the trustee's duty of care (whether through the mechanism of an account or by a payment of equitable compensation), the court seeks to put the beneficiaries into the position they would have been in had the breach of duty not been committed (*Target Holdings v Redferns [1996] AC 421 HL per Lord Browne-Wilkinson*). In principle, where a breach of trust is committed and the beneficiaries are to be compensated through the means of an account or equitable compensation, the common law rules of causation, foreseeability and remoteness do not apply. For example, if a trustee purchases an unauthorised investment, and there are some unforeseen (and unforeseeable) circumstances whereby the value of that investment falls drastically, the beneficiary is entitled to call the trustee to account on the basis that the unauthorised investment had never been purchased, or, if appropriate, to recover equitable compensation in the full amount of the loss. That approach is unquestionably appropriate where the trustee has acted in a manner which is unauthorised. The comments of Lord Browne-Wilkinson in *Target Holdings v Redferns [1996] AC 421 HL* would appear to lend support to the proposition that a similar approach is appropriate in relation to losses arising out of the breach of equitable duties of care and skill, and that as a consequence a 'but for' test of causation applies to losses arising from a breach of trust (including a breach of the trustee's duty of care). Under this test, it is necessary for a beneficiary to show merely that 'but for' the conduct of the trustee, the loss in question would not have arisen. Under the common law tests applicable in relation to the tort of negligence, the test is that of whether the act complained of is the operative cause of the loss.

This distinction is perhaps more easily exemplified than explained. Consider the situation where a trustee invests some of the trust fund in shares in a single company. Let it be assumed that, for reasons which should have been obvious to the trustee, the company in question was a poor investment prospect, and that by investing in it, the trustee has committed a breach of his duty of care. The company ultimately goes into liquidation (and as a consequence the part of the trust fund invested in it is lost), *not* as a result of the factors which indicated that it was a poor investment, but as a result of fraud that was not (and could not have been) known to the trustee. If the trustee had not committed a breach of duty and invested in the shares, the trust would not have lost the money, and on a 'but for' causation test, the trustee is liable for the total amount lost. However, the purchase of the shares was not the operative cause of the loss: the fraud was, and if the 'operative cause' test is applied, then it is at least arguable that the trustee is not liable for the loss, as the cause of the loss was not his breach of duty but the fraudulent conduct of others.

A modern view that has been expressed is that the measure of compensation to which a beneficiary is entitled where the trustee has acted in a manner which is authorised (and therefore within the scope of his powers) but negligent, is similar to the amount recoverable at common law in respect of negligence, and therefore subject to notions of causation, foreseeability and remoteness (see the discussion in *Underhill & Hayton* (sixteenth edition) at pages 852–7). Some support for this proposition may be found in the comments of Millett LJ in *Bristol and West Building Society v Mothew [1998] Ch 1, CA*. The basis for this proposition would appear to be the simple notion that the equitable duty of care is essentially indistinguishable from its common law counterpart in terms of its nature and content, and therefore it would be sensible for equity to follow the law in terms of the recoverability of losses. However, this modern view has not been adopted by the courts in the context of a breach of duty of care by a trustee, and in the recent case of *Hulbert v Avens [2003] EWHC 76 (Ch)* [2003] 12 LS Gaz R 30 the court relied heavily on the analysis of Lord Browne-Wilkinson in *Target Holdings v Redferns*, although it is notable that *Bristol and West Building Society v Mothew* appears not to have been cited in *Hulbert v Avens*.

Whilst there is clearly a move in academic (and some judicial) circles to assimilate the measures of loss for a breach of duty of care by a trustee and negligence at common law, the position remains (for the time being) that the test as set out in *Target Holdings v Redferns* by Lord Browne-Wilkinson is good law, and therefore a trustee will be liable on the basis of a 'but for' causation test for the loss which flows from his breach of duty. As there have not yet been any reported cases in which beneficiaries have recovered compensation from trustees for breach of the statutory duty of care imposed by the Trustee Act 2000, the possibility of the courts using the new duty to further this process of assimilation cannot be ruled out, but until the courts are called upon to decide such cases, the position remains uncertain.

Alternative remedies

6.15 Financial compensation is the usual remedy for breach of duty of care by a trustee, but it is by no means the only remedy that a beneficiary may seek. It may be that whilst the trustee has committed (or continues to commit) a breach of duty, no financial loss has (at the date the beneficiary wishes to take action) been sustained. In such circumstances there would seem to be no bar to a beneficiary bringing a claim for an injunction to compel the trustee to act in accordance with his duty of care (by selling particular investments, for example) or prohibiting the trustee from breaching it (by selling a trust asset at an undervalue, for example). For a general discussion on the procedure for obtaining an injunction, see [REF].

A beneficiary is entitled to apply to the court for removal of a trustee on the basis of the trustee's misconduct (see CHAPTER 8). In principle, a breach or number of breaches of duty of care could form the basis of such a claim. However, unless the breaches are numerous and/or serious, it is unlikely that the court would accede to an application for removal.

As an alternative to removal of the trustee a beneficiary may seek an administration order (pursuant to CPR Part 64) so that the trustees are unable to take steps in the administration of the trust without the permission of the court. Whilst an order for administration used to be a popular remedy for beneficiaries to seek, the modern practice is to treat it as a last resort, and paragraph 3.1 of the Practice Direction to CPR Part 64 now states this practice as '*The court will only make an administration order if it considers that the issues between the parties cannot properly be resolved in any other way*'. It is unlikely that issues arising from breaches of duties of care will be incapable of resolution in any other manner, and therefore such orders are extremely rare in this context. For a commentary on the procedure for obtaining an administration order, see CHAPTER 11.

Costs

6.16 Costs of claims for breach of duty of care will usually follow the event, ie the successful party will have his costs paid by the unsuccessful party. Therefore, if the beneficiary succeeds in establishing a breach of duty he will usually recover his costs from the defaulting trustee. Likewise, a trustee who successfully defends such a claim will usually have his costs paid by the beneficiary.

A claim for breach of duty of care is a hostile dispute between beneficiary and trustee and is therefore not an appropriate case for an order to be made prospectively sanctioning the payment of a party's costs from the trust fund.

Chapter 7

Challenges to an exercise of discretion

Introduction

7.1 The exercise by trustees of their dispositive discretions is frequently uncontentious. Sometimes, however, it is the cause of discontentment or disappointment among the beneficiaries, who may feel that they have received less than they had hoped to receive, or indeed who may have received nothing at all.

It is, of course, the trustees in whom the settlor has vested the power of deciding – in their absolute discretion – which among the class of discretionary objects, or the class of objects of a power of appointment, should receive capital and/or income, and in what shares. The position of discretionary objects, and that of objects of a mere power, differ substantially, but they have this in common: that it is not open to them as of right to attack the trustees' (or appointor's) decision, and substitute for it one which they regard as more acceptable.

On the whole, objects of a mere power have no right to challenge the exercise (or non-exercise) of the discretion at all. If an appointor fails to exercise a power of appointment among a particular class, the objects of it cannot complain. A 'mere power' is perhaps a relative rarity in modern times, giving power without fiduciary obligation. For example, 'to pay the income to my wife for life and thereafter to hold the trust fund as to both income and capital for such of my children, and in such shares, as my wife may by deed or by will appoint, and in default thereof in equal shares for my children living at my wife's death'. The settlor's wife is under no obligation to exercise her power of appointment at all. A power for an appointor to add beneficiaries to a discretionary trust is perhaps a more common example of a non-fiduciary 'mere' power in common use nowadays – even if the power is exercisable only in relation to a limited description of persons (such as the spouses of beneficiaries, or the children of beneficiaries), they cannot generally challenge its exercise in favour of some members of the class, or its non-exercise. If a beneficiary entitled in default of appointment can show that its exercise was a fraud on the power, the court can overturn the exercise (*McPhail v Doulton [1971] AC 424, HL*), but *quaere* whether the disappointed other objects can ever do so.

Conversely, discretionary beneficiaries are always entitled to know that, in reaching the decision that they have made, the trustees have acted honestly, impartially, and consistently with the purposes for which the discretion has been conferred upon them. That is not the same as saying that they are always entitled to know the reasons motivating the trustees. They have a right to be satisfied, however, that the process the trustees have followed in reaching their decision was fair, even if the decision itself was not 'fair' in the eyes of the disappointed beneficiaries.

This chapter, therefore, considers the trustees' obligations in exercising their discretions, and the grounds upon which an exercise of a discretion can be challenged.

The trustees' duties concerning discretions

7.2 Many of the fiduciary duties which attach to all the trustees' functions as such are also relevant in relation to the exercise of their dispositive discretions. There are some additional special obligations with regard to dispositive discretions, as follows:

- a duty to consider, from time to time, whether to exercise the discretion;
- a duty to consider the range of potential beneficiaries among whom the discretion could be exercised;
- a duty to consider the purposes for which the discretion has been conferred on them.

Both in considering whether or not to exercise the discretion, and if they then decide to exercise it to any extent, they must do so in accordance with the following general fiduciary duties:

- the duty to act unanimously;
- the duty to act honestly;
- the duty to act impartially;
- the duty to avoid personal benefit (including the avoidance of personal motives); and
- the duty to take professional advice where appropriate.

It is a central tenet of the law surrounding trustees' discretions that they are not obliged to give reasons for the exercise of their discretion. In *In re Londonderry's Settlement, Peat v Walsh [1965] Ch 918, CA*, Harman LJ said (at pages 928–9): '*trustees exercising a discretionary power are not bound to disclose to their beneficiaries the reasons actuating them in coming to a decision . . . To this there is added a rider, namely, that if trustees do give reasons, their soundness can be considered by the court.*' The judges in *Londonderry* thought that the need for this rule arose out of the fact that the trustees' job would be impossible – and they would be much more reluctant to take on the trusteeship – if every decision was open to challenge by the beneficiaries or review by the court.

It is, therefore, only with reluctance and on clear grounds that the court will interfere in the trustees' exercises of their discretion, or require them to explain the reasons for their decision at all. Another judge in *Londonderry*, Salmon LJ, said (at pages 936–7): '*so long as the trustees exercise [their discretionary power] . . . bona fide with no improper motive, their exercise of the power cannot be challenged in the courts, and their reasons for acting as they did are, accordingly, immaterial*'.

Failure to exercise discretion

General

7.3 Trustees who have a discretion must, as noted, consider from time to time whether they should exercise it, and must consider the full range of beneficiaries among whom they have power to exercise it.

It follows, therefore, that if the trustees are unsure whether they have a discretion, or have doubts as to its extent or meaning, they should take legal advice as to the nature of the discretion, and must then periodically consider whether to exercise it. What they cannot do, either through ignorance of the discretion or through idleness or some other reason, is to put the discretion to one side and fail to consider it at all. The beneficiaries have a right to be considered, which gives them an important power to oblige the trustees actively to consider whether or not to exercise their discretion at all. In *Gartside v IRC [1968] AC 553, HL*, Lord Denning MR said (at pages 566–7): '*Every person who is an object of a discretionary trust has a right in respect of the trust fund . . . He has a right to be considered by the trustees as eligible for a payment to be made to him . . . This right is more than a mere hope or expectation.*' Evidence of such a default might be difficult to find, but beneficiaries who are aware of a discretion, and believe the trustees may be failing to consider it, can call upon them to do so.

In order to consider meaningfully whether or not to exercise the discretion, the trustees must be aware of the extent of the class of beneficiaries. Megarry VC said, in *Re Hay's Settlement Trusts [1981] 3 All ER 786* (at page 791), approving *McPhail v Doulton [1971] AC 424, HL*, that a trustee: '*must make such survey of the range of objects or possible beneficiaries as will enable him to carry out his fiduciary duty. He must find out the permissible area of selection and then consider responsibly, in individual cases, whether a contemplated beneficiary was within the power and whether, in relation to the possible claimants, a particular grant was appropriate*'. The class may be very broad, but it is sufficiently certain if the trustees can say, in relation to any person, whether he is or is not a member of the class (*McPhail v Doulton [1971] AC 424, HL*), and the trustees do not need to be able to draw up a list of the individual beneficiaries (*Re Baden's Deed Trusts (No 2) [1973] Ch 9, CA*).

In many trusts, it is suggested, the class will be limited to a relatively small number of persons who are readily identifiable, such as the spouse, children and grandchildren of the settlor (and perhaps their spouses). The smaller the class, the more it is reasonable to expect that the trustees will have some basic knowledge as to the circumstances of each beneficiary, such that they can consider in context the question of whether or not a distribution is appropriate (or necessary). In larger classes, it is appropriate for the trustees simply to know the extent of the class, to be alive to the possibility of appointing in favour of any of them, and to consider any particular requests or wishes which come to their attention. In either case, they must not improperly overlook the breadth of the class by considering only certain persons within it.

Fettering discretion

7.4 The trustees must not fetter their discretion by refusing to consider exercising it (*Re Gibson's Settlement Trusts [1981] Ch 179*). For example, if trustees decided that, during the life of the settlor and his wife, they would make no distributions to the other beneficiaries (or none unless called upon by the settlor to do so), this would be an improper fetter (and might raise some broader questions about whether the trust was a sham). Similarly, if, having made a distribution to one beneficiary, they have made up their minds that they would not entertain the idea of any more distributions to him, they are fettering their duty to consider him.

Another form of (unacceptable) fetter is where the trustees commit themselves to a long-term policy irrespective of the changes that might in future affect its appropriateness. They should instead structure a shorter-term policy, which they can reconsider and (as appropriate) renew, amend or abandon.

Unanimity

7.5 The trustees must, in whatever deliberations they conduct, and in whatever decision they reach, act unanimously. Beneficiaries are entitled to demand the individual attention of each of the trustees to their duties (*Swale v Swale (1856) 22 Beav 584*). A trustee must not stand aside, allowing the decisions to be made by his fellow trustees, and going along with them for the sake of the appearance of unanimity. It is not improper for him to consider the arguments put to him by the other trustees and to decide that he agrees with them, but total non-participation or 'rubber-stamping' is inconsistent with his trusteeship. In one case, the trustees simply signed everything put before them by the dominant settlor, without ever considering their discretion independently, and the documents signed by them were therefore void (*Turner v Turner [1984] Ch 100*).

Particularly in the context of trusts with individual trustees, it is not unusual for some of them to harbour strong feelings either for or against distributions in favour of certain beneficiaries. A trustee who, in these circumstances, allows himself to be led by the strongly held views of one or more of the other trustees is acting improperly (as they are, if their views amount to bias – see paragraph 7.7 below).

Beneficiary's right to challenge

7.6 The sanction for a beneficiary who believes that the trustees (or any of them) are failing to consider exercising their discretion, and who has failed to persuade them to consider exercising it, is to apply to the court in accordance with the procedure set out in paragraph 7.15 *et seq* below. Similarly, if he believes that a document or decision has not been reached by the unanimous and considered resolution of the trustees, he may apply to have it declared void. The reliefs available to him will vary, and are discussed in paragraph 7.14 below.

Partiality and bias

7.7 Trustees must, in exercising their discretions, act impartially. This implies no right for beneficiaries to be treated equally in terms of the distributions that are made. It simply means that the trustees must not improperly prefer one class of beneficiaries, or one beneficiary, over another or others, and must take an even-handed approach to all of them. In *Edge and others v Pensions Ombudsman and another [2000] Ch 602, CA*, Chadwick LJ said (at page 627): '*Properly understood, the so-called duty to act impartially . . . is no more than the ordinary duty which the law imposes on a person who is entrusted with the exercise of a discretionary power: that he exercises the power for the purpose for which it is given, giving proper consideration to the matters which are relevant and excluding from consideration matters which are not relevant. If [trustees] do that, they cannot be criticised if they reach a decision which appears to prefer the claims of one interest . . . over others. The preference will be the result of a proper exercise of the discretionary power.*'

Personal dislike may prejudice a trustee against a beneficiary, meaning that the trustee does not exercise his discretion properly (or at all). In *Klug v Klug [1918] 2 Ch 67*, for example, one trustee had fallen out with a beneficiary. Her co-trustee wished to make a distribution to the beneficiary, but she would not agree, and the court ordered payment to be made. In fact, it was held that she had refused to exercise her discretion at all, but the position would have been the same if she had tried to distribute the fund to another beneficiary, motivated by the same bias.

Similarly, personal preference is objectionable if it is used as a reason to make distributions to one beneficiary rather than another or others. In one case, a trustee wished to induce a beneficiary (for what she perceived as the beneficiary's own benefit) to take up residence in France, but the appointment designed to enable him to do so was – no matter how well-intentioned – improper (*D'Abbadie v Bizoin (1871) 5 IR Eq 205*).

The beneficiaries affected by an exercise of discretion which they consider to have been motivated by bias or partiality can apply to the court to have it declared void, as not, in fact, being an exercise of the discretion at all (see paragraph 7.14 below).

Improper motives and fraud on the power

7.8 If a trustee exercises a power otherwise than for the purposes for which it was intended, that exercise may be declared void (*Vatcher v Paull [1915] AC 372*). Such an exercise is often called a 'fraud on the power'. This may simply mean that the trustee has considered issues which are irrelevant to the trust in deciding whether or not to make a distribution (such as trying to persuade a beneficiary to move to France, as in paragraph 7.7 above). It may amount to '*a deliberate defeating of what the [settlor] authorised and intended*' (*Re Dick [1953] Ch 343, CA*). A fraud on the power is not necessarily dishonest, but is fraudulent in the sense that it is improper or wrongful because of the motives held by the trustees when exercising their discretion.

Three general indicia of a fraud on the power can be drawn from *Re Crawshay [1948] Ch 123* and *Re Dick*:

- the trustees have made an appointment intended to benefit someone who is not an object of the power, or for a purpose extraneous to the power;
- the trustees' motive must exist at the date of the appointment, even if it is later abandoned, or its object can never be carried into effect; and
- there is no need to establish agreement or even knowledge on the part of the appointee as to the trustees' motive, whatever it might be.

Not every personal benefit by a trustee is a fraud on the power. It is clear that a distribution was improper where the trustee's motive was to benefit himself and he was *not* an object of the discretion (as in *Re Cohen 1911] 1 Ch 37*, where he appointed in favour of his wife so that she could pay some of his debts). However, where he is among the class of potential objects, it is not improper to make a distribution to himself, provided that the process of reaching that decision was properly conducted.

If he harbours an improper motive, however, it is irrelevant whether the trustee intends to benefit himself, or some other person (*Vatcher v Paull [1915] AC 372*). It is equally objectionable if the trustee uses his power to divert funds away from a beneficiary of whom he disapproves.

Similarly, if a trustee purports to make judgments as to what a beneficiary's moral duties might be, or where his betterment lies, that is improper and may be a fraud on the power. In *In re Clore's Settlement Trusts [1966] 1 WLR 955*, it was held that '*it was not open to the trustees to pay away the beneficiary's prospective capital over his head or against his will in discharge of what they consider to be his moral obligations*'. This was also the view in *D'Abbadie v*

Bizoin (1871) 5 IR Eq 205, where the trustee wished to induce the beneficiary for the beneficiary's own benefit to take up residence in France, and in *Re Esteem Settlement, Grupo Torras SA v Al Sabah (No 6) [2001] WTLR 641*, where the trustees were not entitled to conclude that there was benefit to a beneficiary in reducing his debts, where the amount was insufficient to clear them.

Bad faith and dishonesty

7.9 It is often the case that a trustee will simply misdirect himself as to the extent of the beneficial class, or the purposes of the power vested in him, in a way which is entirely innocent or well-meaning (albeit negligent). However, if his conduct is to some degree conscious or deliberate, he may be guilty of bad faith, or may be acting dishonestly. Honesty, in this context, has the objective meaning explained by Millett LJ in *Armitage v Nurse [1998] Ch 241, CA*, namely that the trustee has not acted as an honest person would do in the circumstances.

Many of the examples of bias and improper motives cited in the foregoing paragraphs could be examples of bad faith, or in some cases even dishonesty. Such exercises are always liable to be declared ineffective by the court, but the distinction is that dishonesty or bad faith may also prove to be grounds for removal of the trustee, or for charging the costs of the application to him personally.

Perversity, capriciousness and irrelevance to the settlor's expectations

7.10 *Re Manisty's Settlement [1974] Ch 17* suggests that the beneficiaries are entitled to know that the trustees' discretions would not be exercised in a manner which was perverse, capricious or irrelevant to any sensible expectation of the settlor. Whilst it is perhaps unlikely that such a situation might arise, a suspicion on the part of the beneficiaries that the trustees had acted in such a manner in reaching a particular decision would certainly be grounds for challenging it. It may, in practice, be difficult for the beneficiaries to know what the settlor's expectations were, in the absence of sight of the letter of wishes (as to which, see CHAPTER 4).

Failure to consider the consequences

7.11 It is equally relevant that, when considering an exercise of their discretion, the trustees should think through the potential consequences of their decision. If they do not do so, then the action they take may be set aside. This is the inverse of the 'improper motive' objection, in a sense – it is a results-based objection, not a motive-based objection.

The rationale for this is set out in the case of *Re Hastings-Bass [1975] Ch 25* and is generally called 'the *Hastings-Bass* principle':

- if what the trustee has achieved is unauthorised by the power or discretion vested in him; or
- if it is clear that he *would not* have acted as he did, had he
  - (a) not taken into account considerations which he should not have taken into account; or
  - (b) not failed to take into account considerations which he ought to have taken into account,

then the court may set aside the exercise of the power or discretion. The emphasis in the preceding paragraph is added, but it is the touchstone of the remedy – the applicant (be they beneficiaries or trustees) must be able to demonstrate that the trustee *would not* have acted as he did if he had informed himself as to the potential consequences (such as in *Turner v Turner [1984] Ch 100*, where the trustees merely signed the documents without considering them at all).

The rule has been re-stated and affirmed in a string of cases, such as *Mettoy Pension Trustees v Evans [1990] 1 WLR 1587*. However, it has limitations:

- if the trustees *might* not have acted in the same way had they appreciated the consequences, that is likely to be insufficient (*Stannard v Fisons Pension Trust Ltd [1991] PLR 2, 25 CA*);
- if the trustees failed to act, but would have acted, had they appreciated the consequences of not acting, the court cannot order something to be treated as having occurred which in fact did not occur (*Breadner v Granville-Grossman [2000] WTLR 829*);
- the remedy may be refused if, on the facts, the step complained of was so far in the past, and so many steps have been taken in reliance on its validity, that it would be practically impossible to set the arrangements aside (*Breadner v Granville-Grossman [2000] WTLR 829*); and
- there is widespread commentary that the principle has been taken too far, and that '*it cannot be right that whenever trustees do something which they later regret and think they ought not to have done, they can say that they never did it in the first place*' (per Park J in *Granville-Grossman, approved by AMP (UK) plc v Barker (2000) ITELR 414*).

But, as the law currently stands, if the *Hastings-Bass* criteria are met, then it is irrelevant what the consequence was which is sought to be avoided. The effect may be to rebalance the relative positions of beneficiaries who were wrongly overlooked. There is no (current) objection on public policy grounds if the result of the exercise being found ineffective is that tax which otherwise would have been payable is not now payable (*Green v Cobham [2000] WTLR 1101, Abacus Trust Company (Isle of Man) Ltd v NSPCC [2001] WTLR 953*). (Thus far, the Inland Revenue has declined to be joined to such proceedings so as to be bound by them, however.) The reasoning is that the relevant decision was a nullity from the beginning, as never having been validly reached. It has never taken effect at all, and is thus not 'voidable' but void.

The court's limited role

7.12 In *In re Londonderry's Settlement, Peat v Walsh [1965] Ch 918, CA*, Harman LJ said: '*nobody could be called upon to accept a trusteeship involving the exercise of a discretion unless, in the absence of bad faith, he were not liable to have his motives or his reasons called in question either by the beneficiaries or by the court*'. As noted throughout this chapter, therefore, the courts are generally reluctant to interfere in the exercise by trustees of discretions vested in them.

Certainly, the courts have no power to intervene so as to overturn an exercise which, though honestly reached, is not one which the court (or the beneficiaries) would have reached themselves. As noted at the beginning of this chapter, beneficiaries are occasionally disappointed, but the court's role is not to cure their disappointment in the absence of some more substantial reason. In *Gisborne v Gisborne (1877) 2 App Case 300, HL*, this was explained further, so that, '*where the trustees are willing to exercise the discretion . . . and where the Court allows and declares their right to exercise that discretion, [the Court cannot] go on and express any opinion as to whether the exercise of the discretion by the trustees is . . . wise or unwise*'.

The court's involvement therefore tends to be restricted only to the following situations:

- to confirm the availability of a discretion, and its extent;
- to monitor the trustees' willingness to exercise the discretion (eg *Re Manisty's Settlement [1974] Ch 17*, per Templeman J at page 25: '*The court cannot insist on any particular consideration being given by the trustees to the exercise of the power . . . If a person within the ambit of the power is aware of its existence he can require the trustees to consider exercising the power and in particular to consider a request on his part for the power to be exercise in his favour. The trustees must consider this request, and if they decline to do so or can be proved to have omitted to do so, then the aggrieved person may apply to the court which may remove the trustees and appoint others in their place*');
- to prevent an improper exercise of the discretion (see, for example, *Tempest v Lord Camoys (1882) 21 Ch D 571, CA*, Jessel MR said that: '*it is settled law that when a [settlor] has given a pure discretion to trustees*

as to the exercise of a power, the Court does not enforce the exercise of the power against the wish of the trustees, but it does prevent them from exercising it improperly');

- to ensure that relevant factors were considered, and irrelevant factors excluded ('*there is no doubt that the trustees' decision can be set aside if it can be shown that they failed to consider matters which were relevant, or took into account matters which were irrelevant*' (*Edge and others v Pensions Ombudsman and another [2000] Ch 602, CA,* at page 633)); and

- to review actions for bad faith and dishonesty, and other improper matters (see, for example, *Re Manisty's Settlement [1974] Ch 17,* per Templeman J at page 26: '*The court may also be persuaded to intervene if the trustees act capriciously, that is to say, act for reasons . . . irrational, perverse or irrelevant to any sensible expectation of the settlor*').

The four-fold jurisdiction over discretions

7.13 When it is necessary or desirable for the court to become involved in matters surrounding the exercise of the trustees' discretions, the four methods in which the court can properly assist the trustees and beneficiaries were summarised by Hart J in *Public Trustee v Cooper and others [2001] WTLR 901*:

- where the issue is whether a proposed course of action is within the trustees' powers;

- where the issue is whether the proposed course of action, on which the trustees have in principle decided to embark, is a proper exercise of their powers. The trustees may wish to obtain the court's approval as to the proposed action, for example because the decision is 'particularly momentous';

- where there is a true surrender of discretion by the trustees to the court. The court will only accept a surrender of discretion for good reasons, such as where the trustees are deadlocked but honest (so the deadlock cannot be resolved by removing one recalcitrant trustee) or where the trustees are disabled as a result of conflict of interest; and

- where the trustees have actually taken action, and that action is attacked as being either outside their powers or an improper exercise of their powers.

The first three of these situations tend to be applications made by the trustees, either at their own instance, or perhaps because of overt expressions of concern by the beneficiaries, for the court's directions, as a pre-emptive solution to what might otherwise become a true dispute, as in the fourth quoted situation. However, it is also possible that one or more of the beneficiaries could apply in either of the first two of the above situations for the court's directions to be given, for the benefit of both the trustees and the beneficiaries.

In cases where the fourth type of situation arises, the proceedings are likely to be hostile. Given the court's repeatedly expressed reluctance to review past exercises of trustees' discretion, it is unsurprising that '*those who seek to challenge a decision of [the trustees] should bear the ordinary burden of establishing that the decision has been reached improperly. That is not, of course, to say that the Court . . . cannot draw appropriate inferences from any failure of the trustees to give an explanation when an explanation is called for; nor that the court . . . should not examine critically any explanation that is given. It is, however, to reject the submission that . . . it [is] for the trustees to justify . . . the decision that they took*' (*Edge and others v Pensions Ombudsman and another [2000] Ch 602, CA*, at page 633). The beneficiaries must therefore provide evidence for their belief that the exercise of the discretion should be impugned.

Orders which may be made

7.14 The orders made by the court will vary from case to case:

- if called upon to consider a proposed exercise of a discretion, the court will give directions as to whether the power may properly be exercised;
- if the matter relates to an improper non-exercise of discretion, the court may direct the trustees to consider exercising it;
- if the court believes a past exercise of discretion was tainted by one of the reasons discussed in this chapter, it will declare that the exercise was void from the outset and may then:
  - (i) require nothing further of the trustees (where an exercise of discretion has been overturned entirely); or
  - (ii) require the trustees to consider the discretion anew (or replace the trustees with others who can be relied upon to do so properly);
- only in rare circumstances will the court exercise the discretions in place of the trustees, such as:
  - (i) where the trustees have surrendered their discretion to the court for a proper reason (as in the third case in *Public Trustee v Cooper*, above); or
  - (ii) where the trustees have unreasonably refused to exercise their discretion, and the court believes that they are unlikely to reconsider (*Klug v Klug [1918] 2 Ch 67*);
- in some cases, the court may (either on the application of a beneficiary, or of its own motion) remove a trustee who it believes would be unlikely to exercise the discretions honestly and properly in future (see CHAPTER 8).

Procedure

7.15 Clearly, the nature of the proceedings will vary depending on whether they concern substantial factual issues or not. The following paragraphs consider some options which may be available.

Pre-emptive directions

7.16 Pre-emptive reviews of the trustees' proposed exercise of their discretions – either by the trustees or by the beneficiaries – should be brought under CPR Part 8 (as required by CPR Part 64 and the Practice Directions to that Part). The claim form should contain the following matters:

- a statement that Part 8 applies to the claim;
- a statement that the remedy sought is the directions of the court relating to the proposed exercise of a discretion, or that the trustees seek to surrender their discretion to the court;
- a summary of the legal basis on which that remedy is sought (ie that the trustees are trustees of the settlement and are in doubt as to the existence, extent or appropriate application of their discretion, plus any special features such as conflicts of interest or concerns expressed by the beneficiaries); and
- a statement of truth.

The claimant trustees (or beneficiary) must file and serve a witness statement at the same time as the claim form, containing any evidence on which they (or he) wish to rely. In so doing, it is appropriate to bring to the court's attention all the factors which might be relevant to the decision, whether these advance or harm the course proposed by the trustees. If there are relevant facts which are not brought to the attention of the court, the directions may be flawed, and the trustees will not be protected against beneficiaries' attacks on the exercise of discretion, since it will have been entered into pursuant to directions obtained on a false or incomplete premise.

The matter will then follow the procedure and timetable set out in CHAPTER 2 and APPENDIX 1 until trial.

Challenges of a past exercise

7.17 Challenges of past exercises of a discretion are most likely to be hostile proceedings involving argument as to fact, and perhaps alleging breach of trust. They should in most cases be brought using the procedure in CPR Part 7. As discussed in CHAPTER 2, the Part 7 claim form must contain:

- a statement that Part 7 applies to the claim;
- a description of the remedy sought;
- a summary of the legal basis on which that remedy is sought (unless the claim form is accompanied by a full statement of the claim, which it should be wherever possible); and
- a statement of truth.

The claimant beneficiary must serve the particulars of claim within 14 days of, if not at the same time as, the claim form.

The trustees must *either* serve their defence within 14 days of the service of the claimant's particulars of claim, *or* acknowledge service within those 14 days. If they acknowledge service, they will have an automatic extension of a further 14 days to serve their defence. The parties can agree further extensions of up to 28 additional days for the service of the defence (ie a maximum of 56 days after service of the particulars of claim), but must notify the court in writing of their agreement. The defence should deal with each allegation separately, giving reasons and facts in support of any denials. Usually, matters not specifically denied will be deemed to be admitted, but in the case of an exercise of discretion, where the trustees are not required to provide reasons for the exercise, they need only make it clear in the defence that they have an alternative explanation, do not admit the claimant's allegations, and wish to put the claimant to proof on the allegations.

The procedure and timetable for CPR Part 7 after service of the acknowledgments of service or defences and up to the date of trial are set out in CHAPTER 2 and APPENDIX 2.

Parties

7.18 Since an exercise of the trustees' discretion requires unanimity, it follows that any question over a past or future exercise of the discretion is also one which requires all of them to participate, whether the claim is brought under CPR Part 8 or Part 7. Indeed, CPR Part 64 expressly requires that any proceedings under that Part should involve all the trustees, but makes it clear that the particular circumstances of a case will determine which beneficiaries, and/or which other persons, should be parties to the proceedings. In the context of an application for directions (clearly governed by Part 64), the trustees may, if they are unclear as to whether all or only some of the beneficiaries should be parties, wish to ask the court's guidance as to which other parties should be joined.

Both for a directions application and for contentious proceedings, it is likely to be appropriate that all the beneficiaries who are affected by the exercise of discretion in issue should be joined (or representatives for classes of beneficiaries affected in similar ways), so as to afford all of them the opportunity to state their views.

Costs

7.19 The costs of the parties in directions applications and contentious proceedings are dealt with entirely differently:

- in directions applications, it is usually the case that all costs are ordered to be paid out of the trust fund. In the unlikely event that the trustees are found to have acted unreasonably in bringing the directions application, some or all of their costs may be disallowed (*Tod v Barton [2002] EWHC 265 (Ch), (2002) 4 ITELR 715*);

- in contentious proceedings, the costs usually follow the event, as an unsuccessful beneficiary should not be able to charge the costs of his challenge to the trust fund, and unsuccessful trustees should bear the costs of putting right that which their improper exercise of discretion has brought about; and
- in either case, the beneficiaries may apply for a pre-emptive costs order if the trustees have no power to discharge their costs on an ongoing basis, or have such power but decline to use it (see CHAPTER 3). Particularly where a beneficiary is complaining that the trustees have not exercised their discretion in his favour, he may be unable to afford to launch a challenge on the exercise of the relevant discretion. However, although the court has broad discretion in relation to pre-emptive costs orders, it will usually wish to consider whether the proposed proceedings are in the interests of the trust as a whole when deciding whether or not the trust fund should pay for them. Unlike the situation where there is an alleged breach of trust (see CHAPTER 5), it is perhaps rarely likely to be the case that a hostile claim attacking a past exercise of the trustees' discretion will be for the benefit of the trust fund.

Chapter 8

Proceedings for removal of trustees

Introduction

8.1 There may be many reasons, not all of them hostile, why the beneficiaries might seek the removal of one or more of the trustees of the trust, and a number of different statutory and equitable means by which they can achieve removal in appropriate circumstances. In this chapter, the following matters are discussed:

- the different methods by which removal can be achieved; and
- the grounds which are sufficient in each case to justify removal.

Removal by the beneficiaries themselves

8.2 The general rule is that beneficiaries are not able to force a trustee to retire, nor to remove him from office.

Where all the beneficiaries are of full age and capacity, and between them absolutely entitled under the trust, they can jointly act to bring the trust to an end (*Saunders v Vautier (1841) 4 Beav 115)*. However, this is normally a 'take it or leave it' situation, whereby they have the right either to allow the trust to continue in accordance with its terms, or to bring it to an end. The *Saunders v Vautier* principle does not entitle them to have it both ways, by continuing the trust on their own terms (as to trusteeship or any other matter). They cannot, as a general rule, compel the existing trustees to retire in favour of other trustees of their choosing (*Re Brockbank [1948] Ch 206*).

Section 19 TOLATA

8.3 An exception to this general principle is found in section 19 of the Trusts of Land and Appointment of Trustees Act 1996 (TOLATA 1996). Under that section, unless it has been expressly excluded in the trust instrument (or, for pre–1997 trusts, by a later deed executed by the settlor), where all the beneficiaries are of full age and capacity, and together absolutely entitled, they can direct a trustee to retire, with or without replacement, provided that at least two individual trustees or a trust corporation remain as trustees. The procedure to be followed is this:

- the beneficiaries must give a joint written direction to the trustee(s) to retire (s19(2)(a));
- they must jointly make a written direction to all the trustees to use their power under section 36 of the Trustee Act 1925 to appoint the new trustee(s) specified in the direction (s19(2)(b));
- the trustee(s) directed to retire must enter into a deed of retirement, *provided that* arrangements have been made for the reasonable protection of any interests or rights of his or theirs under the trust, and at least two individuals or a trust corporation remain trustees; and
- if the retiring trustee is not to be replaced (there being sufficient trustees still in place), the continuing trustees must consent by deed to his retirement.

However, this power is only exercisable where the trust instrument does not name any person as having the right to appoint new trustees. In many cases, there may be provision for the settlor, protector or appointor to have the power of appointment of new trustees. The section 19 power will then not be available. It is also not unusual to find the statutory provision in section 36 of the Trustee Act 1925 to be re-stated in the deed, so that the deed makes express provision that the power of appointment of new trustees is to be vested in the trustees for the time being. It is suggested that, in cases where the section 36 provision is expressly repeated, the power of removal under section 19 will not be available to the beneficiaries.

The section 19 power lacks absolute certainty that removal can be achieved without litigation. This is because of the subjective element introduced to that section by implicitly requiring the trustee(s) to be removed to agree that 'reasonable arrangements' have been put in place regarding their rights under the trust. These 'rights' include any rights of remuneration and indemnity available to the trustees in accordance with the terms of the trust. If a trustee is not satisfied that suitable arrangements have been made – and this would also go to the identity of the new trustees, and their appropriateness as indemnitors to the retiring trustee – then the trustee to be removed may insist that the matter is referred to the court.

It is also unclear to what extent the section 19 power may be exercisable by discretionary beneficiaries. Are they 'beneficiaries' for the purposes of TOLATA 1996, where that term is defined (in section 22) as meaning 'any person who under the trust has an interest in property subject to the trust'? Seemingly, yes: *Gartside v IRC [1968] AC 553, HL*, is authority for the fact that a discretionary beneficiary has an interest in the trust, and all the beneficiaries are jointly interested in the property comprised in the trust. Lord Denning MR explained (at pages 566–7): '*Every person who is an object of a discretionary trust has a right in respect of the trust fund . . . He has a right to be considered by the trustees as eligible for a payment to be made to him . . . This right is more than a* mere hope or expectation . . . *It is an interest in the trust fund, though not to any defined part of it. But the group of discretionary objects, regarded as one unit, have an interest in the property as a whole: because all together they are the only persons who have any right to the beneficial enjoyment of the income.*' However, even if the entire class of beneficiaries is identifiable, in existence, and fulfils the usual criteria as to age and capacity, the specific terms of the trust may mean that section 19 cannot apply. For example, the existence of overriding powers of appointment, or default provisions in favour of charities to be selected by the trustees, would be inconsistent with the *Saunders v Vautier* principle which is the root of section 19.

Section 20 TOLATA

8.4 Section 20 of TOLATA 1996 contains a more limited power in cases where a trustee is incapable by reason of mental disorder (within the meaning of the Mental Health Act 1983) of exercising his functions as trustee. Provided that all the beneficiaries fulfil the criteria as to age and capacity, they may direct one of the persons specified in section 20(2) to replace the incapable trustee. The specified persons are the incapable person's attorney under an enduring power of attorney, a receiver appointed over his affairs, or 'a person authorised for the purpose by the authority having jurisdiction' (eg the Court of Protection). Under section 20(1)(b), this power is exercisable if there is 'no person entitled and willing and able' to appoint a replacement for the incapacitated trustee. Whether one or more persons are expressly identified in the trust instrument as having the power to appoint new trustees, or whether only the ordinary power exists under section 36 Trustee Act 1925 for co-trustees to remove one of their number who has become incapable, the section 20 power is available to the beneficiaries if the relevant persons do not take action.

Express terms of compromise

8.5 Finally in the context of the beneficiaries' powers to compel retirement, it is worth noting that the terms of settlement of any dispute may, of course, include a requirement for the trustees (or some of them) to retire. This may be a powerful negotiating tool for the beneficiaries. If the consideration for the trustees' agreement to retire is a forbearance to sue by the beneficiaries, and/or other trustees, such an agreement will be enforceable as a contract if they fail to retire as agreed.

Removal by the protector, appointor or co-trustees

Section 36 Trustee Act 1925

8.6 Section 36 of the Trustee Act 1925 gives power to the person to whom the trust deed gives the power of appointment of new trustees, failing whom the trustees for the time being of a trust, to appoint a new trustee at any time to replace a trustee who (inter alia):

- remains out of the United Kingdom for more than 12 months;
- refuses to act;
- is unfit to act;
- is incapable of acting; or
- is a minor.

It is, therefore, open to the beneficiaries (if any of those circumstances exist) to request the relevant persons to exercise the power of replacement of the trustee in question. This option is, however, clearly only available in limited circumstances, since (unlike section 19 TOLATA 1996) it requires there to be one of the specified objections to the continuation in office of the trustee.

Express power of removal

8.7 As noted in paragraph 8.3 above, where there is provision in the trust deed for specified persons to have the power of appointment of new trustees, section 19 TOLATA 1996 does not apply. *A fortiori*, therefore, it cannot apply if the trust deed gives power of removal to a specified person or persons (except possibly, which would seem unlikely, if such power was not coupled with a power to appoint new trustees in place of the removed trustees and no other persons were given such an express power). It is sometimes the case (particularly so for offshore discretionary trusts) that the trust deed contains power for an appointor or protector to remove trustees. The beneficiaries may consider appealing to such person to exercise their power of removal.

This power is of a fiduciary nature, in that it is exercisable only in the interests of the trust as a whole, and cannot be exercised for the personal motives or benefit of the appointor or protector, or for other improper reasons (*Von Knieriem v Bermuda Trust Company Limited, 'the Star Trusts case' (Supreme Court of Bermuda, 13 July, 1994)*). As it is a fiduciary power, the person in whom such power is vested ought periodically to review the performance of the trustees and consider whether it is in the interests of the trust that someone else be appointed in their place. Grounds on which removal might appear to be in the interests of the trust may include the following situations:

- refusal or unfitness to act by any of the trustees;
- if there is a dispute between the trustees and the beneficiaries;
- if there is a dispute among the trustees; or
- if it appears to the protector or appointor that the trustees are failing in their duties.

Caution, however, is needed where the dispute or failings are the subject matter of extant or pending litigation, or ought to be the subject matter of litigation. It is clearly in the interests of the trust that the trust property should be safeguarded and any trustees in breach should be prevented from committing further breaches. The broader interests of the trust will usually mean that peace is preferable to war. On the other hand, by removing a trustee from office in the midst of pending or actual proceedings, the Protector may cause additional expense and difficulty which is not in the interests of the trust. For example:

- it is likely that whatever proceedings are on foot or contemplated will continue, but that the new trustees will need to be joined to the proceedings, at additional expense and perhaps causing delay to the resolution of the proceedings; and
- in the context of conduct giving rise to a potential claim, it may not be the end of the matter if the wrongdoing trustee is removed. The new trustees may need to commence litigation and care must be taken to ensure that the removed trustee, through the operation of the removal clause (which often provides for a specified kind of release or indemnity), is not unintentionally protected to a greater degree than he would have been if he had remained in office and relied on the exculpation clause alone to protect him.

In cases of difficulty, therefore, the proper course is for the protector or appointor to apply to the court for directions as to whether he should exercise his powers or not, or to await the resolution of the litigation before exercising his powers.

Other options

8.8 It is, of course, open to the beneficiaries to appeal to the trustees themselves, or the protector or appointor, to exercise the relevant power, if they believe there are grounds on which they or he ought to consider exercising it. The trustees or other relevant person must take their views into account when considering whether or not to exercise the power. However, if the beneficiaries do not approach the person(s) having the power of removal, there is no general obligation for such person(s) to consult them before exercising the power.

If there is real doubt over the safety of the assets or the integrity of the trustee in office, a better option than seeking the removal of the trustee(s) may be for the beneficiaries to apply for injunctive relief against the wrongdoing trustee(s) and/or to apply for the trust assets to be paid into court (see CPR 64 PD and CPR 64B PD) or for a receiver to be appointed (see CHAPTER 9).

Removal by the court under statutory powers

8.9 The court has a general power under section 41 Trustee Act 1925 to appoint new trustees in addition to, or so as to replace, the existing trustees, or where there are none. The court may appoint new trustees in any case where it is expedient to do so, and inexpedient, difficult or impracticable to do so without the court's assistance. Section 41(2) contemplates bankruptcy (or insolvency of a company) and the making of an order under the Mental Health Act 1983 as being grounds for exercise of the power, but these grounds are expressed to be non-exhaustive.

Where there is a substantial dispute as to fact, the court may refuse to exercise its power under section 41 (*Re Henderson [1940] 1 Ch 764*). This is because the existence of a dispute as to whether or not there are grounds for removal means that the case for removal cannot plausibly be described as one of 'expediency'. A claim for removal of trustees should not be made under this section as part of a larger dispute, or on arguable grounds such as the breakdown of trust and confidence, therefore.

Cases where the court's statutory power could be used might include situations where the request for removal is coupled with, but dependent upon the outcome of, a claim for breach of trust. The beneficiaries might seek orders in relation to the alleged breach, and an order that, if a breach is shown to have occurred, the trustees be replaced. Since, by that stage of the proceedings, there will be no dispute as to fact, the power might appropriately be used. Alternatively, a separate claim for removal could be made following the finding of liability for one or more breaches.

Removal under the court's inherent jurisdiction

8.10 The court has an inherent jurisdiction 'to supervise, and if necessary to intervene in, the administration of trusts' (per Lord Walker in *Schmidt v Rosewood Trust Limited [2003] UKPC 26*). This includes, in appropriate cases, the power to remove a trustee without replacement, or to appoint a new trustee in substitution for a trustee, even against the wishes of the trustee to be removed and if necessary even without his co-operation (*Re Harrison's Settlement Trusts [1965] 1 WLR 1492*). (Note, however, that a minimum of two trustees or a trust corporation must remain, or the court must appoint a receiver to act *pro tem* pending further order – see CHAPTER 9).

In deciding whether or not to exercise its power, the court will have in mind the interests of the trust as a whole, and the need to ensure that it is properly administered in accordance with its terms and in the interests of the beneficiaries. Consistently with that approach, therefore, the court may consider the following to be sufficient grounds:

- where the trust property is at risk from the trustees' conduct;
- where the trustees appear to be dishonest;
- where the trustees appear to be wanting in good faith;
- where the trustees lack the necessary capacity (including skills or ability) to execute the trusts;
- if there has been a serious breakdown in the relationship of trust and confidence.

It is important to note that the grounds for seeking removal must be serious and substantial. A conflict of interests on the part of one or more trustees may be grounds for removal, but it is only rarely the case that a conflict is so disabling that it is not possible for the trustees to continue in office with the court's directions as necessary (*Public Trustee v Cooper and others [2001] WTLR 901*). Hostility among the trustees can, by itself, be grounds for removing one of their number (or, if it cannot be said that only one trustee is the cause of the problem, all of them). However, in cases such as *Re Wrightson [1908] 1 Ch 789,* it has repeatedly been emphasised that mere animosity between the beneficiaries and the trustees is not sufficient grounds for removal, perhaps especially where the animosity only involves some of the beneficiaries and not others, or where the animosity is based on personal malice or dislike (*Earl of Portsmouth v Fellows (1820) 5 Mad 450*). In *Wrightson*, Warrington J said (at page 800): '*disagreement between the [beneficiaries] and the trustees, or the disinclination on the part of the [beneficiaries] to have the trust property remain in the hands of a particular trustee, is not a sufficient ground for the removal of the trustees. You must find something which induces the court to think either that the trust property will not be safe, or that the trust will not be properly executed in the interests of the beneficiaries. Is that so here, and is it for the welfare of the trust generally, and not merely of the plaintiffs, that these trustees should be removed?*' An example of such a situation can be found in the recent Jersey case of *Parujan v Western Atlantic Trustees Limited (Royal Court of Jersey, 7 March, 2003)*. The trustees in that case were removed in circumstances where there was a total breakdown in the relationship between trustees and beneficiaries, and the trustees had so failed in their duties that the court was led to observe that, 'A trustee should be in the saddle and firmly holding the reins; he should not be running after the horse desperately trying to mount it'.

There is a balance of interests to be borne in mind, therefore. A complete breakdown of trust and confidence is likely to be sufficient if it means that the trustees and beneficiaries, in effect, could not work together in future. In *Letterstedt v Broers (1884) 9 App Cas 371, PC*, Lord Blackburn explained (at page 385): '*It must always be borne in mind that trustees exist for the benefit of those to whom the creator of the trust has given the trust estate . . . If it appears clear that the continuance of the trustee would be detrimental to the execution of the trusts, even if for no other reason than that human infirmity would prevent those beneficially interested, or those who act for them, from working in harmony with the trustee . . . the trustee is always advised to resign . . . If, without reasonable ground, he refused to do so . . . the Court might think it proper to remove him.*'

It may not be putting it too strongly to say that in every case where a trustee finds that, owing to his position, the smooth administration of the trust (including the good relationship of the trustees with the beneficiaries) is being impeded, he ought to consider retiring. The courts have often frowned upon trustees who cling to office, since the office of trustee does not exist for their benefit (see, for example, *Uvedale v Ettrick (1682) 2 Cas in Ch 130*). However, that is not the same as saying that, in every case of hostility, the trustee must retire or be removed. There may be proper reasons for the trustee not to retire, such as those situations identified in *Public Trustee v Cooper and others [2001] WTLR 901* (eg, where the trustee has special skills or knowledge that are valuable to the trust), or in cases where the hostility among the beneficiaries and/or the trustees is so pervasive that his retirement would solve nothing, or where legal proceedings of one kind or another seem likely to occur whether he retires or not.

The court will generally be reluctant to exercise its power unless there appear to be other factors in addition to mere animosity. In *Letterstedt* it was said that: '*friction or hostility between trustees and the [beneficiaries] is not of itself a reason for the removal of the trustees. But where the hostility is grounded on the mode in which the trust has been administered, where it has been caused wholly or partially by substantial overcharges against the trust estate, it is certainly not to be disregarded.*' The additional factor(s) need not, perhaps, be particularly substantial in their own right. In *Cruz de Mercado v Cititrust (Bahamas) Ltd (1986)* (*Butterworths Offshore Cases & Materials* (*1996*) *Vol 1, page 56*), for example, the unresponsiveness of the trustees to the concerns of the beneficiaries was held to be a sufficient additional factor.

The aim, therefore, is to balance the interests of the beneficiaries with those of the trust as a whole, and in this way to avoid a situation where the trust is under the *de facto* control of the beneficiaries, by their being able to demand the dismissal of trustees they dislike or (at the extreme) cannot control.

Application for directions by the trustees

8.11 It is worth noting that, in some cases where a power of removal has been exercised (or purportedly exercised), it may be incumbent upon, or necessary for, the trustee(s) purportedly removed to apply to the court for directions. This was the case in *Von Knieriem v Bermuda Trust Company Limited, 'the Star Trusts case'* (*Supreme Court of Bermuda, 13 July 1994*), where the removed trustees were uncertain as to whether the protector's removal of them was a valid exercise of his power or void (as motivated by extraneous matters, thus a fraud on the power), and therefore whether they in fact remained trustees. Other difficulties could include:

- where fewer than two trustees or a trust corporation would remain in place after the removal;
- where the trustees have reasonable doubts as to the worthiness of the trustee(s) chosen to replace them, and thus are concerned over the safety of the trust assets; or
- where the removal has occurred in the context of a wider dispute or litigation, and the trustees need the reassurance of the court's directions that it is appropriate for them to cease to be trustees.

Procedure

8.12 It is important to note that it is sometimes not necessary to bring proceedings for the removal of a trustee at all. The court can consider removal of its own motion, and may particularly do so in the context of other proceedings where the trustees' conduct is shown to be such that removal seems appropriate (*Re Wrightson [1908] 1 Ch 789*).

It is likely that, in many cases, a claim for removal otherwise than under section 41 or section 19 will be part of larger proceedings for breach of trust, in which event it should be brought under CPR Part 7, the more appropriate procedure to cases where there is a substantial dispute as to fact.

Other cases may be borderline – where the beneficiaries seek removal under section 41 of the Trustee Act 1925, or enforcement of their right of removal under section 19 of TOLATA 1996, the procedure under CPR Part 7 may be used, but if there is no real dispute as to fact, the Part 8 procedure may be equally or more appropriate.

In other cases, there may be no factual dispute underlying the removal application. It may, for example, be brought (perhaps by agreement with the beneficiaries) by the person having the power of removal (ie the protector, appointor or other trustees), either by itself as an application for directions as to whether the power of removal should be exercised, or coupled with an application for directions by those other trustees under CPR Part 8 as to whether the trustee being removed should be sued. The CPR Part 8 procedure is appropriate for claims for any of the following remedies which might be relevant to the removal of a trustee:

- an order requiring a trustee to pay trust money into court;
- an order requiring a trustee to do, or not to do, any act; or
- an order directing any act to be done which the court could order to be done if the trust were being administered or executed under the direction of the court.

The claim form must contain:

- a statement that Part 8 (or, as the case may be, Part 7) applies to the claim;
- a description of the remedy sought;
- a summary of the legal basis on which that remedy is sought (save in the case of Part 7, where a full statement of the claim must be served separately, see below); and
- a statement of truth.

The claimant must, for a Part 8 claim, file and serve the evidence on which he wishes to rely in the form of a witness statement at the same time as the claim form. For Part 7, he must serve his evidence (the particulars of claim) within 14 days of, if not at the same time as, the claim form.

The procedure and timetable for CPR Part 8 are set out in CHAPTER 2 AND APPENDIX 1. The procedure for CPR Part 7 is explained in CHAPTER 2 and APPENDIX 2.

Parties

8.13 Any claim involving a trust brought under CPR Part 8 is required to have all the trustees as parties, and claims under CPR Part 7 will logically also do so, but the question of who the other parties should be will depend upon the facts. The protector or appointor may be an appropriate party in some cases, and it may be necessary to join all the beneficiaries if their interests and views are different.

In rare cases, it is possible that the application for removal may be made on an *ex parte* (without notice) basis. This might be appropriate where there is serious concern over the safety of the trust assets, for example. Proceedings conducted on a without notice basis do, of course, require the trustee(s) to be removed to be named as defendant(s), but the claim form and evidence are not served on them until after the order has been made.

Costs

8.14 It is clear that, in many cases, an application for removal of a trustee will be hostile proceedings, and as such, *Alsop Wilkinson v Neary [1995] 1 All ER 431* is clear authority for the fact that the costs are likely to follow the event. So:

- a trustee who is removed and is found guilty of some misconduct (including unreasonably clinging to office) will usually be ordered to pay the costs of all parties personally;
- a beneficiary who is unsuccessful in his claim may be liable to pay all the costs out of his own pocket (*Fane v Fane (1879) 13 Ch D 228, HC*); and
- only in rare cases, it is suggested, would the costs of a removal application be ordered to be paid centrally out of the trust fund, but the costs of all parties involved in a directions application (eg as to whether an express power of removal should be exercised, or has validly been exercised) may appropriately be paid out of the trust fund.

As discussed in other chapters (for example, CHAPTER 3), paragraph 6 of the Practice Direction accompanying CPR Part 64 provides that the trustees may exercise an express power to agree to pay the costs of the beneficiaries at any time, without the leave of the court, so as to pay the costs of the parties to litigation. If they choose not to exercise the power, or do not have such power, the beneficiaries may apply to the court for a prospective costs order. If the beneficiaries would otherwise be unable to fund the proceedings, the court may (if it thinks fit) make a prospective costs order in relation to the costs of any of the beneficiaries. It is suggested that the interests of the trust as a whole may, in some cases, make it appropriate for steps to be taken at the expense of the trust for the removal of delinquent or wrongdoing trustees. In cases where the opinion of the beneficiaries is divided as to the necessity for the trustees' removal, a pre-emptive costs order seems perhaps less likely to be granted.

Chapter 9

Application for the appointment of a receiver

Introduction

9.1 In cases of substantial risk to the trust assets, or where the trustees (or some of them) are guilty of serious misconduct, it may be appropriate to consider the appointment of a receiver over the trust assets. This is a remedy only for grave and urgent cases, such as where neither the removal of one or more of the trustees, or their replacement wholesale with other trustees, would suffice (*Swale v Swale (1856) 22 Beav 584*), or injunctive relief would be inadequate or irrelevant to the problems at hand.

It is, perhaps, less common nowadays to seek the imposition of a receiver rather than some of the other remedies considered in this book. Some examples of cases where a receiver has been appointed include:

- where the trustee is guilty of 'misconduct, waste or improper disposition' (*Yunghanns v Candoora No 19 Pty Ltd (No 2) [2000] VSC 300*, acknowledging a line of earlier cases);
- where the trustee shows a serious degree of bias towards, or against, a particular beneficiary, such that there are concerns for the safety of the beneficiary's interest (*Yunghanns,* and *Earl Talbot v Hope Scott (1858) 4 K & J 139*);
- where the trustee is insolvent, thus endangering the trust fund (*Mansfield v Shaw (1818) 3 Madd 100*, for example);
- where the trustees, and the affairs of the trust, were in complete disorder (*A-G v Schonfield [1980] 1 WLR 1182*), or the trustees were absent or disagreed among themselves (*Day v Croft (1820) 2 Beav 488*), where the effect is that the trust assets are unprotected;
- where the trustees, in breach of court orders, had secreted funds away abroad (*Clarke v Heathfield [1985] ICR 203, CA*);
- where a worldwide freezing injunction (*Mareva* injunction) had been put in place, and in support of that order (*Derby & Co v Weldon (Nos 3 & 4) [1990] Ch 65, CA*); and
- on the application of a trustee in circumstances where he feared for the safety of the trust assets in the hands of his co-trustee (*Re Fowler (1881) 16 Ch D 723*).

Nature of the application

9.2 It is most often the case that one or more of the beneficiaries will apply for the appointment of a receiver, but the applicant may be a co-trustee who finds he is unable to work with his co-trustee for reasons which appear to him to endanger the trust property.

If the application is made with the consent of all the beneficiaries, then the costs of the receiver will be borne by the trust fund. If, however, only some (or none) of the beneficiaries consent to the appointment, the court may order that the applicant should give an undertaking to bear the costs of the receiver to the extent that they are not ultimately ordered to be paid out of the trust fund or by the defendant trustees. The court may order that the costs of the receivership – and of the application to appoint the receiver – should be borne personally by those trustees whose conduct has necessitated the application (*Wilson v Wilson (1838) 2 Keen 249*).

The application may be made on an *ex parte* (without notice) basis, as was the case in *A-G v Schonfield [1980] 1 WLR 1182*, where the order was coupled with the removal of the trustees. As noted, since the remedy is an equitable one, the aim of which is to safeguard the assets of the trust, the court will take a flexible approach to the nature of the application, and the terms of the order appointing the receiver, depending upon the circumstances of the particular case.

Procedure

9.3 The appropriate procedure for the appointment of a receiver is set out in CPR Part 69, in force since 2 December 2002. This provides that:

- a receiver may be appointed at any time before, during, or after proceedings;
- the receiver must be an individual; and
- the appointment may be made on a without notice basis.

The application must be made under CPR Part 23, the procedure for general applications. The application notice must be served on the receiver, and on each other party to the proceedings (if not made on a without notice basis). The Practice Direction to CPR Part 69 (CPR 69 PD) provides that the application notice must contain:

- the reasons why the applicant believes the appointment is required;
- details of the assets over which the receiver is to be appointed, including estimates of value;
- an explanation of why (if it is the case) the receiver should act without giving security, either at all, or before his appointment; and

- details of the person (if any) that the applicant wishes to nominate, stating why that person is suitable, and exhibiting the written consent of that person to act if appointed.

Whilst the claimant may specify a person whom he wishes to be appointed as receiver, he may in theory leave the appointment to the court. The court is not, in any event, obliged to appoint the person nominated by the claimant, as its main concern is to ensure that the most appropriate person acts as receiver. It will require details of the suitability of any proposed receiver before he is appointed. The court may remove and replace a receiver at any time and may particularly do so if the person initially appointed is not, in fact, suitable for the role.

A receiver appointed by the court must, if ordered to do so (as will often be the case), provide security to cover his acts and omissions as receiver, normally in the form of a bond or guarantee. He must file and serve evidence on all parties to show that he has done so.

The order appointing the receiver, once made, must be served by the applicant upon the receiver, and on such other persons as the court thinks fit, including every party to the proceedings unless the court orders otherwise. The order made will contain details of any charging arrangements (see paragraph 9.7 below).

The role of the receiver

9.4 The role of the receiver will vary from case to case, depending upon the circumstances in which he has been appointed, since it is an entirely equitable remedy (*A-G v Schonfield [1980] 1 WLR 1182*). The court will usually give him directions as to his terms of reference when he is appointed.

The primary purpose of the receiver's appointment is likely to be to overcome a serious risk to the trust assets, or to resolve a situation of disorder in the trust's affairs. This, in turn, is likely to mean that he is charged primarily with a duty to get in, account for and safeguard the assets of the trust. He may be appointed in respect of particular assets only, or in respect of all assets worldwide (as in *Derby & Co v Weldon (Numbers 3 & 4) [1990] Ch 65, CA*).

The receiver may be appointed in place of the trustees, but may be appointed in addition to them. The receiver's duties are usually exclusively in relation to the administration of the trust, and the management of its assets. He does not have any powers in relation to the execution of the dispositive powers, as that is the function of a trustee and not a receiver. It is, therefore, neither inconsistent to retain the trustees with the receiver appointed over the assets, nor to remove the trustees and appoint a receiver to administer the assets pending the appointment of new trustees to execute the dispositive powers of the trust. Indeed, the court's natural reluctance to displace trustees may mean that the preferred order is for the appointment of a receiver to get in the assets pending resolution of how the trust is to be administered and executed in future, and by whom. The risk to the assets having been relieved by the appointment of the receiver, the trustees and beneficiaries are free to resolve any other difficulties that may be confronting them.

The receiver may apply for directions at any time during the currency of his office, on any question or matter in relation to which the court's directions are necessary or helpful to assist him in carrying out his functions. Generally, the court will give directions as to which persons the receiver should join to the application (if any) or upon whom the application for directions and any order containing directions should be served. It is not automatically the case that any person other than the receiver will be present during the application, or entitled to receive notice of it in advance.

An application may be made at any time, by any party (including the receiver) for the discharge of the receiver with or without replacement. The receiver's office is only terminated when the court concludes that he has completed the duties required of him, or that the risk to the trust assets has abated. Merely because one beneficiary applied for his appointment does not mean that his discharge can be secured by the application of the same beneficiary alone (*Bainbrigge v Blair (1841) 3 Beav 421*). On his discharge, provided that he has complied with the terms of any orders requiring him to pay assets under his control into court (or to some specified person) the security he has given for his appointment (see paragraph 9.3 above) will usually be discharged.

Accounts

9.5 As part of the receivership, the receiver may be ordered to produce accounts, typically on a half-yearly basis. Similarly to the trustees' duty to account (discussed in CHAPTER 3), any party to the proceedings may specify items in the accounts to which he/she objects, within a specified time after receiving the accounts. Such items may be liable to be struck from the account.

Parties

9.6 As noted, in urgent cases, the application may be made on a without-notice basis. However, in many cases, it is likely to be appropriate that notice of the application is given to all the trustees, and any other beneficiaries who (although not claimants) may have an interest in the outcome of the proceedings, and whose interests are not already adequately spoken for through a representative beneficiary.

Costs

9.7 As noted above, where the conduct of the trustees has necessitated the appointment of a receiver, the costs of the application itself, and even the costs of the receiver during his term of office, may be ordered to be paid by the trustees personally (*Wilson v Wilson (1838) 2 Keen 249*).

In general, the costs of the application to appoint a receiver are likely to follow the success (or failure) of the application, but it is suggested that, unless the claimant beneficiaries are found to have acted unreasonably in bringing the application, the costs are likely to be ordered to be borne by the trust fund. This is because the circumstances giving rise to a perceived need for a receiver to be appointed will almost certainly be of such an unusual and/or urgent nature that, even if a receiver is not appointed, other reliefs and remedies may be granted in the interests of the trust.

The basis and rates upon which the receiver is entitled to charge, and by whom those charges are to be paid, will be determined by the court at the time of his appointment. Occasionally, the matter may be left open, with the exact amount of his remuneration, and by whom it is to be paid, left to be determined by the court periodically on the application of any party (including the receiver), or at the close of the receivership. Remuneration is on a discretionary basis, and the court will take into account the complexity of the role of the receiver in the particular circumstances, the time dedicated to the role, and the value and nature of the subject matter of the receivership. The court may also refer the receiver's costs to a costs judge for determination (CPR Part 69.7).

Chapter 10

Enforcement of rights under the trust

Introduction

10.1 The beneficiaries of any trust have a multiplicity of rights which are capable of enforcement by the courts if the trustees cannot, or will not, give proper effect to them. Whilst other chapters of this book have focused on enforcement of the trustees' duties (such as the duty to account, considered in CHAPTER 3, and the duty of care, considered in CHAPTER 6), and the sanctions which may be applied if they fail in their duties (removal, in CHAPTER 8, or a challenge to the exercise of their discretions, in CHAPTER 7), this chapter considers the enforcement of some of the most basic rights of the beneficiaries, namely:

- the right to know whether he is a beneficiary of the trust at all;
- the right to know the identities of the trustees;
- the payment of monies due to him under the trust;
- the right to due administration of the trust; and
- the right to procure the winding-up of the trust when the trusts are at an end.

The beneficiary's right to know he is a beneficiary

10.2 A beneficiary of a fixed interest trust has identifiable, definite rights which clearly require him to know that he is a beneficiary. The position with regard to beneficiaries of discretionary trusts is somewhat different, and the position may be less certain.

It has often been said that the principal right of a discretionary beneficiary is that he has a right to be considered by the trustees as eligible for a payment to be made to him. Denning MR went so far as to describe this as '*more than a mere hope or expectation . . . It is an interest in the trust fund, though not to any defined part of it*' (*Gartside v IRC [1968] AC 553, HL*). The enforceability of this right was described in *Re Manisty's Settlement [1974] Ch 17* (per Templeman J at page 25): '*If a person within the ambit of the power is aware of its existence he can require the trustees to consider exercising the power and in particular to consider a request on his part for the power to be exercised in his favour.'*

How, then, is a discretionary beneficiary to enforce his right, if he is unaware that he is a beneficiary? Indeed, if all the beneficiaries are unaware that they are beneficiaries, how is the trust to be enforced at all? The key may lie in Templeman J's use of the phrase 'if he is aware of [the power's] existence'. In order to enforce the trusts, the beneficiary must logically need to be aware of the fact that he is a beneficiary.

In the case of fixed interest trusts, there is considerable case law on the fact that a beneficiary must be entitled to know of his interest, at least when it falls into possession (see *Hawkesley v May [1956] 1 QB 304*, for example). At the other end of the scale, in relation to mere powers – even if they are of a fiduciary character – it has been held that the trustees are under no obligation to inform the possible objects of that power of its existence (*Re Manisty's Settlement Trusts [1974] Ch 17*). The intermediate position is not wholly clear. It would seem logical (following *Manisty*) that trustees of trusts with a very broad discretionary class need not notify every potential object of the discretion that he is capable of benefit. However, in the case of most family discretionary trusts, it is suggested that the class will be of a manageable, limited size, and that the members of the class ought to know (at least from when they attain their majority) of the trust's existence and that they are among the beneficial class. Cases such as *Spellson v George (1987) 11 NSWLR 300*, and *Chaine-Nickson v Bank of Ireland [1976] IR 393* have indicated that this is the proper approach. Trustees (or indeed settlors) who are reluctant for the beneficiaries to know of the existence of the trust, and their potential interest, until (if ever) they are in receipt of a distribution may be vulnerable to accusations that the trust is a sham, or that the trustees have failed to consider the entire beneficial class.

A beneficiary who knows of or suspects the existence of the trust can require the trustees to confirm whether or not he is a beneficiary. If he receives no response, or an unsatisfactory response, he may apply to the court under the procedure in CPR Part 8, for a determination (in accordance with CPR Part 64) as to the nature of his interest (if any) in the trust. A trustee who is found to have acted unreasonably in refusing the beneficiary the information requested – or, worse, who has untruthfully denied that the enquirer is a beneficiary, knowing that he is – will be personally at risk as to the costs of the application (see, for example, the Jersey case of *Hogg v Williamson (Royal Court of Jersey, 7 August 2003, unreported)*).

Payment of funds due to a beneficiary

10.3 Where funds are due to a beneficiary, it is clear that he must have the right to enforce the payment to him of the sums due. This may be necessary where payment is due to the beneficiary in respect of:

- income due to him as life tenant or annuitant;
- distributions of income and/or capital which the trustees of a discretionary trust have resolved to pay to him; or
- where he has attained a vested interest in capital.

Fixed interest in income

10.4 Where there are trusts to pay the income of the settlement to A for life, and then to pay the trust fund (as to both income and capital) to B, or where the trust fund is held for C and D subject to the payment of the sum of £20,000 per annum to E, the rights of A and E are to receive the income due to them. However:

- E's right is an absolute right to receive £20,000 per annum (which may be payable in monthly or quarterly instalments); but
- A's right is to receive all the income of the trust on an arising basis (though, again, it may be payable in instalments for administrative convenience), subject to:
  - the trustees' duty to deduct expenses properly to be borne out of income (ie expenses of a recurring nature);
  - the trustees' right to reimbursement out of both income and capital against all expenses properly incurred in the administration of the trust (section 31(1) of the Trustee Act 2000) provided that they repay any sums due to the income account out of the capital account, and vice versa, as soon as is practicable (*Carver v Duncan [1985] AC 1082, HL*); and
  - the trustees' lien for contingent or future liabilities for which a retention of income is appropriate (perhaps because the capital value of the trust may be insufficient) (*X v A [2000] 1 All ER 490*).

Procedure

10.5 It is an important principle that the trustees must not simply wait to be asked to pay funds to the beneficiary who is entitled to them. They have a positive duty to ensure that the right sums (of capital or income) are paid to the proper recipients at the earliest opportunity (*Hawkesley v May [1956] 1 QB 304*; *Ministry of Health v Simpson [1951] AC 251, HL*). They are not entitled to hold the funds longer than is reasonably necessary to pay them to the proper recipient. If they delay:

- E's right to receive his £20,000 (or, depending upon the terms of the trust as to instalments, £5,000 per quarter) is, if unsatisfied, the subject matter of a pure debt claim, which may be enforced under the procedure in CPR Part 8 to obtain an order to compel the trustees to pay him (see CPR Part

64). It is unlikely to involve factual argument, so that the CPR Part 7 procedure is less likely to be relevant; and

- A's right to obtain his money may depend upon more complex arguments as to what is properly due to him, and what expenses the trustees may properly deduct (or make allowance for out of the income). His claim should be brought under CPR Part 7 if he argues that deductions have been improperly made, or there are other disputes as to fact. He may use CPR Part 8 if he seeks a more open-ended order that the trustees should pay him whatever sums are properly due to him (perhaps coupled with an order for account).

Discretionary distributions of income or capital

10.6 The trustees of a discretionary trust cannot be compelled to exercise their discretion in any particular way, but can only be required to consider exercising it (*Re Manisty's Settlement [1974] Ch 17*). However, once they have determined to do so, or the court has ordered that they should do so (see CHAPTER 7), then (subject to the consent of any relevant person, such as the protector) they must pay the funds over to the beneficiary or to the person in whose favour payment is to be made for his benefit. In the unlikely event that they fail to make a payment that is due, a beneficiary in this position can compel the payment to be made (under CPR Part 8, as an order requiring the trustees to do a positive act, or a direction that the beneficiary is entitled to receive a particular sum).

Conversely, the beneficiary can also restrain a payment being made which he does not believe is for his benefit, though expressed to be. For example:

- if the trustees have failed to consider the potential tax consequences for him, he (or they) may apply to have the exercise of discretion set aside under the *Hastings-Bass* principle (*Re Hastings-Bass [1975] Ch 25, CA*), using either the procedure in CPR Part 7 or the CPR Part 8 procedure (depending on the circumstances); or
- if the trustees have purported to make judgments as to what the beneficiary's moral duties might be, or that a payment is for his betterment, the beneficiary may prevent the payment being made for his purported benefit (as in *Re the Esteem Settlement, Grupo Torras SA v Al Sabah (No 6) [2001] WTLR 641*, where the trustees wrongly concluded that it was for the benefit of a beneficiary that money should be applied to reduce his debts, even though the value of the trust fund was insufficient to clear them, which might have been construed as a benefit to him). The claim here is for an order (under CPR Part 64) that the trustees should *not* make the payment, and the claim is brought under the CPR Part 8 procedure.

Beneficiary who has attained a vested interest

10.7 As noted in paragraph 10.5, the trustees must not simply wait to be asked to pay funds to the beneficiary who has become entitled to them, and must take active, prompt steps to pay the correct amount of capital (and/or income) to the beneficiaries to whom they are due (*Hawkesley v May [1956] 1 QB 304*; *Ministry of Health v Simpson [1951] AC 251, HL*).

A beneficiary who has attained an absolute and vested interest in possession in the trust is entitled to have the trust property transferred to him (*Saunders v Vautier (1841) 4 Beav 115*). He must have attained the age of majority, or have married under that age, if his interest is not contingent upon his surviving to a greater age specified in the trust deed (*Re Somech [1957] Ch 165*, and section 21 of the Law of Property Act 1925). In some cases, the interest of one beneficiary will vest ahead of others' interests, such as in a trust for 'my children who attain the age of 21 and if more than one, in equal shares'. A beneficiary whose interest is only one of several prospective interests can nonetheless call for an equal (or *aliquot*) share of each of the trust assets, without waiting for all the interests in the trust to vest (*Re Marshall, Marshall v Marshall [1914] 1 Ch 192*; *Re Sandeman's Will Trusts [1937] 1 All ER 368*; *Stephenson v Barclays Bank Trust Co Ltd [1975] 1 WLR 882*). This right is subject to certain limitations:

- the trustees' lien for costs and expenses;
- any need to bring previous advances into account for hotchpot;
- impossibility of physical division, or any special restrictions arising because of the nature of the trust property (such as land, or shares in a private company); and
- any exercise by the trustees of their powers of appropriation.

The trustees cannot generally refuse to transfer assets to a beneficiary whose interest has vested in possession. For example, in *Re Sandeman's Will Trusts*, there was an express direction in the trust instrument that the trustees must retain the trust property unsold. It was held that the direction did not entitle the trustees to retain the property as against the absolute beneficial owners of them. In *Moss v Integro (1997/98) 1 OFLR 427*, the trustees wrongly relied on a clause stating that the trust would terminate at the end of the perpetuity period or by their earlier execution of a deed (which they declined to do). It was held that the description of the trust period could not affect the underlying entitlements of the beneficiaries, and did not therefore mean that the trust could not terminate on an earlier date by operation of law.

The trustees cannot refuse to transfer the beneficiary's share to him on the grounds that there is some theoretical or remote risk that the value of the trust may fall in future, at the expense of the other beneficiaries. The beneficiary's entitlement is to his fair share of the trust assets at their then market value, which must take into account all the relevant circumstances (including, presumably, any reasonably foreseeable risk of depreciation). If the trustees distribute to him in the belief that it is proper to do so at that value on that date, then they are not liable if, thereafter, the trust's value is unexpectedly diminished, to the detriment of other beneficiaries (*Re Hurst (1892) 8 TLR 528, CA*). If, however, there are reasonably foreseeable (albeit remote or contingent) liabilities which may affect the trust fund, the trustees can exercise their lien over the beneficiary's share of the trust so as to retain it (or part of it), as well as those parts in which no interest has yet vested, because it would be unfair to allow that beneficiary to take his share, leaving the undistributed funds to bear the risks alone (see, for example, *X v A [2000] 1 All ER 490*).

Procedure

10.8 A beneficiary who believes that the trustees have improperly or unreasonably refused to transfer his equal share of the trust fund can apply to the court for an order under the procedure in CPR Part 8 (as indicated by CPR Part 64) declaring that the trustees should pay his share to him. The costs of such an application may (if the trustees have acted unreasonably) be charged to the trustees personally. If, however, there are genuine difficulties (for example, in knowing how to divide particular assets) the costs are likely to come out of the fund, in which case they are deducted before calculating what is due to the claimant beneficiary.

The right to due administration of the trust

10.9 The beneficiaries of a trust have the right to ensure that the trust is properly administered and executed, including, if necessary, calling upon the court's assistance. The court may, with appropriate orders, bring about a situation more likely to result in the proper execution of the trusts, and/or supervise the due administration of the trusts. Different approaches may be appropriate, depending upon the nature of the problem:

- where the trustees themselves are deadlocked or in dispute, removal of one or more of the trustees may be of assistance (see CHAPTER 8);
- where the trust property is at risk, or the affairs of the trust are in disarray, the appointment of a receiver to identify and collect in the trust assets may resolve the problem (see CHAPTER 9);
- either the beneficiaries or the trustees may apply for the court's directions as to how to deal with a particular situation or difficulty (see CHAPTER 7 and CHAPTER 11); or
- where the problems are pervasive, and would not be cured by the removal of a trustee, or where no other remedy is likely to prove expedient, the court may (on the application of the trustees or the beneficiaries) make an administration order over the trust.

This fourth category of remedies – an administration action – is available only in circumstances of unusual difficulty, as its effect is extremely restrictive. It takes effect in relation to the whole of the fund (or the part of it over which the administration order is made) so as to suspend the trustees' powers of administration over the trust entirely. The trustees must seek the leave of the court for any exercise of any administrative power (*Re Viscount Furness [1943] Ch 415*) including the power of investment (*Bethell v Abraham (1873) LR 17 Eq 24*) and the power to pursue or defend legal proceedings (*Jones v Powell (1841) 4 Beav 96*).

An administration action does not suspend the trustees' ordinary duties in relation to the trust, so that they must still actively consider what administrative steps ought to be taken, but cannot implement those actions without the court's authorisation (unless they are actions which relate to a part of the fund not covered by the administration order). Similarly, the order does not prevent the trustees from exercising dispositive discretions or powers, although the court's approval may be required if the proposed exercise would involve the exercise of an administrative function (eg sale of shares to satisfy a distribution) or might otherwise trespass on the areas subject to the administration order.

The purpose of the administration order being made is so as to ensure that, until the court's further order (which will usually be made when the difficulties have been resolved), the trustees do not act without the court's approval. This is both a safeguard for the beneficiaries, and reassurance for the trustees, who may be dealing with a trust the affairs of which are seriously disordered, or which is endangered by litigation or insolvency, or the assets of which are of such an unusual or speculative nature that the court's assistance is required to deal with them appropriately.

Procedure

10.10 Any of the beneficiaries, or indeed the trustees themselves, may commence proceedings under CPR Part 8 (which CPR Part 64 indicates is the correct procedure) calling for the administration of the trust under the supervision of the court and identifying the unusual circumstances which indicate that such a remedy is required.

Since the court will only make the order if it considers that it is in the interests of the trust to do so, the costs of a successful application are likely to be paid out of the trust fund, as are the costs of the ongoing administration proceedings. The costs of the application itself may be relatively insubstantial, as the trustees' duty (if they are not the claimants) is to remain neutral, and await the court's assessment of whether such an order would benefit the trust or not. The costs of the administration proceedings themselves may, however, be extremely substantial, as they may continue for several months or years, with applications to the court required periodically, whenever the trustees require new directions as to how to proceed.

In the unlikely event that the application is refused, and the applicants are found to have acted unreasonably, costs may be ordered against them personally. However, this seems unlikely, only from the practical perspective that it is difficult to imagine such a restrictive order being sought in the absence of compelling difficulties.

When the court concludes – either of its own motion, or on the application of any party – that the difficulties which gave rise to the need for administration under the court's supervision have abated, or been resolved, it will make a further order discharging the administration order. The aim is to achieve this as soon as is practicable, so that the trust does not continue to suffer any longer than is reasonably necessary the expense, and relative inconvenience, of the trustees' powers being suspended.

The right to secure the winding-up of the trust

10.11 The 'rule in *Saunders v Vautier*' is widely known as providing authority for the principle that a trust may be brought to an end by all its beneficiaries acting jointly, provided that they are all in existence, over 18 and have full capacity.

In *Saunders v Vautier (1841) 4 Beav 115, 49 ER 282* the testator had left certain shares upon trust to accumulate the income until the claimant attained the age of 25, and then to transfer them to the claimant absolutely (or, if he had died before then, to his executors). On attaining the age of majority (then 21), the claimant argued that the shares should be immediately transferred to him, because he (and no other person) was absolutely entitled to them, whether or not the income continued to accumulate. It was held that, whatever the express terms of the trust, a beneficiary who has an absolute indefeasible interest is entitled to call for the transfer of the trust assets to himself as soon as he has capacity to give a valid receipt to the trustees. By extension, a trust with more than one beneficiary may be brought to an end by all the beneficiaries acting jointly (even discretionary trusts), provided that they all meet the criteria for *Saunders v Vautier. (See also Re Smith [1928] Ch 915, IRC v Hamilton-Russell [1943] 1 All ER 474, CA*; *Stephenson v Barclays Bank Trust Co Ltd [1975] 1 All ER 625*; *Wharton v Masterman [1895] AC 186 HL*).

Some types of trust in relation to which the beneficiaries could seek termination under *Saunders v Vautier* include:

- a trust for A for life, remainder to B – A and B could agree to bring the trust to an end by capitalising A's income interest, but not where there are substitutive trusts in case B predeceases A, or B's interest is otherwise defeasible, unless all the substitute beneficiaries also agree (*Re Bellville's Settlement Trusts [1964] Ch 163*);
- a discretionary trust for the benefit of the settlor, his wife and his (named) children – whilst the settlor might be unlikely to wish to bring the trust to an end, after he dies, if all the children have attained 18 (or the relevant age of majority under the proper law of the trust), they can bring the trust to an end with the widow's consent, or after her death, jointly by themselves;
- a trust for the benefit of the settlor's children who attain 25, in equal shares – when the settlor dies (so that there can be no more children

capable of being born) and all the children attain 18, seemingly (provided there are no substitutive trusts) they need not wait until they all attain 25 if they all agree that the trust should be ended sooner (as in *Saunders v Vautier* itself).

Clearly, this option is not available where some of the beneficiaries do not consent or are incapable of consenting. Where a beneficiary is a minor, his parent or guardian cannot consent on his behalf. The attorney (under an enduring power) or receiver of a person suffering from mental incapacity (within the meaning of the Mental Health Act 1983) may be empowered by the Court of Protection to give consent, but cannot do so in the ordinary course.

As is made clear in the examples above, where there are substitutive gifts in the event of the beneficiaries failing to attain the vesting age, their consent is also required to terminate the trust at an earlier date. Seemingly, if there is a power of appointment in favour of a specified class, exercisable before the vesting date, the consent of each member of that class might also be required. Where there is a mere power of addition of beneficiaries, that would not be an impediment, provided that the power has not been exercised so as to include a person not competent to give consent as at the date when the beneficiaries seek to terminate the trust.

Procedure

10.12 As noted in paragraph 10.7 above, the trustees cannot refuse the request of the beneficiaries to transfer the assets to them (*Re Sandeman's Will Trusts, Moss v Integro (1997/98) 1 OFLR 427*), subject to the payment of all the costs and expenses properly chargeable to the trust fund, and reasonable protection against future risks (in the form, perhaps, of an indemnity, coupled with a retention of funds if there is an identifiable risk). If reasonable protection cannot be given against future or contingent liabilities, the trustees may retain some or all of the trust fund until (if ever) the liability is discharged or abates (*X v A [2000] 1 All ER 490*).

If the trustees refuse to wind up the trust, either they or the beneficiaries can apply to the court for an order under the procedure in CPR Part 8 (as CPR Part 64 indicates is the correct Part). The order sought would be for directions, or a declaration, as to whether the trustees should terminate the trust or not, or as to the beneficiaries' absolute interest to take the trust assets. If the trustees have acted unreasonably, the costs of that application may be charged to them personally. It is possible that they may have genuine difficulties, however, such as knowing whether the rule in *Saunders v Vautier* applies at all, or being certain of reasonable protection against future or contingent liabilities (as in *X v A and others*). In such cases, the costs are likely to be ordered to be paid out of the trust fund prior to its being distributed to the beneficiaries.

Chapter 11

Enforcement of external claims against the trust

Introduction

11.1 In CHAPTER 10, the enforcement of the beneficiaries' rights under the trust was considered. This chapter considers the enforcement against the trust of claims which are external to the trust, that is, of claims which exist independently of the trust but where a remedy, or the only remedy, available to the claimants, is enforcement against the trust of which they are beneficiaries. These claims may include:

- the rights of spouses, either in the context of divorce, or under the relevant foreign matrimonial property system (known as community of property) to which their marriage is subject;
- the rights of members of a non-UK domiciled settlor's family (most commonly, his spouse and children) to claim fixed shares of his estate in accordance with the law of his domicile;
- the rights of creditors to recover against trust assets, or to have the trust set aside in some circumstances; and
- claims that the trust is a sham.

Whilst some of these rights and claims – and many others – could potentially belong to persons other than beneficiaries, this chapter concentrates (unless the wording appears more general) on such claims and rights in the hands of persons who are beneficiaries.

Claims by spouses

11.2 As noted in paragraph 11.1 above, there are three principal contexts in which the spouse of the settlor may wish to challenge the validity of the trust, or its terms:

- the court may be invited, in the context of a divorce, to consider setting the trust aside or varying its terms, or to take its value into account when considering the assets 'available' to one of the spouses;

- a spouse may claim that, under the law of the jurisdiction to which his/her marriage to the settlor is subject, a community of property regime applies, such that he/she co-owned the assets purportedly settled into the trust by the settlor as sole owner; or
- a spouse may claim, following the death of the testator, that a will trust makes insufficient provision for her, and ask that it be varied.

Divorce

Inherent jurisdiction of the court

11.3 In the context of division of matrimonial assets, the court has an inherent discretion to take into account the value of assets available to either spouse. Form E, which is required to be completed by each spouse, requires the person completing the form to provide a sworn, truthful and complete statement of the assets available to them. This includes (in Part 2 of the Form):

- details of any interest under a trust (including a discretionary trust);
- an estimate of the value of that interest; and
- details of when it may be realisable.

If the party completing the form believes (which may particularly be the case for discretionary trusts) that the interest has no value, or may never be realisable, but they must provide reasons for that belief. The court looks at the substance, not the form, of the situation, and may nonetheless take into account the value of assets it believes to be 'available' to either spouse, including where the facts suggest that any request made by the beneficiary spouse to the trustees of a discretionary trust for a distribution is likely to be granted (*Thomas v Thomas [1995] 2 FLR 668*).

Although the trust itself will not necessarily be set aside (unless it falls within section 37 of the Matrimonial Causes Act – see paragraph 11.4 below), the court may consider it appropriate, when ordering the division of assets, to take into account the value of assets held in the trust. In deciding whether or not to do so, the court may make other orders including, for example:

- an order that the trustees of the trust should prepare accounts and disclose them, with copies of accounting materials, to the beneficiary who was the respondent spouse (*Re Lombardo Settlement (Royal Court of Jersey, 5 December 1990, unreported)*);
- an order to disclose any letter of wishes which would indicate how the trust assets are intended to be applied (*In the matter of the Rabaiotti 1989 Settlement [2000] WTLR 953*); and
- an order joining the trustees (or any other relevant person) to the proceedings so as to bind them (*T v T (Joinder of third parties) [1996] 2 FLR 357*).

Section 37 Matrimonial Causes Act

11.4 Section 37 of the Matrimonial Causes Act 1973 contains power for the court to set aside transactions, such as trusts, which it appears have been entered into by either spouse with the intention of reducing the assets available to provide financial support to, or a 'clean break' settlement with, the claimant spouse, or maintenance payments for children. A trust may be affected in the following situations:

- the court may order the restraint by injunction of a proposed disposal of assets, including the creation of a settlement, if it appears likely that one spouse is intending to enter into a transaction of this sort;
- where the transaction was entered into within three years prior to the application, there is a rebuttable presumption that the requisite intention was present;
- where the transaction was entered into three years or more prior to the application, the burden is on the claimant spouse to show that the requisite intention existed.

The effect of a trust being set aside in these circumstances is that it is void *ab initio*, with the result that the trustees must be holding the trust assets upon resulting trusts for the defendant settlor (but subject to the terms of any order which may require the trustees to pay some or all of the assets to the claimant spouse or another person).

Section 24 Matrimonial Causes Act

11.5 The court may also make orders for the variation of any 'nuptial settlement' under section 24(1) of the 1973 Act, whether or not the settlement:

- was created before or after the marriage; or
- is subject to English law (subject to questions of enforceability of the judgment in the relevant jurisdiction – see CHAPTER 16 – the court's powers extend to foreign settlements: see, for example, *E v E (Financial provision) [1990] 2 FLR 233*).

A 'nuptial settlement' is one:

- which has been made by any person (not only one of the spouses);
- which '*makes some form of continuing provision for both or either of the parties to a marriage*' (*Brooks v Brooks [1996] AC 375*); and
- where the marriage of the disputing parties is '*a fact of which the settlor takes account in framing the settlement*' (*Joss v Joss [1943] P 18*; *Melvill v Melvill and Woodward [1930] P 159*).

A variation may be ordered to as to provide for one of the spouses, or to partition the trust fund in any shares the court thinks fit.

Community of property

11.6 Community of property applies to the parties to a marriage (or long-term relationship), to varying degrees, in many civil law jurisdictions in Europe, the USA and parts of Africa. The matrimonial domicile – which determines the law governing the marriage, and hence whether a community of property regime applies – is that of the state in which both parties were domiciled at or immediately after their marriage, or, failing this, the law of the state with which the parties, and their marriage during its subsistence, had the closest connection. In many states, the community can be limited or excluded by pre-nuptial agreement entered into by the spouses. The spouses may also change matrimonial domicile to a state which has different rules or, like most common law countries (such as England and Wales), which has no community property rules at all. (Interestingly, following the landmark decision in *White v White 1 [2001] All ER 1, HL*, the courts' approach to the division of assets on divorce in England and Wales is now to start from a presumption of equality, and consider factors which should reduce the share of either spouse. This is an approach which, in its effect at the end of the marriage, might appear to differ little from community of property, but significantly does not impose any similar concepts during the subsistence of the marriage.)

In the absence of a pre-nuptial agreement or an agreed change of law, the applicable community regime will attach to the worldwide assets of the couple. A settlor whose marriage or relationship is subject to community of property rules may not be the sole beneficial owner of the assets which he wishes to settle into trust. He will therefore be unable to dispose freely and by himself of the assets subject to the community. This may extend even to land, even if the jurisdiction where the land is sited does not itself have a community regime (see *De Nicols v Curlier [1900] AC 21, HL*, (where the court held that community of property applied to all the couple's movables worldwide); and *Re De Nicols, De Nicols v Curlier [1900] 2 Ch 410* (where the community also applied to UK immovables)).

It is possible, therefore, that a spouse may claim at any time (but often in the context of divorce) that a settlement has been created or funded with assets which, in truth, did not belong to the settlor, and that the claimant spouse has an interest in those assets as tenant in common (using English law terminology to describe the most usual position under foreign community laws). Many offshore jurisdictions have enacted legislation expressly designed to avoid the bringing of claims of the invalidity of a trust which are *solely* based on foreign matrimonial property regimes (although, see later in this chapter, it may be possible, on the facts, to attack the trust as a sham). However, English law has no such prohibitive rules.

It is arguable whether it is inconsistent for a claimant spouse to say, on the one hand, that she had an interest in the assets settled into trust as tenant in common with her husband, and on the other hand to continue to assert her rights as a beneficiary in respect of any assets properly settled. The court may not, for example, allow her to claim disclosure of documents to her as a beneficiary without restrictions on the extent to which (if at all) she could use it as evidence of her proprietary claim to assets held in the trust (*Lemos v Coutts & Co (Cayman) Ltd (1992–93) CILR 5)*.

The claim is, however, a hostile challenge to the trust, as a proprietary claim to the assets purportedly held on the trusts of the settlement. As such, the claim should be brought by a claim under CPR Part 8. The procedure is discussed in paragraph 11.17 below. A better course is often for trustees who are aware of a possible claim to apply to the court for directions as to the true beneficial ownership of the funds they hold (*Finers v Miro [1991] 1 All ER 182)*, ie, whether they are holding those funds on the express trusts, or as trustees for the claimant spouse. This is also discussed at paragraph 11.17.

Claims by widows and widowers

11.7 If a testator made a will trust which provided only a life interest, or discretionary interest, to a spouse whose entitlement on divorce would have included an outright sum, it is possible that the court might extend her rights under the Inheritance (Provision for Family and Dependants) Act 1975.

In a pre-*White* case where the widow had a life interest in the matrimonial home and in a sum of money, she did not succeed in her application for an absolute interest (*Re Clarke [1991] Fam Law 364*). In another case, *Davis v Lush (15 January 1991, unreported, CA*), a wife's appeal failed where she had already been granted a life interest in the whole of her husband's estate. An application by the widow to enlarge her interest under a will trust is perhaps more likely to be available since *White v White [2001] 1 All ER 1, HL which introduced a greater presumption towards equal division of assets on divorce. In principle, there appears to be no reason why the treatment of assets at the end of a marriage should differ substantially merely because in one case it ends by divorce, and in another case, by the death of one spouse. One case which supports this trend is Bheeku v Watson [2001] unreported, where the widow – who had issued divorce proceedings shortly before her husband's death – was awarded 44% of the worldwide estate except for assets in the country of her husband's domicile.*

Other claims by family members

11.8 In common law jurisdictions (such as England and Wales), every person is free to dispose of his property as he chooses, whether during his life or on his death, and may disinherit his children and/or other family members and dependants at will (subject to claims under the Inheritance (Provision for Family and Dependants) Act 1975). Conversely, as well as applying community of property, most civil law jurisdictions tend to restrict the extent to which a person may dispose of his assets (ie the property which belongs to him after application of the relevant community of property rules). Usually, he is obliged to provide for specified classes of family members in fixed shares which they must receive outright, and may be able to dispose freely of as little as one-fifth of his estate. The rights of children in particular to inherit a fixed share of the testator's estate are entrenched in civil law and cannot be overridden. Often, the rules can only be disapplied if the excluded person has committed one of a limited number of specified offensive acts towards the deceased (eg murder, abandonment, etc).

The notional 'estate' to be divided among the heirs is often grossed-up to include not only the worldwide assets possessed by the person at his death, but also assets given away by him during his lifetime, either during a specified time before his death, or occasionally without limit of time. A form of hotchpot applies so as to require each family member to account for assets already received by them when calculating the sum to which they are entitled on the person's death.

It may be argued by the settlor's family (or even, rarely, by the settlor himself, as in the *Thyssen* litigation in Bermuda) that the creation of the trust was unlawful under the law of the state of which he was a domiciliary (or habitual resident, or citizen, as may be the relevant factor under private international law, which is beyond the scope of this book). Generally such claims are made on the footing that, under the law of the civil law jurisdiction to which the settlor or testator was subject, one or more of the following arguments applies:

- a community of property regime applied to his marriage (see 11.6 above);
- on his death, his children (and sometimes also the spouse, and perhaps other relatives, eg parents) are indefeasibly entitled to a fixed share of the deceased's assets ('forced heirship rights'), and the purported creation of a trust the terms of which are in any degree inconsistent with those rights is void;
- trusts are simply not recognised, and therefore the creation of a trust is to be regarded as a beneficial gift to the trustees, which (whether or not they are family members) may be an obvious offence against community property and forced heirship rules if the amount settled into trust exceeded the share of his estate of which the settlor was competent freely to dispose; and/or
- (in certain cases) the creation of trusts of any kind by the citizens (or habitual residents or domiciliaries, as the case may be) of the relevant state was expressly prohibited by that state's law (as is the case in Monaco, for example).

Such claims are likely to affect trusts in the following ways:

- the devolution of immovable property (*inter vivos* or on death) is governed by the law of its situs. Since English law has no forced heirship concept, an English court might be reluctant to allow claims by heirs to a share in, say, English land held in trust, by virtue of foreign forced heirship laws, although the court might do so if the value of the English immovables represented a substantial proportion of the testator's estate (but there is no authority on this point);

- dealings with movable assets are governed (for English law purposes) by the law of the owner's domicile (though other countries may look to citizenship or habitual residence). An English law trust of movable assets is therefore potentially subject to challenge on the grounds that it offends against the laws to which the owner was subject; and
- as noted in paragraph 11.6, above, many offshore jurisdictions have enacted legislation which prohibits the bringing of claims that a trust is invalid, such claims being *solely* based on foreign matrimonial property and/or forced heirship rights. This does not necessarily prevent the bringing of claims (if the facts support such an allegation) that the trust is void as a sham (see further below in this chapter).

A claim based on foreign-forced heirship rights is a proprietary claim to the trust assets, and should be brought using the procedure in CPR Part 8 (discussed at paragraph 11.17 below). So, too, is a claim that the law of the settlor's domicile prevented him creating a trust, since in effect, the heirs are claiming that they would be absolutely entitled to the trust assets under his intestacy (or to a share of them, under his will).

Notably, the beneficiaries cannot usually advance a claim to attack the trust whilst at the same time claiming rights as beneficiaries under it. In *Lemos v Coutts & Co (Cayman) Ltd (1992–93) CILR 5*, this inconsistency meant that the trustees tried to put the claimant beneficiaries to an election, to prevent them from claiming as beneficiaries the disclosure of documents for the purposes of attacking the trust. In ordering disclosure of information (in effect, without prejudice as to whether the trust was found to be valid or not), the court required the claimant beneficiaries to give undertakings as to the use of the information disclosed to them, such that it could not be used in the forced heirship proceedings.

Creditors' claims

11.9 It is possible that a beneficiary of a trust may have a claim as creditor which affects the trust. This may happen in two ways:

- where he stands as creditor against the trust itself; and
- where he is a creditor of the settlor.

Creditor of the trust

11.10 Under English law as it currently stands, a creditor of the trust has no direct rights against the trust assets unless he has a properly enforceable charge over specified assets. Since the trust has no legal personality, the trustees must contract personally, and a creditor's rights are therefore against the trustees.

However, in limited circumstances (such as where the trustee is insolvent or untraceable), the creditor may be entitled to be subrogated to the trustee's right of reimbursement from the trust assets (*Staniar v Evans (1887) 34 Ch D 470*; *Re Blundell (1888) 40 Ch D 370*; *Re Raybould [1900] 1 Ch 199*; *Boscawen v Bajwa [1996] 1 WLR 328*). The creditor's right in such circumstances cannot be better than the right of the trustee himself. Since the trustee's right of reimbursement may be limited or lost to the extent that the trustee is himself indebted to the trust fund, by being liable to make good losses caused by breaches of trust for which he is liable, the creditor is subject to any restrictions on the right of the trustees through whom he claims (*McEwan v Crombie (1884) 25 Ch D 175*).

The Trust Law Committee Report '*Rights of creditors against trustees and trust funds*' (1999) makes the following recommendations for a future change in the law regarding creditors' rights in respect of trusts:

- '*10.3(a) Subject to any contrary intention in the trust instrument, where a trustee's entry into a contract with a creditor was in breach of his equitable duties this shall not prevent such creditor having a right of indemnity out of the trust fund unless he was dishonest.*
- (*b*). . .
- *10.4 Where an individual, who is a trustee . . . contracts with a person "as trustee" . . . he shall be rebuttably presumed not to contract otherwise than in such capacity and be liable personally no further than the value of the trust fund . . . at the time the other person requests payment*'.

As the law stands, however, the creditor must claim through the trustee. The procedure is likely to be that in CPR Part 7, because of the often complex issues involved in seeking subrogation to the rights of another person. The procedure to be followed is set out in CHAPTER 2 and APPENDIX 2.

Creditor of the settlor

11.11 Claims by creditors of the settlor's may affect the trust in two principal ways identified in the Insolvency Act 1986, if the trust is within the classes of transaction which may be set aside in the event of an individual's insolvency:

- transactions at an undervalue made within the previous five years; and
- transactions at an undervalue entered into at any time with the intention of defrauding creditors.

Transactions within a specified period before insolvency

11.12 The creation of a trust is almost invariably a transaction at an undervalue. Sections 339–342 of the Insolvency Act 1986 concern transactions at an undervalue entered into by an individual during a specified period prior to bankruptcy. The provisions are as follows:

- section 339 gives the court broad powers to make orders for '*restoring the position to what it would have been if the individual had not entered into*' a transaction at an undervalue, including gifts and all other transfers for a consideration less than the value transferred. This clearly includes the creation of a trust, the addition of funds to a trust, or other dealings such as loan transactions with a trust;
- section 340 contains similar powers to deal with bankrupts who have given preferences to creditors, and may, for example, affect a trust to which a settlor or beneficiary has repaid a loan in preference to paying his other creditors in advance of his insolvency;
- section 341 sets out the relevant period prior to bankruptcy during which a transaction at an undervalue can always be set aside. This is three years. A transaction entered into three to five years before bankruptcy may also be set aside, unless it can be shown that the transferor was not insolvent at the time of, nor did he become so as a result of, the transaction;
- if the court sets aside a transaction, it has broad powers to make orders relating to the property affected. For example, the court has power to '*require any property . . . to be vested in the trustee of the bankrupt's estate*', or to '*require any person to pay, in respect of benefits received by him from the individual, such sums . . . as the court may direct*' (section 341(1)). In other words, the trustees could be required to pay over the trust assets to the settlor's trustee in bankruptcy, and other beneficiaries could be required to restore assets they have received from the trust.

Transactions defrauding creditors

11.13 Sections 423–425 of the Insolvency Act 1986 contain separate provisions relating to any transactions at an undervalue entered into at any time with the intention of defrauding creditors. In the event of the transferor's insolvency, the trustee in bankruptcy of the transferor can challenge a trust which appears to have been created with such a motive. Furthermore, section 424 permits a challenge '*in any other case, by a victim of the transaction*'.

To set aside the creation of a trust, or a transfer of assets into a trust, the claimant must show that the transferor, in entering into the transaction, had as his purpose the aim of '*putting assets beyond the reach of a person who is making, or may at some time make, a claim against him*' or '*otherwise prejudicing the interests of such a person*' (section 423(3)). Where the transferor has more than one purpose, the court will assess, on the facts, whether the avoidance motive was uppermost in his mind, or sufficiently substantial that the transaction should be impugned. In *IRC v Hashmi (executor of Ghauri) [2002] EWCA Civ 981 [2002] 2 BCLC 48, CA*, there was evidence that the settlor had intended to provide for his son but, in creating a trust for his benefit, was aware that the transaction would put the property beyond his creditors' reach. There was held to be no overwhelming evidence that, at the date when he created the trust, the settlor intended exclusively to benefit his son, and accordingly his dominant purpose must have been to ensure that the beneficial interest in the property passed out of his estate. This was confirmed on appeal, although the test was held to be slightly different, namely that the avoidance motive need not be the only or the dominant purpose, but must be a 'real or substantial purpose'.

The court has similar powers under section 425 to those under section 341 (see paragraph 11.12 above) to make orders relating to the subject matter of transactions which are set aside. In *Hashmi,* above, the trust was set aside.

Sham

11.14 If a trust is shown to be a sham, the trust instrument will never have had any effect, and the trustees can never have been holding the trust assets on the express terms of the sham trust instrument. The expression 'sham trust' is used in two separate contexts:

(a) 'unilateral sham', where the settlor alone has no intention of creating a trust at all. It is doubtful whether this can truly be called a 'sham' (per Diplock LJ in *Snook*, referred to below), since the trust simply fails for want of intention to create a trust, one of the 'three certainties' fundamental to the creation of a valid trust (*Knight v Knight (1840) 3 Beav 148, 49 ER 58*); and

(b) 'bilateral sham' or 'common sham', where there are '*acts done or documents executed by the parties . . . which are intended by them to give to third parties or to the court the appearance of creating. . . legal rights or obligations different from the actual legal rights or obligations (if any) which the parties intended to create*', the essence being a common intention of all parties to the transaction or document that it should not have the effect it appears on its face to have (*Snook v London and West Riding Investments Ltd [1967] 2 QB 786 per Diplock LJ*).

The express retention of some powers of consent, veto, and appointment of trustees by the settlor on the face of the trust instrument does not necessarily make the trust a sham, since the document and the conduct of the parties are consistent, and the settlor may well have a duty to exercise the powers he has retained in a fiduciary manner (such as, for example, powers of appointment of new trustees). However, the retention of an excessive number of powers of consent or veto may indicate a lack of comfort with, or understanding of, the trust concept (which may result in failure of the trust for want of certainty), or may be evidence of a sham. Other indicia of a sham are often thought to include:

- the settlor retaining physical control of the trust assets;
- the settlor referring to the trust assets as his own;

- the existence of a letter of wishes which merely asks the trustees to give effect to any wishes expressed by the settlor from time to time (and after his death, those of another nominated person);
- the custom on the part of the settlor of telephoning or writing to the trustees with detailed instructions (for example, 'buy 10,000 BT shares at 110p or better', or 'please pay £5,000 to my son'), which the trustees commonly follow, often without evidence of separate consideration; and
- the existence of an expressly retained power for the settlor (as such, and not for example as protector) to remove trustees.

Perhaps the best-known example of a (common) sham trust was in *Rahman v Chase Bank Trust Company (CI) Ltd (1991) JLR 103*, where the settlor expressly retained certain powers over the trust, but in additional to those expressly retained powers he actually exercised a degree of control over the trust assets which was not contemplated by the wording of the trust deed. The judgment of the Royal Court of Jersey was that, '*from the date on which [Rahman] purported to constitute the settlement he exercised dominion and control over the trustee in the management and administration of the settlement . . . he treated the assets comprised in the trust fund as his own and the trustee as though it were his mere agent or nominee*'.

Effects of sham

11.15 The question of whether the existence of a sham is fatal to the whole trust depends on the circumstances of a particular case:

- the sham may affect part only of the conduct or documents complained of (perhaps, for a trust, in relation only to certain additions of property, or some only of the terms of the trust), while the rest of the document or transaction is valid (*Hitch v Stone [2002] EWCA Civ 63*);
- where the settlor's intention is that a trust will only become valid on the occurrence of a contingency, it remains a sham if the validating of the trust would prejudice others. In *Midland Bank v Wyatt [1995] 1 FLR 697*, a trust of the family home was only intended to have effect in the event that the bank foreclosed on the mortgage. For obvious reasons, when the bank did so, the trust was not perfected, since the interest of the bank would have been prejudiced;
- a sham trust may not be perfected by death. A settlor may intend to continue to enjoy (and perhaps control) the assets during his life, intending the express trusts to have no real effect until his death. For a person domiciled in England and Wales, every disposition to take effect on death must comply with the formalities for the execution of a will, as set out in section 9 of the Wills Act 1837. (Settlors subject to the laws of some other jurisdiction must comply with the relevant formalities, which may be less stringent than the requirements of English law.) If it does not comply with the relevant requirements, the trust may be void as an insufficiently

formally executed testamentary document (*Re Pfrimmer's Estate [1936] 2 DLR 123 (Manitoba), Cock v Cooke (1866) LR 1 P&D 241*).

However, a likely result of a finding of sham by the court is that the settlor retains the full beneficial ownership of all the trust assets, such that the trustees hold them on resulting trusts for him alone.

This is a further situation where the claim, as a hostile one against the validity of the trust, which goes to the question of the beneficial interest in the 'trust assets', ought to be brought using the procedure in CPR Part 8, discussed at paragraph 11.17 below.

Other proprietary claims to the trust assets

11.16 In addition to the claims under community of property and forced heirship principles discussed elsewhere in this chapter, a claim may be made by any third party (whether or not related to the settlor) based on an assertion that the assets of the trust belong to them and not to the settlor (see, for example, *Alsop Wilkinson v Neary [1995] 1 All ER 431*). Again, this is a claim which must be brought under CPR Part 8, as a claim to be beneficially entitled to the 'trust assets'.

Procedure

11.17 The claims discussed in this chapter have in common, despite their varying causes, the fact that they are all hostile, and mainly proprietary, claims to the trust assets.

If they become aware of a possible proprietary claim, the trustees must not actively defend the claim without the leave of the court. The trustees are entitled to refuse to distribute capital (or income) where there are pending claims which cast doubt as to their title to any trust asset (*Neale v Davies (1854) 5 De GM&G 258, 43 ER 869*; *Moss v Integro*). Indeed, it would seem sensible to take no steps to dispose of any assets prior to the matter being heard before the court, since the effect of such a claim being asserted is that the trustees become aware that they may not be holding the trust assets (or some of them) upon the expressly declared trusts, but may be holding them upon resulting trusts for the claimant. The trustee is at risk of personal liability if he takes any steps which are inconsistent with whatever may turn out to be the true beneficial ownership of the trust assets.

It is notable that the trustees' duty, when faced with a proprietary claim to the trust assets, is to remain neutral and to present the court with all the facts and information known to them, but without purporting to prefer the settlor's version of the truth to that of the claimant (see *In re Bank of America Trust Co*

(Jersey) Limited (1995) JLR n29, for example, where the trustee was required to remain neutral even though the effect was to leave the claim undefended). This goes to the question of costs, discussed below.

Nor, consistently with the trustees' duty not to set up *jus tertii*, may they actively encourage a third party claim to the trust assets, nor notify a potential claimant of his right to claim against the trust (*Twigg & Franks v Mason (1916) 50 Ir LTR 173, HL*).

It is sensible for trustees in this situation to apply to the court at the earliest opportunity (as in *Finers v Miro [1991] 1 All ER 182, CA*) for directions as to the true trusts upon which they hold the assets. The court has a broad discretion to make orders which will help resolve any dispute as to title, or indeed, may direct the trustees to continue dealing with the trust assets in accordance with the trust instrument, there being no *prima facie* evidence of wrongdoing (*Moss v Integro (1997/98) 1 OFLR 427*).

Whether the initiative is taken by the trustees, or a hostile claim is launched by the beneficiaries (as creditors, or as a proprietary claim to the trust assets), the appropriate procedure to be used is also that in CPR 8. As explained in CHAPTER 2, CPR Part 64 makes this clear by providing expressly that certain trust-related claims *must* be commenced using the Part 8 procedure. The two Practice Directions which accompany that Part (CPR 64 PD and CPR 64B PD) explain that such claims may include:

- claims relating to a beneficial interest in any property subject to a trust;
- claims regarding the rights or interest of any person claiming to be beneficially entitled under a trust; and
- applications for directions by the trustees.

The appropriate procedure, and sample timeline, for CPR Part 8 proceedings are set out in CHAPTER 2 and APPENDIX 1.

Costs

11.18 Trustees faced with a proprietary claim should, as noted throughout this chapter, remain neutral, and present the court with all the relevant information available to them (whether or not it advances either argument). If they do this, then it is likely that the costs order will be as follows:

- if the claimant is successful, the trustees will nonetheless be entitled to take their costs out of the trust fund; and
- if the claimant is unsuccessful, the costs may be ordered to be paid by the claimant, since it is unjust that the trust fund should bear the costs of an unsuccessful claim.

If the trustees do not remain neutral, then they may be personally at risk as to costs if the arguments they advance (for whichever side they choose) are unsuccessful. It would be unfair to burden the trust fund with the costs of the trustees if the trustees have, in breach of their duty not to set up *jus tertii*, either:

- argued against the claimant, and it is later found that the trust assets belong to him; or
- sided with the claimant, and the trust is found valid in respect of all the trust assets.

There is considerable discretion as to the claimant's costs. The claimant may be ordered to pay his own costs (and those of other parties) if his claim is unsuccessful. If his claim is proved, however, he may be able to claim his costs against the settlor (if still alive, and if he is the person who has purported to settle assets which he had no right to settle) or against the trustees (if they have behaved unreasonably). Otherwise, the costs may be paid out of the trust assets, if there is no other party who has argued against his claim and against whom it is reasonable to charge the costs of the proceedings. The case of *d'Abo v Paget (2000) The Times, 10 August* was one where costs were ordered out of the trust fund. The judge said: '*These are proceedings which in the ordinary course would have been brought by the trustees . . . If [the claimant] had not instituted the proceedings, the trustees would have had to do so in order to establish the interests of the beneficiaries.*'

As discussed in other chapters (see CHAPTER 3, for example), there is power under CPR Part 64 for the court to order costs to be paid pre-emptively out of the trust fund. Where the claim is a proprietary one, however, it appears less likely that such an order would be made, since to do so might be to prejudge the likely outcome of the case. *Quaere* however whether, if the beneficiaries and the claimants are the same (but in different capacities), such an order could appropriately be made.

Chapter 12

Applications for directions

Introduction

12.1 In CHAPTER 1, the *Alsop Wilkinson* categorisation of trust-related litigation was set out, as follows:

- '*Trust disputes*', which relate to the trusts on which the trustees are holding the assets;
- '*Beneficiaries' disputes*', which are 'internal' claims by the beneficiaries relating to the propriety of actions taken (or omitted to be taken) by the trustees, or which they may take in future; and
- '*Third party disputes*', that is, claims by or against the trustees involving only third parties, such as contractual disputes.

(From *Alsop Wilkinson v Neary [1995] 1 All ER 431*.)

In the context of any of these types of claim, it may be appropriate for the trustees to seek the directions of the court, for example in the following cases:

- claims for interpretation of the trust instrument, or the powers of the trustees;
- hostile claims by family members or third parties that the assets of the trust belong to them and are not held on the (purported) express trusts at all (see CHAPTER 11);
- where there are questions over the management or administration of the trust, or the exercise of the powers, duties and discretions of the trustees;
- where the trustees propose to incur costs at the expense of the trust fund to bring, or defend, proceedings for the benefit of the trust.

Whatever the nature of the proceedings or question to which the directions application relates, the directions proceedings themselves have in common the fact that the trustees' duty is to apply to the court in a neutral manner, and to bring to the court's attention all the facts and information they have, so as to assist the court in determining the correct course of action or the truth of a situation. They must not spend trust money on arguing for, or against, any particular view.

The reason for including this topic in a book on beneficiaries' actions is two-fold:

- many of the actions discussed in this book which are available to the beneficiaries will, at some point, require the directions of the court to be given to the trustees, so as to make the directions application an integral part of the claim process; and
- the beneficiaries themselves have an important right, not to be overlooked, to seek the directions of the court if the trustees have not done so, or refuse to do so (see, for example, *In re Buckton [1907] 2 Ch 406*, where Kekewich J said: '*although the application is made, not by trustees . . . but by some of the beneficiaries, yet it is made by reason of some difficulty of construction, or administration, which would have justified an application by the trustees*').

Directions regarding an exercise of powers or discretions

12.2 Trustees who are in any doubt regarding a possible exercise of any of the powers or discretions vested in them by the trust deed or by the general law can apply to the court for directions. This may happen in one of three types of situation identified by Hart J in the case of *Public Trustee v Cooper and others [2001] WTLR 901*:

- '(*1*) *the first category is where the issue is whether some proposed action is within the trustees' powers . . . A question of that sort must be decided in open court and only after hearing argument from both sides;*
- (*2*) *the second category is where the issue is whether the proposed course of action is a proper exercise of the trustees' powers where there is no real doubt as to the nature of [those] powers . . . but, because the decision is particularly momentous, the trustees wish to obtain the blessing of the court for the action on which they have resolved . . . In a case like that, there is no question of surrender of discretion;*
- (*3*) *the third category is that of surrender of discretion properly so called. There the court will only accept a surrender of discretion for a good reason, the most obvious good reasons being either that the trustees are deadlocked* (*but honestly so, so that the question cannot be resolved by removing one trustee rather than another*) *or because the trustees are disabled as a result of conflict of interest;*

(*Cases within* (*2*) *and* (*3*) *are similar in that they are both . . . traditionally heard in chambers in which adversarial argument is not essential though it sometimes occurs . . .*)'.

(Hart J identified a fourth category, namely where trustees have acted, and their actions are attacked by the beneficiaries in hostile litigation. In such cases, the directions of the court are not required, so much as a pronouncement on whether or not their actions can be impugned.)

The discretions as to which the trustees may require the guidance of the court are discussed in CHAPTER 7, but the trustees may also use this form of application for directions as to the exercise of any of their administrative powers, and must do so if the trust is subject to an administration order (see CHAPTER 10). They may be seeking interpretation, confirmation, or resolution of a deadlock where they honestly cannot decide what to do.

As noted in *Cooper*, the court will only rarely accept a surrender of discretion, as opposed to giving the trustees guidance on the extent of, or appropriate application of, their powers and discretions. Indeed, the court may refuse to accept a surrender of discretion where the circumstances are not sufficiently unusual to justify it (see, for example, *Re Allen-Meyrick's Will Trusts [1966] 1 WLR 499*, where the court required the trustees, rather than seeking the court's exercise of their discretion as to a long-term policy they could not decide upon but did not need to formulate, to exercise their own discretion from time to time).

If the trustees refuse to apply for directions on a particular matter, the beneficiaries may apply to the court, joining the trustees as defendants, and request the directions of the court as to the matter in question. This will be binding on the trustees (if the directions are mandatory) or, at the least, will constitute guidance as to an exercise of their discretion which they would disregard at their own risk as to the costs of any further application.

Directions where the trustees have conflicts of interest

12.3 Hart J's third category (in *Public Trustee v Cooper and others [2001] WTLR 901*) is that of 'surrender of discretion'. As he explained, the court will only accept a surrender of discretion for a good reason. One such good reason is where the trustees are disabled as a result of conflict of interest.

The judge noted what he called 'a surprising lack of English authority on the consequences of trustees acting or purporting to act in situations . . . where actual or potential conflicts are alleged to exist'. He observed that, in such situations, the burden is upon the allegedly conflicted trustee to show that his conflict has not caused him to act in a way which is for his own benefit, such that it can be set aside.

How, then, can a trustee's conflict be managed so as to avoid difficulty? Unlike in companies, where a director can declare an interest or conflict, and may take no part in a decision in relation to which his conflict disables him, the position of trusts is different. Trustees of a private trust – unlike directors of a company, or charitable trustees – are required to act unanimously, and this means that the conflicted trustee cannot simply 'rubber-stamp' a decision made by his fellow trustees. As discussed in CHAPTER 7, the beneficiaries are entitled to the active participation of every trustee in reaching the unanimous decision.

Hart J went on to identify three ways of managing a conflict:

- *'the trustee concerned [may] resign. This will not always provide a practical or sensible solution. The trustee concerned may represent an important source of information or advice to his co-trustees or have a significant relationship to some or all of the beneficiaries such that his or her departure as a trustee will be potentially harmful to the interests of the trust estate or its beneficiaries';*

- *'the nature of the conflict may be so pervasive throughout the trustee body that they, as a body, have no alternative but to surrender their discretion to the court'; or*

- *'the trustees may honestly and reasonably believe that, notwithstanding a conflict affecting one or more of their number, they are nevertheless able fairly and reasonably to take the decision. In this case, it will usually be prudent, if time allows, for the trustees to allow their proposed exercise of discretion to be scrutinised in advance by the court . . .'.*

If the trustees do not apply to the court, either by way of surrender of discretion, or for a 'blessing', then they run the risk that one or more of the beneficiaries may later attack the exercise of the power or discretion. The beneficiaries are not entitled as of right to have every exercise of a power or discretion where one or more of the trustees was conflicted set aside. However, the allegation that it was an imperfect exercise places the burden on the conflicted trustee(s) to justify the exercise of their discretion and to demonstrate that their decision was one which any reasonable body of trustees might have taken, and further, that it was not in fact influenced by the conflict.

An ongoing conflict – whether pre-existing before the relevant trustee took on his office, or arising afterwards – is usually sufficient to mean the resignation of the trustee is to be recommended, so as to avoid the expense and inconvenience of applications to the court. However, as Hart J foresaw, there may be situations where the experience or skills of the trustee are of particular value to the trust. This was not the case in *Wight v Olswang (1999) The Times, 18 May*, CA where Mummery LJ found that the solicitor trustee did not merely fail to sell, or actually retain, the shares – he refused to entertain a bid on the ground of his conflict of interest. The solicitor trustee should have taken steps to ensure his replacement by a trustee who would not have been so hampered.

Beddoe applications

12.4 If trustees wish to embark on litigation, or are faced with a claim that they wish to defend, it has long been recognised that they ought first to apply to the court for directions for leave to do so at the expense of the trust fund. There are three principal reasons for this:

- to ensure that they can appropriately charge their own costs of the litigation, win or lose, to the trust fund (subject to any other costs order that might be made);

- to ensure that they can pay the costs of their successful opponent to the trust fund (if ordered against them); and

- to protect the trustees against any future claim by any of the beneficiaries that, in paying any or all of these costs from the trust fund, they were acting improperly.

The case of *In Re Beddoe, Downes v Cottam [1893] 1 Ch 547, CA* provides the best-known authority for this need for what is often called a '*Beddoe* application'. In that case, Lindley LJ said (at page 557): '*A trustee who, without the sanction of the Court, commences an action or defends an action unsuccessfully, does so at his own risk as regards the costs, even if he acts on counsel's opinion; and when the trustee seeks to obtain such costs out of his trust estate, he ought not to be allowed to charge them against his [beneficiaries] unless under very exceptional circumstances. If, indeed, the judge comes to the conclusion that he would have authorised the action or defence had he been applied to, he might, in the exercise of his discretion, allow the costs incurred by the trustee out of the estate; but I cannot imagine any other circumstances under which the cost of an unauthorised and unsuccessful action brought or defended by a trustee could be properly thrown on the estate.*'

The sorts of claims for which *Beddoe* applications are appropriate are:

- claims by the trustees against third parties, or vice versa, which do not amount to proprietary claims against the trust assets;

- proprietary claims against the trust assets where the trustees reasonably believe that the evidence very strongly supports one analysis rather than the other (eg *Barclays Private Bank & Trust v Bhander (No 2) [1998–99] 1 ITELR 46*);

- claims for the recovery of trust assets; and

- claims by the body of trustees against one of their number, or against beneficiaries (as to which, see paragraph 12.6 below).

Claims for which *Beddoe* applications are not appropriate, by virtue of the fact that it is unlikely that the costs would ever be ordered to be paid out of the trust fund, include:

- proprietary claims against the trust fund (in the ordinary course, where there is no compelling evidence either way, as in *In re Bank of America Trust Co (Jersey) Limited (1995) JLR n29*, where the trustee was required to remain neutral even though the effect was to leave the claim undefended);

- claims for breach of trust; and

- claims for removal of the trustees, or the imposition of a receiver, in either case at the instance of the beneficiaries.

Procedure

12.5 The *Beddoe* procedure was summarised by Bowen LJ in *Re Beddoe.* The trustees must:

- take out an originating summons (now a claim form under CPR Part 8);
- state the point under discussion, giving all the facts and information, including any which would support their intended case, or work against it (for if they do not disclose facts which are relevant, the *Beddoe* order they have obtained may be ineffective);
- ask the Court whether the point is one which should be fought out or abandoned.

In deciding whether the order should be granted, the court will weigh up the merits of the case (usually, an opinion of counsel is required as to the merits of the case), the reasonableness of the course of action proposed to be taken, and the likelihood of the proposed course of action being successful. The court may also consider what costs order(s) might be made at the end of the matter in issue. (*Alsop Wilkinson v Neary [1995] 1 All ER 431*). Consultation with beneficiaries is often appropriate, and the court will wish to know to what extent this has taken place, and its results.

The court will commonly (if it authorises the trustees to proceed) give the trustees leave only to proceed up to a specified point of the proceedings, such as close of pleadings, before returning to the court for further directions as to whether to continue.

In cases of urgency, the trustees may proceed with their action or defence without first obtaining the leave of the court, but would be prudent to seek a *Beddoe* order at the earliest opportunity (either simultaneously, or immediately afterwards). They will be proceeding at risk of having to pay their own costs (and those of other parties if so ordered) if their course of action is unsuccessful, and not later approved by the court. Therefore, in purely practical terms, the sooner the court's approval is sought, the less likely it is that they will have incurred substantial costs which may be for their own account. However, an early *Beddoe* application also goes to the question of reasonableness and prudence, which may be factors that the court takes into account when considering whether it is appropriate to allow them to charge their costs to the trust fund.

What the trustees may not do (as Lindley LJ had indicated in *Re Beddoe)*, is rely on legal advice alone in ordinary cases without special urgency. In *Singh v Bhasin [1999] WTLR 275*, the trustees had taken an opinion of counsel that there was a good defence to a claim, but did not seek a *Beddoe* order. When their defence failed, it was said that they were not entitled to take their costs from the trust fund unless the court could be satisfied that, had they applied for a *Beddoe* order, the court would have authorised them to proceed with the defence.

Re Moritz applications

12.6 In paragraphs 12.4 and 12.5, the *Beddoe* procedure was considered in its general form. However, a special procedure applies when the trustees, or beneficiaries, seek the leave of the court to sue one or more of the trustees. It is also used where the proposed action is against one or more of the beneficiaries or (occasionally) where the proposed course of action is to defend hostile proceedings brought by a beneficiary against the trust.

In Re Moritz, deceased [1960] Ch 251 is authority for the fact that the *Beddoe* procedure is available in special form where the prospective defendant(s) are likely to be present in court. In that case, Wynn-Parry J explained that, while it may be proper and necessary to join the parties against whom the proposed action is to be taken, those parties should not be present in court (either in person, or through solicitors or counsel) when the matter is debated, and they should not be provided with the evidence which the court is asked to consider.

This approach was endorsed for potential claims or defences against beneficiaries in *In re Ojjeh Trust [1992–3] CILR 348*, where the question put to the court related to legal proceedings instituted by the beneficiary outside the jurisdiction. The beneficiary was excluded from the relevant parts of the hearing.

Applications by beneficiaries on behalf of the trust

12.7 As noted in paragraph 12.1, where the trustees have declined to bring an application for directions, the beneficiaries may be able to apply for directions instead. Similarly, where the trustees refuse to bring legal proceedings against one of their number, or some third party, for the benefit of the trust, the beneficiaries (or any of them) may apply under the *Beddoe* procedure for leave to stand in the shoes of the trustees, and to bring the claim on behalf of the trust (see, for example, *In re Buckton [1907] 2 Ch 406* and *d'Abo v Paget (2000) (The Times, 10 August))*.

In *Wallersteiner v Moir (No 2) [1975] QB 373, CA*, it was said that, '*Seeing that, if the action succeeds, the whole benefit will go to the company, it is only just that the shareholder should be indemnified against the costs he incurs on its behalf. . .If the action fails . . . assuming that the shareholder had reasonable grounds for bringing the action – that it was a reasonable and prudent course to take in the interests of the company – he should not himself be liable to pay the costs of the other side . . . [and] should be indemnified by the company in respect of his own costs even if the action fails . . . In order to be entitled to this indemnity, the shareholder soon after issuing his writ should apply for the sanction of the court in somewhat the same way as a trustee does* (*In Re Beddoe*)*. . . the shareholder should apply ex parte to the master for directions, supported by an opinion of counsel as to whether there is a reasonable case or not . . ..*'

The whole of this chapter may, in appropriate circumstances, be read as if it were the beneficiaries applying for directions and not the trustees.

Procedure

12.8 The procedure in CPR Part 8 would logically be the most appropriate procedure to use when applying for the court's directions. Indeed, the two Practice Directions which accompany CPR Part 64 (CPR 64 PD and CPR 64B PD) expressly provide that, among the trust-related claims which *must* be commenced using the Part 8 procedure, are:

- claims relating to a beneficial interest in any property subject to a trust;
- claims regarding the rights or interest of any person claiming to be beneficially entitled under a trust;
- claims for any of the following remedies:
  - (i) an order requiring a trustee to do, or not to do, any act;
  - (ii) an order approving any transaction (eg sale, purchase, or compromise); or
  - (iii) an order directing any act to be done which the court could order to be done if the trust were being administered or executed under the direction of the court;
- applications for directions by the trustees,

any of which could be the subject matter of the various directions applications discussed in this chapter.

The claim form must contain:

- a statement that Part 8 applies to the claim;
- a statement that the remedy sought is the directions of the court;
- a summary of the legal basis on which that remedy is sought, ie the particular matter which requires directions and why it is that the trustees are unable to decide the matter without the court's assistance; and
- a statement of truth.

The claimants must file and serve the evidence on which they intend to rely, in the form of a witness statement, at the same time as the claim form.

The defendants have 14 days in which to acknowledge service of the claim form, and (unless the time is extended – see APPENDIX 1) must file and serve their evidence in the form of a witness statement at the same time as they acknowledge service.

The matter will then proceed in accordance with the procedure and timetable set out in CHAPTER 2 and APPENDIX 1 until trial. The order then made will authorise (or, as the case may be, require) the trustees to take the particular course of action specified, or direct the trustees as to the true trusts upon which they are holding the assets to which a proprietary claim has been made.

Parties

12.9 Whilst all the trustees must be parties to the application, the beneficiaries need not all be parties (either personally or by representation). Only those who wish to be parties, or whose interests will be affected by the proposed actions, need be joined (CPR Part 64.4(1)). It may occasionally be appropriate to join other parties, such as the protector, if the proposed course of action will affect them. (See CHAPTER 2 for a discussion of the appointment of representative beneficiaries and litigation friends.)

Costs

12.10 Trustees should strive to be jointly represented wherever possible, so as to reduce the overall costs. In *Gaunt v Taylor (1840) 2 Beav 346*, Lord Langdale MR noted that trustees are generally only allowed one set of costs. However, there will be exceptions to that general rule, such as:

- where one trustee has a personal interest which conflicts with his fiduciary duty;
- if one of several trustees can admit facts which the others believe not to be true; or
- if the matter in relation to which directions are sought relates to proposed legal proceedings against one or more of the trustees.

Clearly, in such cases the trustees cannot be jointly represented, but the question of whether they are entitled to two sets of costs depends on the circumstances of the case. The question will be whether there were reasonable grounds for them to be separately represented. If so, more than one set of costs may be allowed (or part of the costs). If they have acted unreasonably in being separately advised, or if one of the separately represented parties departs from the usual requirement for neutrality, then some or all of their costs may be disallowed.

In *In re Buckton [1907] 2 Ch 406*, Kekewich J identified two main types of directions application:

- '*In a large proportion of [cases] . . . the applicants are trustees . . . who ask the Court to construe the instrument of trust for their guidance, and in order to ascertain the interests of the beneficiaries, or else ask to have some question determined which has arisen in the administration of the trusts. In cases of this character I regard the costs of all parties as necessarily incurred for the benefit of the estate, and direct them to be taxed as between solicitor and client and paid out of the estate*';

- '*There is a second class of cases differing in form, but not in substance, from the first. In these cases . . . although the application is made, not by trustees . . . but by some of the beneficiaries, yet it is made by reason of some difficulty of construction, or administration, which would have justified an application by the trustees . . . To cases of this class I extend the operation of the same rule as is observed in cases of the first class.*'

Generally, therefore, the usual form of costs order in respect of an application for directions is that the costs of all parties are to be paid out of the trust fund. It is only if the person(s) applying for directions are found to have acted unreasonably in seeking directions which are unnecessary that the costs may be ordered against them personally (as in *Tod v Barton [2002] EWHC 265 (Ch), (2002) 4 ITELR 715*).

As discussed in other chapters (see, for example, CHAPTER 3), pre-emptive costs orders may be available if it appears to the court that any party would otherwise be unable to participate in the proceedings. CPR Part 64 gives the court a broad discretion to make pre-emptive costs orders if the trustees have no power to pay the parties' costs out of the trust fund, or are unwilling (or uncertain as to whether) to exercise such power. This subject is more generally discussed in CHAPTER 3, but in the context of directions proceedings, it is often likely to be in the interests of the trust that any party who wishes to appear should be able to do so.

Chapter 13

Liability of trustees

Introduction

13.1 There is a further important issue to be considered in the context of any potential claim, in addition to the questions of what claims may be brought against trustees, and what remedies may be available to make good the loss or damage suffered by the trust and/or its beneficiaries. This third main question, namely whether the trustees are liable to make good any loss or damage in a particular case (whether or not a remedy is available in principle) is, however, dealt with only after considering any defences that the trustees may have, or whether there is any other reason why they should be excused or relieved from liability. It is also worth considering whether there may be other persons upon whom liability can be fixed. A former trustee, or any other person who has been closely connected with the breach, may be liable for dishonest assistance in a breach of trust (see CHAPTER 14).

This chapter therefore considers the following questions relating to the issue of whether a claim will be enforceable against the trustees:

- Is the trustee liable in principle for the act or omission causing the loss or damage?
- Can the beneficiaries enforce the claim against some other person?
- Is the claim time-barred, or barred in equity?
- Are the beneficiaries prevented from bringing the claim by reference to their role in, or knowledge of, the breach?

Before considering these other aspects of liability and enforceability, it is worth considering whether the trustees' reliance on legal advice can operate as a defence.

Reliance on legal advice

13.2 Trustees who are uncertain as to how to proceed have a duty to seek legal advice to resolve their difficulty. However, it has long been established that reliance on legal advice is not, in itself, sufficient to excuse trustees from liability for a breach of trust which they commit (even if that breach results from incorrect legal advice) (*Doyle v Blake (1804) 2 Sch & Lef 231*). It is always open to trustees to apply to the court for directions as to any matter affecting the trust and, if they choose not to do so, but act in reliance on legal advice alone without the further reassurance of the court's directions, they may be held liable if what results from that course of action is a breach.

Nor can a trust deed validly remove the obligation to seek legal advice (or the directions of the court). A clause which purports to give trustees the absolute right to determine any question before them will be struck out as an invalid attempt to oust the jurisdiction of the court (*Re Tuck's Settlement Trusts [1978] Ch 49, CA*). It is permissible to give the trustees power to determine questions of fact, however.

The question of whether trustees have taken legal advice, and relied upon it (even if it is wrong) will be taken into account by the court in determining whether or not, in all the circumstances, the trustees should be excused from liability under the statutory provisions discussed in paragraph 13.21 below. It may also be a relevant factor in determining whether they have acted reasonably and/or in good faith, for the purposes of any express exculpatory provisions (see paragraphs 13.12 to 13.20 below).

Trustee's liability for own acts

13.3 The basic rule is clear – a trustee must abide by the terms of the trust deed, and the provisions of the general law, and, in so doing, he must act in the best interests of the beneficiaries. If he deviates from the terms of the trust, and a loss results, or if he breaches his fiduciary duties and makes a profit for himself (even where the trust suffers no loss), he is always, subject to any defences or reliefs available to him, liable for the consequences of his own acts and defaults. It is not sufficient for him to say that he did not know that what he was doing was a breach, or that he was induced to commit the breach by someone else, or that he went along with the other trustees.

The deviation or breach itself, therefore, is enough to create potential liability on the part of the trustee to make good the damage caused (or profit gained). In *Royal Brunei Airlines Sdn Bhd v Philip Tan Kok Ming [1995] 2 AC 378, PC*, Lord Nicholls put it thus (at page 390): '*So far as the trustee himself is concerned the legal analysis is straightforward. Honesty or lack of honesty is not the test for his liability. He is obliged to comply with the terms of the trust. His liability is strict. If he departs from the trust terms he is liable unless excused by a provision in the trust instrument or relieved by the court.*'

However, there are practical, reasonable limits on the liability of the trustee. In *Re Chapman [1896] 2 Ch 763, CA*, Lindley LJ explained it thus: '*a trustee is not a surety, nor is he an insurer; he is only liable for some wrong done by himself, and loss of trust money is not per se proof of such wrong . . . Trustees acting honestly, with ordinary prudence and within the limits of their trust, are not liable for mere errors of judgment.*' Not every loss, therefore, is an actionable loss, even when it can be attributed to a particular act or omission on the part of the trustees. Later parts of this chapter consider in detail whether the trustees have defences available to them, or can be relieved from liability on some other ground, but it is an important starting principle that a loss may not, in fact, be anyone's fault at all.

Where more than one trustee is liable for the breach, their liability is joint and several, but the court has power (either under the Civil Liability (Contributions) Act 1978, or under its inherent jurisdiction) to make such orders as are just and equitable in all the circumstances for the proportionate liability of each of the trustees who have been found liable.

Trustee's liability for acts of others

13.4 It is generally the case that a trustee is liable only for his own acts and omissions, and not those of his fellow trustees or of predecessor or successor trustees (*Townley v Sherborne (1633) Bridg 35*). This principle was also enshrined in section 30(1) of the Trustee Act 1925, which used to provide expressly that each trustee was liable only for his own acts and defaults. However, that protection was removed by Trustee Act 2000. There is now no presumption of non-liability for the 'innocent' trustee – rather, the burden is on him to show that he acted reasonably. In so doing, the 'innocent' trustee will need to establish:

- that he did not himself, in allowing the breach to be committed, commit a breach of his own;
- that he did not turn a blind eye to the conduct of his fellow trustees;
- that he took no steps which were designed to facilitate the breach occurring.

The trustee's own independent breach

13.5 In *Townley v Sherborne*, the case concerned the receipt by only one of the trustees of sums due to the trust. It was held that, not only were his fellow trustees not liable to account for sums received by him, but that, absent any fraud or wrongdoing on their part, they had not committed a breach of trust by permitting the moneys to be paid to him alone. In other situations, however, it is easy to see that a trustee might himself commit a breach of trust by allowing a situation to exist where another or others were able to commit a breach. For example, if one trustee took no active role in the management of the trust through his own default, then he might be held liable, by virtue of that default, if his fellow trustees (who took an active role) were thereby able to cause loss or to misappropriate trust assets.

Similarly, if new trustees became aware of breaches by the former trustees (which they ought to do, if they fulfil their obligation to acquaint themselves with the affairs and assets of the trust – *Harvey v Olliver (1887) 57 LT 239*) then they should consider whether to sue them. If they do not pursue the former trustees, without reasonable grounds, they may be liable for their own breach of trust in failing to get in the trust assets, of which the right to recover damages for the breach in question is one (*Hobday v Peters (No 3) (1860) 28 Beav 603*).

Turning a blind eye

13.6 A trustee who closes his eyes to what his fellow trustees are doing (or not doing) may render himself liable for the consequences of their action (or inaction). An apparently 'innocent' trustee who has, for example, signed trustee resolutions or other documents by which the breach has been facilitated, while seemingly unaware of his fellow trustees' intentions, could be liable for wilful default, or (if he turned a blind eye despite his suspicion as to what might be happening) a dishonest breach of trust.

In this context, '*acting dishonestly, or with a lack of probity . . . means simply not acting as an honest person would in the circumstances*' (*Royal Brunei Airlines Sdn Bhd v Tan [1995] 2 AC 378, PC*, per Lord Nicholls at page 389). That test is a purely objective one. Lord Nicholls was explicit, however, in distinguishing negligence from dishonesty: '*Carelessness is not dishonesty. Thus for the most part dishonesty is to be equated with conscious impropriety*', and further, '*Imprudence is not dishonesty, although imprudence may be carried recklessly to lengths which call into question the honesty of the person making the decision . . .*'.

Taking steps to facilitate a breach

13.7 Even where a trustee has not acted dishonestly, he may nonetheless have taken steps which were intended to facilitate a breach of trust. Faced with a request, for example, to make an investment which he believes to be outside his powers, if he refuses (as he ought to do), it would be a breach of trust for him then to retire in favour of another trustee who it is intended, or hoped, will be more amenable to the request. This situation was discussed in *Head v Gould [1898] 2 Ch 250,* where Kekewich J said (at page 272): '*[The question is] did they denude themselves of the trust funds under circumstances that warranted any reasonable belief of the insecurity of the trust funds in the hands of those to whom they committed them?*'

Whilst Kekewich J set a high bar for claimant beneficiaries by saying, at pages 273–4: '*In order to make a retiring trustee liable for a breach of trust committed by his successor you must show . . . that the very breach of trust which was in fact committed was not merely the outcome of the retirement and new appointment, but was contemplated by the former trustee when such retirement and appointment took place*', there is some scope in an earlier passage of his judgment for believing that the liability of retiring trustees is potentially wider. At pages 268–9 of the report, he said: '*It is the duty of trustees to protect the funds entrusted to their care, and to distribute those funds or hand them over to their successors intact . . . This duty is imposed upon them as long as they remain trustees and must be their guide in every act done by them as trustees. On retiring from the trust and passing on the trust estate to their successors . . . they are acting as trustees, and it is equally incumbent upon them in this ultimate act of office to fulfil the duty imposed on them as at any other time. If therefore they neglect that duty and part with the property without due regard to it, they remain liable . . . for the consequences properly traceable to that neglect.*' It appears, therefore, that even if the later breach was not expressly contemplated, the retirement of the former trustee without due regard to the safety of the trust assets, and the interests of the beneficiaries, could render him liable if losses later occur by reason of the new trustees' inherent unsuitability.

This duty would, it appears, extend to situations where the trustee is removed (a power which, in modern trust deeds, is often vested in his fellow trustees, or a Protector or Appointor). If he has grounds to doubt that the continuing or replacement trustees will safeguard the trust assets, or act in the interests of the beneficiaries as a whole, then it may be incumbent upon him to apply to the court for directions as to how to proceed (see CHAPTER 12).

Liability of directors of corporate trustees

13.8 Whilst, in past times, it was common to have trusted individuals such as friends and professional advisers to act as trustees, it has (since at least the growth of the trust industry in the 1960s) increasingly frequently been the case that professional trust companies are appointed as trustees. The enforcement of a claim against such companies rarely presents any practical difficulties, as they are likely to be required by their local regulatory body to carry adequate insurance and, in any event, are likely to have substantial assets of their own. However, in the (ever-decreasing number of) unregulated jurisdictions, this may not always be the position, and a small professional trust company may, in reality, have few assets and little (if any) insurance cover. A bigger difficulty, perhaps, is presented by family trust companies, which are incorporated for the particular purpose of acting as trustee of one or more family trusts. These companies are unlikely ever to have any assets, and are not usually regulated (and therefore not required to carry insurance).

An award of damages for breach of trust against such an insubstantial and/or uninsured trust company could, on its face, appear unrecoverable. In some cases, it is possible that the claimant beneficiaries may have little option but to take the losses, and to fall back on their right to ask the court to replace the trustees with others who will have greater care of the assets in future.

In some cases, however, it may be possible to bring a so-called 'dog-leg' claim against the directors of the trust company, assuming that they have assets against which redress could be obtained. This possibility was raised in the judgment of Nicholls LJ in *Royal Brunei Airlines v Tan [1995] 2 AC 378, PC*, when discussing the potential liability of advisers to the trustees, such as solicitors, bankers, and so on: '*[the third party advisers] have undertaken work for the trustees. They must carry out that work properly. If they fail to do so, they will be liable to make good the loss suffered by the trustees in consequence. This will include, where appropriate, the loss suffered by the trustees, being exposed to claims for breach of trust.*'

This passage of Lord Nicholls' judgment was approved in *HR v JAPT [1997] PLR 99*, where the claimants sought, on a number of different footings, to bring claims against the directors of a trust company, and not the company itself, for the reasons discussed above. Lindsay J expressly declined to find that the directors of a trust company owe any direct fiduciary duties to the beneficiaries of a trust of which the company is trustee. Nonetheless, he said (referring to *Tan*), '*Whilst Lord Nicholls was not dealing with third parties whose involvement was as or merely as directors of a corporate trustee, it is hard to see . . .why such a defendant should ipso facto be less vulnerable to an indirect or, as it was called in the case, a "dog-leg" claim by beneficiaries than some more extraneous stranger such as a solicitor or banker whose . . . knowledge of the trusts [would be likely to be] less extensive than that of such a director.*'

The essence of the 'dog-leg' claim before Lindsay J, which he was considering in the context of a strike-out claim, was that:

- the directors of the trust company owe that company a fiduciary duty;
- encompassed within that duty is a duty not to act in a way which would expose the company to liability to third parties;
- if, in breach of that duty, their conduct exposes the company to such liability, the company itself would have a claim against them;
- such a claim would represent an asset of the company;
- in satisfaction of their claim against the trust company for breach of trust, the beneficiaries are entitled to claim every asset of the company; and therefore,
- the beneficiaries should be entitled to pursue the claim against the directors, if the company has insufficient other assets to satisfy the claim.

In an earlier Australian case, *Young v Murphy (1994) 13 ACSR 722,* the directors of a corporate trustee were said not to be liable as they owed no particular fiduciary duty in respect of one trust of the many of which that trust company was trustee. In *HR v JAPT*, Lindsay J distinguished *Young v Murphy,* partially on the facts, as the trustee in *HR* was trustee of only a single trust. However, in principle, *Young v Murphy* could now be irrelevant, as there appears to be no reason why (on the arguments raised in *HR v JAPT*) liability should not be enforced against the directors of a trust company with more than one trust, since their duties to the trust company are the same, whether it is trustee of one trust or many.

Time limitation through statute and equity

13.9 A trustee accused of breach of trust may be able to rely on a statutory time limit or may plead equitable relief on the grounds of prejudicial passage of time.

Limitation Act 1980

13.10 The statutory time limits relevant to trust-related actions are found in the Limitation Act 1980, which provides:

- An action to recover trust property, or in relation to a breach of trust, cannot be brought more than six years after the right of action accrued (section 21(3)), which means:

  (i) the date of the breach or misappropriation; or, if later,

  (ii) (for claims based on mistake or fraud, or where the facts giving rise to a claim have been fraudulently concealed by the defendant) the date on which the beneficiaries discovered the breach, or could reasonably have discovered it by making enquiries (section 32(1)); or, if later,

  (iii) the date on which the claimant beneficiary's interest fell into possession if, at the time of the breach or misappropriation, his interest was only a future interest; or, if later,

  (iv) the date on which the beneficiary attained or recovered capacity to sue, having previously been under a legal disability, eg because he was a minor or a patient within the meaning of the Mental Health Act 1983, but has now recovered from the relevant legal disability (section 28(1));

- For claims based on negligence, where the facts are not known at the time when the right of action arose, the time limit is the longer of (a) six years from the date when the right of action arose, and (b) three years after the date when the claimant had the necessary facts available to him to bring the claim, and the right to bring it (section 14A), provided that the claim is brought within 15 years of the last date on which the negligence is alleged to have occurred to which the loss or damage is attributable (the 'long-stop limit' in section 14B);

- A claim against a trustee beneficiary who has been overpaid is limited, after the expiry of six years, to the amount of the excess, provided that he has acted honestly and reasonably;

- An action to recover trust property (or its proceeds) obtained dishonestly by the trustee himself exists without limit of time (section 21(1)(b));

- No time limit applies to an action based on fraud, or fraudulent breach of trust (section 21(1)(a));

(i) A claim for account by itself exists without limit of time (*A-G v Cocke, and Nelson v Rye [1996] 2 All ER 186*), but a claim for the payment of any sums due after taking the account has the same time limit as the nature of the breach or default giving rise to the loss (section 23). However, section 36(1) expressly preserves the duty of the court under section 2(7) of the Limitation Act 1939 to consider, in relation to a claim for account, whether or not a defence under the doctrine of laches (see further below) would have been available to the defendant prior to the 1939 Act. This introduces an element of uncertainty in relation to the absolute right of the beneficiaries to claim an account, which is potentially helpful to the trustees who might be prejudiced by a claim for account in relation to long-past matters, but is nonetheless unsatisfactory (as pointed out in *Cia de Seguros Imperio v Heath (REBX) Limited [2001] 1 WLR 112, CA*);

(ii) Matters not covered by the Limitation Act 1980 thus include any claim for breach of fiduciary duty which is not a breach of trust (ie a breach of any duty to which other fiduciaries are subject, and not only trustees), such as a breach of the self-dealing rule (*Tito v Waddell (No 2) [1977] Ch 106*) (see CHAPTER 5) (but see *Cia de Seguros Imperio v Heath (REBX) Limited [2001] 1 WLR 112, CA*, where breach of fiduciary duty was thought to be within the scope of the six-year rule).

A trustee who wishes to rely on the provisions of the Limitation Act 1980 as a defence must expressly plead his reliance (CPR 16 PD.13.1).

The aim of the statute was explained most clearly by Millett LJ in *Cave v Robinson, Jarvis & Rolf [2002] 2 All ER 641*, namely that a defendant '*should be spared the injustice of having to face a stale claim, that is, one with which he never expected to have to deal*'. Clearly, if the cause of his not expecting to have to deal with the claim was that he had fraudulently concealed its existence, it can be seen that he cannot rely on the Limitation Act 1980 to help him. In other cases, however, the passage of time is likely to mean that documents have been innocently and routinely destroyed, and the memories of those involved in the breach may be less clear, and the Limitation Act 1980 protects defendants from the unfairness that would result from a claim being brought in such circumstances.

Laches

13.11 Similar thinking exists in the equitable doctrine of laches. The passage of time may mean that the claim (even if not barred by the Limitation Act 1980) should in all fairness not be allowed to be pursued. The remedy is wholly discretionary and, as such, its application is less certain, but more flexible, than the provisions of the Limitation Act 1980. Mere passage of time, by itself, is not likely to be sufficient to assist the defendant. What is required is unreasonable delay or sloth on the part of the claimant, such that there would be unfair prejudice to the defendant to allow the claim to proceed.

There must be a demonstrable link between the delay, and the prejudice it is claimed would occur – so, for example, if a beneficiary, knowing of the facts relating to the claim, allowed time to pass knowing that the trustee routinely undertook destruction of old documents, the beneficiary might later be prevented from bringing his claim. In *Nelson v Rye [1996] 2 All ER 186*, the trustee successfully argued, in just such a situation, that he would be prejudiced by his inability to provide evidence. The relief was granted, and Laddie J held that: '*Factors [to be taken into account] include the period of the delay, the extent to which the defendant's position has been prejudiced by the delay, and the extent to which that prejudice was caused by the actions of the plaintiff . . . and whether the balance of justice or injustice is in favour of granting the remedy or withholding it.*' In *Stafford v Stafford (1857) 1 De G & J 193* (in fact a case where the trustees pleaded acquiescence, discussed at paragraph 13.12 below), 15 years elapsed before the beneficiary (who had known in advance of the breach) took action. Such a situation would now fall within the ambit of the Limitation Act 1980 (discussed above), but in those days the trustees relied upon the court's equitable jurisdiction to refuse the claim.

The role of beneficiaries in a breach of trust

13.12 When seeking to ascertain whether the trustees are liable for the loss or damage resulting from the breach of trust, it is important to consider what role in, or knowledge of, the breach the beneficiaries themselves had. The types of involvement or knowledge which may be relevant can be summarised as follows:

- procuring a breach of trust;
- consenting to a breach of trust (before the fact);
- releasing the trustee from liability for a breach of trust (after the fact);
- acquiescing or concurring in a breach of trust (before or after the fact).

Procuring a breach

13.13 It is logical that a beneficiary who instigates or procures a breach of trust should not later be able to complain that it has occurred. Very often, trustees in such a situation will require the beneficiary to indemnify them in relation to any proposed action taken at his request which appears to them to be likely to be a breach. Even where no express indemnity is available, the instigation of the breach by the beneficiary will nonetheless operate as an absolute discharge for the trustees in relation to any complaint by that beneficiary, unless of course they have gone beyond what even that beneficiary requested them to do.

However, where there are other beneficiaries, the trustees are not protected, as against the claims of the 'innocent' beneficiaries, by reference to the instigation of the 'guilty' beneficiary. In those circumstances, the court may use its power under section 62 of the Trustee Act 1925 to impound the interest of the beneficiary who procured the breach, so as to meet the claims of the beneficiaries who were not involved (and see also *Fuller v Knight (1843) 6 Beav 205, Bolton v Curre [1895] 1 Ch 544*). The trustees' liability is limited to the excess of the claims above the value of the beneficiary's impounded interest, and they may be able to claim even that excess against his personal assets by counterclaiming against him under CPR Part 20.

Consent

13.14 Section 62 of the Trustee Act 1925 also gives power to the court to impound a beneficiary's interest where he has consented to a breach, provided that the consent was in written form. However, the trustees need not rely on section 62 unless they are seeking to impound the beneficiary's interest, which is largely irrelevant to discretionary trusts where no beneficiary has an interest. Provided that the consent can be proved to have occurred, it need not be in written form in order to afford a complete defence to the trustees against the claim of the consenting beneficiaries. Again, however, others may not have consented, or may not have given an operative consent, and the trustees will remain liable to each of them, without the benefit of a counterclaim against the beneficiary who did consent (unlike a procuring beneficiary).

In order to be valid and operative, the consent must have been given by the beneficiary:

- at a time when he was not a minor, and not under any other legal disability (eg being a patient under the Mental Health Act 1983);
- knowing of the full facts and circumstances surrounding the breach, although he need not know that it was a breach; and
- of his free will, not being under any undue influence or duress

(*Fletcher v Collins [1905] 2 Ch 24, CA*).

It is irrelevant whether or not the consenting beneficiary has personally benefited from the breach, so long as all these factors are present, and it would not be just and equitable to allow the beneficiary to claim against the trustees (*Re Pauling's Settlement Trusts [1961] 3 All ER 713).*

An interesting example of the degree to which knowledge is relevant is found in *Bolton v Curre [1895] 1 Ch 544*, where a beneficiary who instigated a breach was liable to have his life interest impounded to make good the loss; but another beneficiary who consented to a deliberate breach of trust by the trustee, not knowing that it was a breach, was not liable to have her life interest impounded (but could not claim against the trustees).

Release

13.15 In some cases, the beneficiaries may have released the trustees from liability for a breach of trust that has previously occurred. In such circumstances, those beneficiaries clearly have no claim against the trustees, provided that the requirements as to capacity and knowledge above are satisfied. Such releases, being individual, have no bearing on whether or not the trustees are liable in respect of the claims of other beneficiaries who did not release them.

Acquiescence

13.16 A more complex situation arises where a beneficiary, knowing of all the facts of a proposed breach, or a past breach, does nothing at all. He has neither instigated it, nor consented to it, and he has not released the trustees from liability. He simply 'sits on his hands'. In these circumstances, if he later claims against the trustees for the breach in question, equity may come to the assistance of the trustees through the doctrine of acquiescence, which operates in a similar way to that of laches (discussed in paragraph 13.9 above).

The trustees may be able to demonstrate that the beneficiary's conduct was such that it is fair to assume that he silently consented to, or did not object to, the breach, and ought not now to be allowed to pursue them for it. Mere passage of time is not enough, although gross delay may be an indicative factor if trustees are pleading acquiescence, or indeed laches, which, as noted, has similar characteristics (see paragraph 13.9 above).

Unlike laches, it is possible that situations may exist where the trustees may wish to claim that acquiescence is shown on grounds other than passage of time, such as (for example) if the trustees were intending to distribute funds and the beneficiary (despite knowing of an earlier breach) said nothing until after they had done so (*French v Hobson (1803) 9 Ves 103* – but not where only part of the funds were distributed, as in *Re Cross (1882) 20 Ch D 109, CA*). In *Lindsay Petroleum v Hurd (1874) LR 5 PC 221*, actually a case principally concerning laches, the judge described a situation where '*it would be practically unjust to give a remedy, either because the party has by his conduct done that which might fairly be regarded as equivalent to a waiver . . . or where by his conduct and negligence he has . . . put the other party in a situation in which it would not be reasonable to place him if the remedy were afterwards to be asserted*'. This could perhaps more appropriately be used to define acquiescence, where time alone is not always relevant.

Trustees who are also beneficiaries

13.17 A trustee who is also a beneficiary, and who participates in a breach of trust, is liable to be treated as if he was a beneficiary who had procured that breach (see paragraph 13.10 above). The whole of his interest may be impounded to satisfy the claims of the other beneficiaries, ahead of any contribution from his co-trustees.

Exculpation clauses

13.18 It is almost invariably the case that a trust deed contains an exculpation clause (also called exemption clauses, exoneration clauses, indemnities, and relieving clauses). A typical clause will read something like this:

> 'In the professed execution of the trusts hereof, no Trustee [other than a remunerated Trustee (1)] shall be liable for any loss or damage arising to the trust fund by reason of any investment made in good faith or for the negligence or fraud of any agent employed in good faith by any of the Trustees, whether or not such employment was strictly necessary or expedient, or by reason of any mistake or omission made in good faith, or by reason of any other matter or thing whatsoever except wilful and individual fraud or dishonesty on the part of the Trustee who it is sought to make liable [or, in the case of a remunerated Trustee, his own negligence (2)]'.

(The words in square brackets, of which it should be pointed out that (1) and (2) are alternatives, tend to be a more recent trend, explained by Lord Millett's view in *Armitage v Nurse,* discussed below, that these clauses are otherwise weighted too far to the advantage of professional trustees.)

The aim of such clauses is to excuse or relieve the trustees for liability for a breach that *has been proved to have occurred.* There is therefore an important distinction between the operation of such clauses, and other clauses that may prevent the trustee from becoming liable at all, by removing or limiting a duty. These latter types of provision include so-called 'anti-*Bartlett*' clauses, the aim of which is to remove entirely the trustees' duty (established by *Bartlett v Barclays Bank Trust Company Limited [1980] Ch 515*) to intervene in the management of companies in which the trust has a controlling interest. It is common for trust deeds to contain clauses which counter or restrict some duty of the trustees, and particularly with non-UK trusts, there may be a multiplicity of clauses which may even limit or remove the duty to provide information to beneficiaries, and other significant duties, although *Armitage v Nurse [1998] Ch 241, CA* suggests that there may be some limits on the extent to which the trustees can be relieved of 'core obligations' (discussed below). If the proceedings relate to an alleged breach of a duty which is covered by such an 'anti-duty' clause contained in the trust instrument, there will have been no breach, as there was simply no duty capable of being breached. Accordingly, the claimant beneficiary's claim will have failed at the outset, and the court will not need to consider the effectiveness of the exculpation provisions.

Where there are no such anti-duty clauses, and where a trustee has been shown to have breached his duty, causing loss, attention will turn first to the availability of any of the defences and excuses discussed in the preceding paragraphs of this chapter, and then (if no such defences or excuses are available) to the exculpatory provisions in the trust deed, to see whether the trustee is excused from liability or not. In reality, attention is likely to turn to any such provisions at a much earlier stage, since if the clause is likely to be effective to relieve the trustee from liability, there will be little point in pursuing the trustee to prove that a breach has occurred for which (whether or not other defences are available) he cannot be held liable. In all probability, one of the very first steps that will be taken by the claimant's legal advisers is to turn to the exculpation clause to determine whether the claim should be brought at all, and how it should be framed (and what evidence is required) in order to ensure that the breach pleaded is not within the classes of breach for which the trustee will be relieved by that clause.

The question of whether or not a breach is one which is covered by the exculpation clause is usually construed strictly against the trustee. If there is any doubt as to whether the wording covers the breach, therefore, or where two or more clauses appear contradictory, the trustee will not be relieved from liability on a generous interpretation – rather, the ambiguity will be construed against him.

Public policy considerations

13.19 It is important to note that such clauses are not (under the present law) liable to be disregarded as unconscionable or contrary to public policy as a general rule. There are some public policy considerations – for example, a clause would be repugnant if it purported to exclude liability for dishonest breaches of trust or fraud (and in the US, for gross negligence – see *Browning v Fidelity Trust Company 250 F 331 (3rd Cir 1918)* – see also below).

In *Armitage v Nurse [1998] Ch 241, CA*, this point was examined (and rejected) by Lord Millett, giving rise to his now-famous pronunciation (at pages 253–4) that: '. . . *there is an irreducible core of obligations owed by the trustees to the beneficiaries and enforceable by them which is fundamental to the concept of a trust. If the beneficiaries have no rights enforceable against the trustees there are no trusts. But I do not accept the further submission that these core obligations include the duties of skill and care, prudence and diligence. The duty of the trustees to perform the trusts honestly and in good faith for the benefit of the beneficiaries is the minimum necessary to give substance to the trusts, but in my opinion it is sufficient.*'

Lord Millett did acknowledge the widely held view that such clauses are weighted very heavily in favour of the trustee, and the body of opinion that it ought not to be the case that a professional, remunerated trustee could exclude liability for gross negligence. Indeed, the law of many jurisdictions (such as, for example, Jersey) expressly prohibits a professional trustee from relying on a clause excluding gross negligence. However, as Lord Millett pointed out, that is not the position under English law at present, and the intervention of Parliament (not the courts) is required to change that position. *Law Commission Report No. 171* is a consultation paper on Trustee Exemption Clauses and invited practitioners' comments on proposals including whether professional trustees should be permitted to exclude liability for breach of trust, or to rely on anti-duty clauses or extended powers clauses if it is unreasonable for them to do so in the circumstances. It additionally proposes that all trustees should have power to purchase indemnity insurance at the expense of trust. Its results should become clear in 2004, but, as matters stand, it is in the hands of individual draftsmen as to what is contained in the trust deed, and market practice still means that many professional trustees are protected in relation to their trusteeship of private trusts to a degree that (it might be thought) would not be acceptable in ordinary terms of business for paid professional services.

Conflict between duty and exculpation clause

13.20 Exculpation clauses cannot be disregarded or struck out on the footing that they cause a conflict between the trustees' duty to the beneficiaries and their likely release for any breaches covered by the exculpation clause. No conflict can arise, because the exculpation clause does not remove the duty, but rather relieves the trustees from liability for breaching it (see paragraph 13.18 above). The trustees' duty remains the same. Indeed, a trustee who acted deliberately or carelessly, with one eye on the exculpation clause to relieve him if his act should be a loss-making breach, would almost certainly not be able to rely on the typical exculpation clause, since he would not have been acting in good faith (*Horabin v British Overseas Airways Corpn (1952) 2 All ER 1016*, for example).

The argument has also been rejected that such clauses confer a benefit on the trustee which conflicts with his duty not to profit from his trusteeship. In a case where the draftsman was a solicitor who later became a trustee (*Bogg v Raper (1998) 1 ITELR 267, CA*), Millett LJ said: '*[the clause] does not confer a benefit on the persons responsible for advising the Testator on the contents of his Will. In the first place it does not discriminate between the persons who advised the Testator in connection with his Will and other persons who become executors or trustees and who have had no part in the preparation of his Will. In the second place, it does not confer a benefit on the executors and trustees but defines the extent of their potential liabilities. Unlike a trustee charging clause, it does not enable the executors and trustees to profit from their position; but it protects them from loss thereby. The inclusion of the Clause does not, therefore, conflict with the rule that, in the absence of clear words, a trustee may not profit from his trust.*'

Wording of the clause

13.21 Turning back to the wording of the typical exculpation clause first quoted in paragraph 13.18 above, it is helpful to examine each of the phrases on which attention has been focused in a series of highly significant cases over the past five years or so (see paragraphs 13.22 to 13.25 below). It is also essential to consider what the clause does *not* cover (see paragraph 13.26 below).

'In the professed execution of the trusts . . .'

13.22 The court will not contort words beyond their ordinary meaning to permit the beneficiaries' claim to succeed. For example, in the case of *Walker v Stones [2001] QB 902, CA*, Sir Christopher Slade dismissed the claimants' argument that the words '*In the professed execution of the trusts and powers hereof*' (which generally preface exculpation clauses) should prevent the trustee from being relieved from conscious and deliberate acts which he knows to be beyond his powers. As Sir Christopher said, '*the suggested construction of clause 15 would thus confine its operation to unconscious or accidental, as opposed to conscious, breaches of trust . . . On its true construction [the clause] must apply so as to exonerate the trustees, save to the extent excluded by the clause . . . for anything done by them in the purported execution of the trust and powers . . . that is to say even though in fact not done in the execution of the powers*'.

'Actual fraud'

13.23 In *Armitage v Nurse [1998] Ch 241, CA*, it was held that 'actual fraud' in the context of an exculpation clause has a particular meaning, which goes beyond even deliberate breaches of trust or the level of conscious risk-taking that equity might regard as improper (ie equitable fraud). Millett LJ explained this in full (at page 251):

> 'By consciously acting beyond their powers (as, for example, by making an investment which they know to be unauthorised) the trustees may deliberately commit a breach of trust; but if they do so in good faith and in the honest belief that they are acting in the interest of the beneficiaries their conduct is not fraudulent . . . The expression "actual fraud" in clause 15 is not used to describe the common law tort of deceit . . . it simply means dishonesty. I accept the formulation put forward . . . on behalf of the respondents which . . . is that it "connotes at the minimum an intention on the part of the trustee to pursue a particular course of action, either knowing that it is contrary to the interests of the beneficiaries or being recklessly indifferent whether it is contrary to their interests or not".'

Actual fraud is thus to be distinguished from other kinds of wrongdoing which may be described as 'equitable fraud'. Clauses which are not qualified in the manner of *Armitage*, and which refer simply (as in the example at paragraph 13.18 above) to 'individual fraud', may not protect a trustee against a charge of equitable fraud. That term was defined in *Kitchen v RAF Association [1958] 2 All ER 241* as '*conduct which, having regard to some special relationship between the two parties concerned, is an unconscionable thing for the one to do to the other*'. If the conscience of equity can be said to be disturbed with regard to the conduct of the trustees, therefore, and if they are not protected by an

Armitage-type exclusion clause which excludes liability for all but 'actual fraud', then they may nonetheless be liable.

'Dishonesty'

13.24 Honesty is usually taken to mean not acting in a way in which an honest person would act in the circumstances. For the purposes of trustee exoneration clauses, in *Armitage v Nurse,* Lord Millett explained the meaning of dishonesty as follows (at page 251):

> 'It is the duty of a trustee to manage the trust property and deal with it in the interests of the beneficiaries. If he acts in a way which he does not honestly believe is in their interests then he is acting dishonestly. It does not matter whether he stands or thinks he stands to gain personally from his actions. A trustee who acts with the intention of benefiting persons who are not the objects of the trust is not the less dishonest because he does not intend to benefit himself. In my judgment clause 15 exempts the trustee from liability for loss or damage to the trust property no matter how indolent, imprudent, lacking in diligence, negligent or wilful he may have been, so long as he has not acted dishonestly.'

This view has been endorsed, with some qualification, in *Walker v Stones [2001] QB 902, CA* where Slade J, considering Lord Millet's judgment that even a deliberate breach is not dishonest if the trustee honestly believes it is in the interests of the beneficiaries, said: '*In the case of a solicitor-trustee, a qualification must . . . be necessary to take account of the case where the trustee's so-called "honest belief", though actually held, is so unreasonable that, by any objective standard, no reasonable solicitor-trustee could have thought that what he did or agreed to do was for the benefit of the beneficiaries*.' Slade J also pointed out that a trustee's honest belief that something is 'in the interests of the beneficiaries' should probably be construed as requiring the trustee to believe honestly that the intended act was 'not at the expense of the financial interests of the beneficiaries'. This would put a greater onus on the trustee to show that he considered the possible financial consequences of the act, rather than being able merely to say that the act was in the beneficiaries' broader interests.

'Wilful default'

13.25 Although this phrase is not, in fact, used in the typical exoneration clause quoted at paragraph 13.18 above, it is common, particularly in some older exculpation clauses, to find wilful default expressly included among the concluding words identifying the breaches for which trustees are not to be relieved. 'Wilful default' has a particular meaning in the context of a claim for account (see paragraph 3), where it connotes a passive breach of trust, and no intentional wrongdoing or breach of trust need be shown. 'Wilful default' for the purposes of exculpation clauses indicates deliberate or reckless wrongdoing on the part of the trustee in failing to fulfil his duties or otherwise committing a breach by omission. In *In re Forest of Dean Coal Mining Company (1878) 10 Ch D 450*, Jessel MR said (at page 451): '*Wilful default no doubt includes the case of a trustee neglecting to sue, though he might by suing earlier have recovered [a trust asset] – in that case he is made liable for want of due diligence.*'

What the clause does not cover

13.26 As well as the matters such as fraud, wilful default, and dishonesty in respect of which the trustees' liability is expressly preserved by the exculpation clause, there are other matters from which a trustee is unlikely to be relieved by a standard exculpation clause, such as:

- the duty to account to the beneficiaries is, as described in CHAPTER 3, a perpetual duty from which the trustee cannot be excused, and Lord Millett stated (in *Armitage v Nurse*) that any attempt to exclude that duty would have been repugnant to the trust;
- a trustee who has misappropriated trust assets for his own use remains liable to restore them to the trust fund (see CHAPTER 3);
- a trustee who, in breach of his fiduciary duties, makes a profit, is liable to account for that profit to the trust, whether or not the trust has suffered a loss (again, see CHAPTER 3);
- such clauses do not, on the typical wording illustrated in clause 12.12, currently excuse a trustee from breach of statutory duty, namely the duty of care in section 1 of the Trustee Act 2000 (see CHAPTER 5).

Where a relieving provision is qualified by the words 'in good faith', a trustee who has not acted in good faith in relation to the relevant act would probably not be protected, even if he has not been dishonest or committed actual fraud. Despite the catch-all wording at the end of the clause ('or by reason of any other matter or thing whatsoever . . .'), it appears that the clause should properly be read so that the presence of good faith is an express proviso to each of the mentioned breaches being relieved, and its absence means that they are not relieved at all. In other words, a trustee is to be excused from:

- any loss or damage arising to the trust fund by reason of any investment *provided that the investment was* made in good faith;
- for the negligence or fraud of any agent *provided that he was* employed in good faith by any of the trustees, whether or not such employment was strictly necessary or expedient;
- by reason of any mistake or omission *provided that it was* made in good faith;
- or by reason of any *other* matter or thing whatsoever except wilful and individual fraud or dishonesty,

(emphasis added). The distinction is perhaps a fine one, as the absence of good faith is usually to be equated with equitable fraud, but it may relieve the claimant beneficiaries of the need to show actual dishonesty on the part of the trustees.

Statute-based relief from liability

13.27 A trustee who is not otherwise excused or relieved of liability can call upon the court to excuse him under section 61 of the Trustee Act 1925, which contains an additional relieving provision. This relief can only be used in the limited circumstances set out in that section:

> 'If it appears to the Court that a trustee . . . is or may be personally liable for any breach of trust . . . but has acted honestly and reasonably, and ought fairly to be excused for the breach of trust and for omitting to obtain the directions of the Court in the matter in which he committed such breach . . . the Court may relieve him wholly or partly from personal liability for the same.'

This section is rarely required to be called upon in modern times, because of the prevalence of trustee exculpation clauses. Because of the four-fold requirement of the section (the trustee must have acted honestly *and* reasonably *and* it must be fair to excuse him, not only for the breach, but for failing to seek directions from the court), this provision cannot usually be called upon where an express exculpation clause was available, but the breach is not excused by its terms. Clearly, if the express clause is anything like the example given in paragraph 13.18 above, the failure to excuse the trustee under its terms is likely to mean that he has been guilty of bad faith or dishonesty or fraud, which it is most unlikely would be excused under section 61.

However, the section has recently been considered in the case of *Re Evans (deceased) [1999] 2 All ER 777*, where the defendant executrix had distributed the entire estate to herself, as one of two beneficiaries, having obtained a missing beneficiary insurance policy in respect of her brother, the other beneficiary, who had last been heard of some 30 years earlier. She did not, however, obtain a *Re Benjamin* order authorising her to distribute on the assumption that he must be dead. Four years later, he did re-appear, and whilst the policy was sufficient to cover the capital sum due to him, it did not cover the interest owing to him. The executrix was relieved under section 61 to the extent that her brother's loss could not be made good out of the sale of the one remaining undistributed asset of the estate.

In essence, in considering whether or not to grant the relief, the court considers whether the balance of justice ('ought fairly to be excused') is in favour of the beneficiaries bearing the loss, or the trustees. Factors which the court may take into account in deciding whether the trustees have acted reasonably will include whether the trustees took legal or other professional advice (*Roome v Edwards,* but relief is not automatic even where he has relied on advice – see *Marsden v Regan [1954] 1 All ER 475, CA*). Arguably, a professional trustee is less likely to be excused under this section, since his expected standard of conduct is higher than that of a lay trustee (see, for example, *Re Pauling's Settlement [1961] 3 All ER 713*).

This discretionary relief is only sparingly granted, as other cases illustrate. In *Hobday v Peters (No 3) (1860) 28 Beav 603*, the trustees were excused (under the predecessor to section 61) for failing to take action to protect the trust property, where the only option would have been to sue an impecunious defendant. In *Re Smith (1902) 86 LT 401*, the trustee was excused where her solicitor's clerk made off with trust assets. He was able to do so because the solicitor wrote the cheques out and his clerk delivered them for the trustee to sign. The trustee was negligent, but innocent, in allowing this practice, and it was fair to excuse her.

Notably, however, section 61 does not confer power on the court to excuse a trustee from liability for a future breach of trust in contemplation (*Re Tollemache [1903] 1 Ch 457*).

'No contest' clauses

13.28 In the context of trustees' liability, it is also worth considering the effect and effectiveness of so-called 'no contest' clauses. Such clauses purport to exclude from benefit any beneficiary who challenges the validity of the trust or (more rarely) any beneficiary who issues proceedings in relation to the trust. Accordingly, if valid, they might mean that a beneficiary who wished to bring a claim might (depending on the facts) cease to have any standing and/or would cease to be a beneficiary.

These types of clauses are not *per se* repugnant, if they are expressed in terms that the beneficiary's interest survives until (if ever) he applies to the court. However, conditions of any kind which are imposed *in terrorem* – such as conditions providing for termination *if* someone marries, or (as in this case) *if* they issue proceedings, are void. The essence of a valid clause, therefore, is one which has trusts over in the specified circumstances, and does not merely forfeit the interest of the beneficiary concerned (*Re Whiting's Settlement [1905] 1 Ch 96*). Where the trustees have a discretion as to whether or not to invoke the termination of a beneficiary's interest, they must take care not to exercise it in circumstances which could be seen as self-protection, or indeed an invalid attempt to oust the jurisdiction of the court.

Instructions by the settlor or third parties

13.29 It is worth considering to what extent, if at all, it is a defence to an allegation of breach of trust against the trustees for them to say that they acted on the instructions of another person.

Where the trust deed does not expressly allow this, the compliance by the trustees with the instructions of another (frequently the settlor) is in itself a breach of trust, as it is improper for them to surrender their own discretions, which they ought to exercise personally, to a stranger. In such cases, it is no defence to them to say that they acted in accordance with his instructions, and they are unlikely to succeed in joining the settlor to the proceedings by making a Part 20 claim against him – absent an express power in the trust deed, he is unlikely to owe them any duty of care in relation to the actions he has directed them to take.

If the trust deed expressly reserves power to the settlor, or gives power to another person, to give directions to the trustees (for example, on investment matters), they are nonetheless relieved from liability for the consequences of acting in accordance with those directions only if the provision is coupled with an express requirement that the trustees *must* act as directed. If there is no such requirement, the trustees remain liable to exercise their own discretion (and take advice) as to whether the direction is a good and appropriate one. They may seek to join the relevant person by bringing a counterclaim under Part 20, so that the question of liability as between them is one to be determined by the court.

Chapter 14

Rights against third parties

Introduction

14.1 In addition to the beneficiaries' rights, considered elsewhere in this book, to bring claims against the trustees, or directly against the trust fund, and the rights they have to ask for the court's guidance on areas of doubt or difficulty, they may have additional rights to claim against third parties.

In this chapter, the following types of claim are considered:

- claims against the settlor;
- claims against the protector;
- claims against third parties who have received assets of the trust;
- claims against third parties who have been closely connected with a breach of trust;
- claims against former trustees; and
- claims against third parties for disclosure of documents held by them.

Claims against the settlor

14.2 When the settlor creates the trust then (even if he is himself a beneficiary) he retains few, if any, responsibilities in relation to the trust and its assets. He may have expressly retained certain powers for himself, which may be of a fiduciary character (such as powers of appointment of new trustees, or investment consultancy powers) or may be personal powers (such as the power to select or remove members of a protector committee – see *IRC v Schroder [1983] STC 480*). He remains answerable, however, for the creation of the trust, the transfer of assets into the trust, and any actions he actually takes in relation to the trust, whether or not expressly contemplated by the trust deed.

It is possible that, in some circumstances, the settlor may have information about the trust or its trustees which the beneficiaries wish to obtain. This was considered in the case of *Murphy v Murphy [1998] 3 All ER 1*, where the son, who believed he was a beneficiary of a trust, had fallen out with his father. The son did not know any details of the trust, not even the identity of the trustees, but believed it to exist. Neuberger J said: '[there are] *two different types of circumstances in which the court can order a defendant, who is not otherwise an appropriate party to proceedings, to identify the name and address of a third party. The first type of case is where the defendant has . . . become "mixed up in" the wrongdoing of the proposed defendant and the plaintiff has a claim in respect of that wrongdoing . . . Secondly, there is what I shall call "the equitable jurisdiction".*' (The first such kind of jurisdiction is discussed at paragraph 14.16 below.)

In relation to the equitable jurisdiction, Neuberger J said that, where a claimant has an equitable interest in property and wishes to force an innocent third party to divulge the identity of the person in whom the trust property is held, the court must be able to assist him, because: '*If all the discretionary beneficiaries wished . . . to know the identity of the trustees of a settlement, and the settlor . . . refused to tell them, it would be surprising indeed if the court had no power to compel him to do so.*'

In other cases, it may be that the settlor's ongoing interference in the running of the trust has caused, or will shed light on, losses in the trust fund. For example, where the settlor has been accustomed to giving investment advice (or even directions) to the trustees, and the trust instrument does not expressly permit him to do so, the trustees may follow his instructions in breach of trust. If a loss results, the beneficiaries may wish to claim:

- against the settlor as well as, or instead of, the trustees (for example, for dishonest assistance, as in paragraph 14.13 below);
- against the trustees, but with the benefit of information that only the settlor can provide, such that they require a non-party disclosure order against him (see paragraph 14.16 below); or
- if the facts support it, that the trust is a sham (see CHAPTER 11).

It is of course no defence to an allegation of breach of trust against the trustees for them to say that they acted on the instructions of another person, where the trust deed does not expressly allow this. For this reason, it is perhaps unlikely that the trustees would succeed in joining the settlor to the proceedings by making a Part 20 claim against him – absent an express power in the trust deed, he is unlikely to owe them any duty of care in relation to the investments he has directed them to make.

Claims against the protector

Fiduciary role of the protector

14.3 There has been a considerable amount of debate as to whether protectors are fiduciaries or not. It is nowadays generally accepted that their role must be fiduciary, since the alternative – that their powers are personal, and can be exercised (or not) entirely at their whim – seems inconsistent with the existence of a protector role, usually designed as a check on the activities of the trustees for the benefit of the beneficiaries. In *Von Knieriem v Bermuda Trust Company, 'the Star Trusts case' (Supreme Court of Bermuda, 13 July 1994, unreported)*, it was held that the protector was obliged to exercise its powers in a fiduciary manner (distinguishing *Rawson Trust v Perlman (Supreme Court of the Bahamas, 25 April 1990, unreported)* where the protectors were beneficiaries and were held on the facts not to be fiduciaries). In another case, *Re Osiris Trustees Ltd v Goodways Ltd (2000) 2 ITELR 404*, it was held that the power of appointment of new trustees was one which could only be exercised for the benefit of the trust as a whole, and in the interests of its beneficiaries.

The duties of a fiduciary were explained fully in *Bristol and West Building Society v Mothew [1996] 4 All ER 698*, where Millett LJ set out the principles which govern the role of a fiduciary, as follows: '*A fiduciary must act in good faith. He must not place himself in a position where his duty and his interest may conflict; he may not act for his own benefit or the benefit of a third person without the informed consent of his principal.*' Similarly to a trustee, therefore, the protector must consider the interests of the beneficiaries when exercising every power vested in him as protector. In practical terms, therefore, considering the powers commonly likely to be available to the protector, his position is as follows:

- many of his powers are likely to be powers of consent or veto in relation to proposed exercises of the trustees' powers, such as their dispositive powers. He has no power to oblige the trustees to make any particular decision – his role is a passive one, requiring him only to give or withhold his consent when provided with a decision that the trustees wish to implement. In considering whether to grant his consent or not, he must have in mind the interests of the trust and not his own interests, or any other matters extraneous to the trust;

- he may also have proactive powers which he possesses independently of the trustees, such as powers of removal or appointment of trustees. The protector must from time to time give active consideration as to whether or not the best interests of the trust require him to use them. This may involve, for example, considering the performance of the trustees and whether they remain suitable trustees for the trust, in all the circumstances. Further, he must (if he exercises them at all) exercise them for the benefit of the trust and its beneficiaries and not for any extraneous or personal purposes (see, for example, the *Star Trusts* case, where the court considered whether the protector had removed the former trustees in order to benefit the settlor);

- the protector may additionally have powers which are non-fiduciary in nature, such as power to direct investments (as in *Re Hart's Will Trusts [1943] 2 All ER 557*, where this was held to include power to direct them to purchase investments from himself). More common, perhaps, within this category are the powers of addition or exclusion of beneficiaries. Such powers are, logically, incapable of being exercised in a fiduciary manner, since it would rarely be in the interests of the trust to add or remove a beneficiary (although arguably, it might seem to be in the interests of the trust to remove a beneficiary whose residence or domicile may give rise to taxation problems for the trust, for example); and

- generally, it is doubtful whether a protector has a duty to consult the beneficiaries on any matter. If he does so, or if they communicate wishes or views to him, he must, however, take those into account in reaching his decision on the matter before him.

Types of claim against protector

14.4 In what contexts, therefore, might beneficiaries have a right to attack the protector or his decisions? They might wish to take steps with regard to any of the following matters:

- to compel the protector to consent or veto an exercise of a power by the trustees;
- to assert that he ought to, or ought not to, exercise his independent proactive powers;
- to attack the protector's exercise, or non-exercise, of any power.

Enforcement or prohibition of exercise of power of veto

14.5 It may occasionally be the case that the protector is slothful in confirming whether he consents to, or does not consent to, a proposed exercise of a power by the trustees to which his consent is required. Seemingly, and consistently with the fiduciary nature of his powers of consent and veto, the protector must indicate his consent (or refusal) within a reasonable time. It does not appear to be open to him to do nothing. If he does not give his consent or veto within a reasonable time, therefore, either the trustees or the beneficiaries may apply to the court to compel him to exercise his power (perhaps in the form of an 'unless' order, giving a period of time within which he must exercise the power). In this sense, the protector's position is unlike that of a trustee exercising (or refusing to exercise) a discretion, as considered in CHAPTER 7, since the court has no power to compel a trustee to exercise his discretion, but only to consider exercising it.

However, the sanction available to the beneficiaries in the case of a protector who refuses to act is (it would appear) the same as that available in respect of a trustee who refuses to act – removal. Whilst there appears to be no authority on the point, the court's inherent jurisdiction over trusts must include power, if it appears expedient in the interests of the trust, to remove a protector. In the Isle of Man case of *Steele v Paz (1995) (Butterworths Offshore Cases & Materials, Vol 1, page 338*), where a schedule in the trust deed in which the protector's name should have been inserted had inadvertently been left blank, the court found that, by analogy with the maxim that 'equity will not allow a trust to fail for want of a trustee', the court must have power to appoint a protector where the trust was immobilised without the protector's consent being available to the trustees' exercises of their powers (as was also the case in *Re an Irrevocable Trust [2000] 2 ITELR 842*). By extension, the removal of a protector must similarly be an option within the court's general discretion.

Actions in relation to the protector's proactive powers

14.6 Where the protector has some proactive power of his own, which does not only become operative as a result of some proposed exercise of the trustees' powers, such as the power of removal and/or appointment of trustees, his options (and his duties) are broader than for his powers of consent and veto. As noted above (in paragraph 14.3), and by analogy with trustees' exercises of their discretions (discussed in CHAPTER 7), the beneficiaries have a right to expect that the protector will:

- leave out of consideration any personal motives or other matters which are not relevant; and
- throughout the process, act in the interests of the trust and its beneficiaries.

It is unlikely that the beneficiaries can compel a protector to use a power in a particular manner. For example, if the beneficiaries believed that one or more of the trustees was unsuitable, they could not compel the protector to exercise his power of removal. Their options include:

- requesting the protector to seek directions as to whether or not he should exercise his power; or
- seeking to attack the purported exercise, once made (see paragraph 14.7 below).

It is possible that the beneficiaries may seek to prevent a particular exercise of a power, such as, for example, where they become aware of a proposed exercise which they believe to be improperly motivated. They may choose to put the protector on notice that they would regard such an exercise as open to challenge, and the protector himself may use the opportunity to seek the court's directions where he believes a proposed exercise is likely to be regarded as contentious (see, for example, *In re the Omar Trust [2000] WTLR 713*). In cases where the beneficiaries have reasonable grounds for believing that the protector would ignore any request or notice given to him, they may apply for an injunction against the protector, without notice, to prevent him from exercising his powers without the leave of the court.

Attack on an exercise of the protector's power

14.7 In the same way that beneficiaries have a right to know, in relation to trustees' exercise of their discretions, that in reaching the decision that they have made, the trustees have acted honestly, impartially, and consistently with the purposes for which the discretion has been conferred upon them, the beneficiaries must have a right to expect similar standards of the protector. As discussed in CHAPTER 7 in relation to trustees, the beneficiaries have a right to be satisfied that the process the protector has followed in reaching a decision was fair, even if the outcome itself was not 'fair' in the eyes of the beneficiaries.

In some senses the protector has a heavier burden applied to him in seeking to show that a particular decision to veto was fairly reached. As noted above (see paragraph 14.1), his powers of consent and veto are intended to act as a check on the trustees. Since the trustees' duties are also fiduciary, if they have concluded (for example) that a distribution is appropriate, having regard to the range of possible objects and their respective needs and interests, it is perhaps likely to be difficult for the protector to make out a good case for refusal.

As was said in *Bristol and West Building Society v Mothew [1996] 4 All ER 698*, '*the various obligations of a fiduciary merely reflect different aspects of his core duties of loyalty and fidelity. Breach of fiduciary obligation, therefore, connotes disloyalty or infidelity*'. Any exercise of the protector's powers of consent and veto may therefore be impugned as a breach of fiduciary duty if, on the facts:

- the protector failed to take into consideration all the matters that he ought to have taken into account, or took into account things he ought not to have taken into account (as in *Re Hastings-Bass [1975] Ch 25*); or
- the protector's exercise of his power was motivated by bad faith or extraneous matters, such that it was a fraud on the power (*Vatcher v Paull [1915] AC 372*).

It is suggested that the appropriate procedure to be followed, and the matters to be taken account in bringing a challenge to the protector's exercise of his power of consent or veto, are similar to those set out in CHAPTER 7 in relation to challenges to exercises of the trustees' discretions.

The protector's rights of reimbursement and indemnity

14.8 It is rarely the case that a trust instrument will provide expressly for the protection of the protector, by way of remuneration, reimbursement of costs, or indemnity.

The protector has no general right to be remunerated. Unless the trust deed expressly provides for him to be paid, therefore, his position is not covered by the Trustee Act 2000 (which allows for the remuneration of trustees in certain circumstances where no, or insufficient, express provision is made by the trust deed), and he is expected, in line with the general rule for trustees, to act gratuitously. A protector who purports to charge for his own time and services should not be paid by the trustees, absent such express provision. If they make payment to him, it is a breach of trust.

The protector's right to be reimbursed is more complex. Section 31 of the Trustee Act 2000, which entitles a trustee to reimburse himself for expenses properly incurred by him in acting on behalf of the trust, does not create any similar right for other fiduciaries. In general terms, a protector is unlikely to find it necessary (and accordingly, proper) to incur expenses in the discharge of powers of consent and veto, and clearly, unlike the trustees, he has no authority to contract on behalf of the trust, such that he should require an indemnity against out-of-pocket expenses or other liabilities. However, in some circumstances, it is apparent that a protector may require legal advice as to the extent of his powers, or the appropriateness of exercising (or refraining from exercising) them. Since he does not have physical control of the trust assets, he has no possessory lien to secure any right of reimbursement that might be found to exist. A trustee's lien does not, however, need to be possessory in order to be effective (since the trustee would be entitled to recoup sums due to it from a successor trustee – *Re Pauling's Settlement (No 2), Younghusband v Coutts & Co [1963] 1 All ER 857*). Is the protector's position similar – does he in fact have a lien, albeit not a possessory one? The answer would appear to be that the protector has no lien of any kind, but is reliant upon the court's inherent jurisdiction to authorise the payment (or repayment) of sums properly incurred on behalf of the trust. If the court considers that the protector has acted reasonably in seeking advice as to his powers, then whether or not the court ultimately agrees that the protector was right to exercise his powers in the manner that he did (or to refrain from exercising them), the protector's costs may be ordered to be paid out of the trust fund. *Quaere* whether the trustees have power to discharge the protector's costs on a pre-emptive basis without the court's approval, however.

Similarly, a protector has no general right to be indemnified or excused from liability for any acts or omissions which cause loss to the trust fund. Trust deeds rarely contain such protection for the protector, and it seems unlikely that section 61 of the Trustee Act 1925 would allow the court to excuse him, since it refers so expressly to trustees. If a protector has, by his own act or omission in breach of his fiduciary duty, caused loss or damage (including additional expense, or loss of opportunity) to the trust fund, it would appear that his liability for the breach of fiduciary duty giving rise to that loss or damage is strict and that he would not be entitled to be excused in the absence of an express exculpation clause.

Claims against third parties connected with a breach

14.9 It may be the case that, in connection with a breach of trust, some third party can be identified upon whom liability can justly be imposed. The court does not lightly fix a third party with liability – it has long been established that, in order to be liable as an accessory to a breach of trust, the third party must have received trust property or been involved, to a degree which can be regarded as dishonest, in the breach by the trustee. The origin for these two bases of liability are the much-quoted dictum of Lord Selborne LC in *Barnes v Addy (1874) LR 9, CA 244* (at pages 251–2):

> '[The responsibility of a trustee] may no doubt be extended in equity to others who are not properly trustees, if they are found . . . actually participating in any fraudulent conduct of the trustee to the injury of the cestui que trust. But . . . strangers are not to be made constructive trustees merely because they act as the agents of trustees in transactions within their legal powers, transactions, perhaps of which a court of equity may disapprove, unless those agents receive and become chargeable with some part of the trust property, or unless they assist with knowledge in a dishonest and fraudulent design on the part of the trustees.'

Third party liability may therefore be imposed upon the third party in one of two principal ways:

- the third party may be liable for knowing receipt of trust assets derived from a breach of trust. This head of liability is concerned with the liability of a third party for recipient of trust property or its traceable proceeds; or
- the third party may be liable for dishonestly assisting in a breach of trust. This head of liability is concerned with the liability of an accessory to a trustee's breach of trust. Liability as an accessory is not dependent upon receipt of trust property. It arises even though no trust property has reached the hands of the accessory. It is a form of secondary liability in the sense that it only arises where there has been a breach of trust.

The level of knowledge required for liability for knowing receipt and dishonest assistance has lead to a large number of reported cases. The elements of each head of liability are briefly summarised below. For convenience of order, this section of this chapter considers:

- firstly, dishonest assistance in a breach of trust;
- secondly, knowing receipt; and
- thirdly, the rules on tracing.

Dishonest assistance

14.10 Any person who has been connected with a breach of trust may be liable for dishonest assistance in a breach of trust. Or, as Lord Nicholls put it in *Royal Brunei Airlines v Tan [1995] 2 AC 378, PC*, at page 386: '*A trust is a relationship which exists when one person holds property on behalf of another. If, for his own purposes, a third party deliberately interferes in that relationship by assisting the trustee in depriving the beneficiary of the property held for him by the trustee, the beneficiary should be able to look for recompense to the third party as well as the trustee.*'

In the case of former trustees, liability might arise where (for example) they have retired as trustees with the intention of facilitating the commission of a breach by the continuing or replacement trustees. More generally, liability of any third party assistant in a breach may arise in a number of ways, which may (but need not necessarily) amount to a fraudulent conspiracy.

It is not necessary that the third party should be in possession of, or ever have received, any assets representing trust assets or their traceable proceeds (*Royal Brunei Airlines v Tan [1995] 2 AC 378, PC*). However, the current state of the law is that it is necessary to prove dishonesty on the part of the assistant. The current test for knowledge on the part of the assistant to the breach of trust was set out in the recent House of Lords judgment in *Twinsectra v Yardley [2002] 2 AC 164 at 171, CA* (apparently approving and applying the PC decision in *Tan*): '. . . *it must be established that the defendant's conduct was dishonest by the ordinary standards of reasonable and honest people and that he himself realised that by those standards his conduct was dishonest.*' It is, therefore, a test of 'conscious dishonesty' comprising both an objective element and a subjective one.

This form of liability can extend to any person who has assisted in a breach, since it can occur in any situation where:

- a breach of trust or of fiduciary duty has occurred. The original breach of trusts need not itself have been dishonest (*Tan,* distinguishing *Belmont Finance Corp Ltd v Williams [1979] Ch 250, CA*; now followed by *Twinsectra Ltd v Yardley [2002] 2 AC 164, CA*);
- that breach can be linked to a loss to the trust fund; and
- a third party has participated or assisted to some material degree in the breach such that his conscience is affected by equity (*Grupo Torras SA v Al-Sabah (No 5) [2001] Lloyds Rep Bank 36, CA).*

The result of a finding of constructive trusteeship based upon dishonest assistance is that the defendant third party can be affixed with personal liability for the whole of the loss, or (if there is no loss, or if the gain is greater) the whole of the gain that he has obtained, in either case limited by reference to the assistance he has given to the breach as a whole (*Grupo Torras SA v Al-Sabah (No 5) [2001] Lloyds Rep Bank 36, CA).*

Knowing receipt

14.11 In *El Ajou v Dollar Land Holdings plc [1994] 2 All ER 685*, Hoffman LJ stated that the essential elements of 'knowing receipt' were (at page 700): '. . . *a disposal of* [the plaintiff's] *assets in breach of fiduciary duty; secondly, the beneficial receipt by the defendant of assets which are traceable as representing the assets of the plaintiff; and thirdly, knowledge on the part of the defendant that the assets received are traceable to a breach of fiduciary duty.*'

Although the courts have been troubled as to the level of knowledge required on the part of the recipient in order to establish liability for knowing receipt, the current state of the law is that it is not a requirement of this claim that the claimant should have to show dishonesty on the part of the recipient (*Bank of Credit and Commerce International v Akindele [2001] Ch 437*, approving the earlier Court of Appeal decision in *Belmont Finance Corpn Ltd v Williams Furniture (No 2) [1992] 1 All ER 393*). As Nourse LJ put it in *BCCI v Akindele [2001] Ch 437 at 455*: '*. . . just as there is now a single test of dishonesty for knowing assistance, so ought there to be a single test of knowledge for knowing receipt. The recipient's state of knowledge must be such as to make it unconscionable for him to retain the benefit of the receipt. A test in that form, though it cannot, any more than any other, avoid difficulties of application, ought to avoid those of definition and allocation to which the previous categorisations have led. Moreover, it should better enable the courts to give common sense decisions in the commercial context in which claims in knowing receipt are now frequently made . . .*'

Nourse LJ also cited with approval the observations of Vinelott J in *Eagle Trust plc v SBC Securities Ltd [1993] 1 WLR 484* (at page 497), where he said: '*What the decision in Belmont (No 2) shows is that in a "knowing receipt" case it is only necessary to show that the defendant knew that the moneys paid to him were trust moneys and of circumstances which made the payment a misapplication of them. Unlike a knowing assistance case it is not necessary . . . to show that the defendant was in any sense a participator in a fraud.*'

If one reads the obiter remarks of Lord Millett in *Twinsectra [2002] 2 AC 164*, at 194, it is possible to see a judicial drift towards strict liability for receipt of assets derived from a breach of trust: '*Liability for "knowing receipt" is receipt-based. It does not depend on fault. The cause of action is restitutionary and is available only where the defendant received or applied the money in breach of trust for his own use and benefit: see Agip (Africa) Ltd v Jackson [1990] Ch 265. There is no basis for requiring actual knowledge of the breach of trust, let alone dishonesty, as a condition of liability. Constructive notice is sufficient, and may not even be necessary. There is powerful academic support for the proposition that the liability of the recipient is the same as in other cases of restitution, that is to say strict but subject to a change of position defence.*'

The Court of Appeal in *BCCI v Akindele* examined the same point in a less positive light:

> 'We were referred in argument to "Knowing Receipt: The Need for a New Landmark", an essay by Lord Nicholls of Birkenhead in "Restitution Past, Present and Future" (1998), a work of insight and scholarship . . .Most pertinent for present purposes is the suggestion made by Lord Nicholls, at page 238, in reference to the decision of the House of Lords in *Lipkin Gorman v Karpnale Ltd [1991] 2 AC 548*: "In this respect equity should now follow the law. Restitutionary liability, applicable regardless of fault but subject to a defence of change of position, would be a better-tailored response to the underlying mischief of misapplied property than personal liability which is exclusively fault-based. Personal liability would flow

> from having received the property of another, from having been unjustly enriched at the expense of another. It would be triggered by the mere fact of receipt, thus recognising the endurance of property rights. But fairness would be ensured by the need to identify a gain, and by making change of position available as a defence in suitable cases when, for instance, the recipient had changed his position in reliance on the receipt."
>
> No argument before us was based on the suggestions made in Lord Nicholls's essay. Indeed, at this level of decision, it would have been a fruitless exercise. We must continue to do our best with the accepted formulation of the liability in knowing receipt, seeking to simplify and improve it where we may. While in general it may be possible to sympathise with a tendency to subsume a further part of our law of restitution under the principles of unjust enrichment, I beg leave to doubt whether strict liability coupled with a change of position defence would be preferable to fault-based liability in many commercial transactions, for example where, as here, the receipt is of a company's funds which have been misapplied by its directors. Without having heard argument it is unwise to be dogmatic, but in such a case it would appear to be commercially unworkable and contrary to the spirit of the rule in *Royal British Bank v Turquand (1856) 6 E & B 327* that, simply on proof of an internal misapplication of the company's funds, the burden should shift to the recipient to defend the receipt either by a change of position or perhaps in some other way. Moreover, if the circumstances of the receipt are such as to make it unconscionable for the recipient to retain the benefit of it, there is an obvious difficulty in saying that it is equitable for a change of position to afford him a defence.'

As the law currently stands, however, if the beneficiaries can identify a third party who has received trust assets (or their traceable proceeds) for his own benefit in breach of trust, *knowing* of the breach of trust, then the beneficiaries are entitled to reclaim them (or their traceable proceeds) for the benefit of the trust.

The essential prerequisite for recovery is that the assets must remain traceable. Whilst a detailed explanation of the tracing rules are beyond the scope of this book, they are briefly summarised in the following paragraphs 14.12–14.14.

Tracing generally

14.12 In the recent House of Lords decision in *Foskett v McKeown and Ors [2001] 1 AC 102* (at pages 127–8), Lord Millett eloquently explained the meaning of tracing as follows:

> 'The process of ascertaining what happened to the plaintiffs' money involves both tracing and following. These are both exercises in locating assets which are or may be taken to represent an asset belonging to the plaintiffs and to which they assert ownership. The processes of following and tracing are, however, distinct. Following is the process of following the

same asset as it moves from hand to hand. Tracing is the process of identifying a new asset as the substitute for the old. Where one asset is exchanged for another, a claimant can elect whether to follow the original asset into the hands of the new owner or to trace its value into the new asset in the hands of the same owner. In practice his choice is often dictated by the circumstances.

[...] The transmission of a claimant's property rights from one asset to its traceable proceeds is part of our law of property, not of the law of unjust enrichment. [...] Property rights are determined by fixed rules and settled principles. They are not discretionary. They do not depend upon ideas of what is "fair, just and reasonable". Such concepts, which in reality mask decisions of legal policy, have no place in the law of property.

A beneficiary of a trust is entitled to a continuing beneficial interest not merely in the trust property but in its traceable proceeds also, and his interest binds every one who takes the property or its traceable proceeds except a bona fide purchaser for value without notice.

[...] Tracing is thus neither a claim nor a remedy. It is merely the process by which a claimant demonstrates what has happened to his property, identifies its proceeds and the persons who have handled or received them, and justifies his claim that the proceeds can properly be regarded as representing his property. Tracing is also distinct from claiming. It identifies the traceable proceeds of the claimant's property. It enables the claimant to substitute the traceable proceeds for the original asset as the subject matter of his claim. But it does not affect or establish his claim. That will depend on a number of factors including the nature of his interest in the original asset. He will normally be able to maintain the same claim to the substituted asset as he could have maintained to the original asset. If he held only a security interest in the original asset, he cannot claim more than a security interest in its proceeds.'

Traditionally there have been different rules for tracing in law and equity. Although the House of Lords questioned the logic of this, they did not go so far as to sweep away the long-recognised distinction between common law and equitable tracing which still remains relevant (*Shalson and Ors v Russo and Ors [2003] EWHC 1637 (Ch)).* The different rules are discussed in paragraphs 14.13 and 14.14 below.

Common law tracing

14.13 The common law tracing rules require the legal title to the asset of which the trust has been deprived to be identifiable in the hands of its recipient. For beneficiaries seeking to trace trust assets into the hands of third parties, there is the logical difficulty that they may have no standing to pursue a common law tracing claim at all, since they will not be the legal owners of the assets involved. More commonly, therefore, this form of tracing is available to the trustees of the trust.

In any event, the common law rules of tracing rapidly fail in practice, except in the simplest cases. This is because the common law tracing rules do not permit tracing through a mixed fund where the victim's money has been mixed with that of the recipient or of other victims. In one case, money transferred through the New York clearing system could not be traced at common law as the sum of money sought to be traced had been mixed with the money of others in the clearing system. It could, however, be traced in equity under its more flexible tracing rules (*Agip v Jackson [1991] Ch 547, CA).*

Equitable tracing

14.14 Tracing funds in equity is far more flexible than at common law and equity has long recognised the ability to trace into and through a mixed fund. Tracing in equity requires that the claimants establish a fiduciary relationship, because of the requirement that the claimant must have an equitable title to the asset being claimed. The House of Lords decision in *Foskett v McKeown* did not dispense with this long established requirement: *Shalson and Ors v Russo and Ors [2003] EWHC 1637 (Ch)*. This will easily be established where a beneficiary is claiming property originating from a trust, although it often acts as a bar to tracing in other claims.

Where, for example, a chattel has passed out of the trust in breach of trust, and has been sold by the recipient, the claimant may elect (as noted in paragraph 14.13 above) either to follow the chattel into the hands of its new owner, or to trace into the proceeds received by the original recipient of the chattel. The position is more complex where the traceable proceeds of a breach of trust have become mixed with other assets. Equity, however, gives the claimant a pro rata charge on the asset into which the proceeds have been converted (*Re Diplock [1948] Ch 465, CA*). Thus, in *Foskett*, the beneficiaries could trace monies misappropriated from the trust into the proceeds of a life insurance policy, where some only of the premiums of that policy had been paid out of trust monies. However, the proceeds of a breach of trust can generally not be traced through an overdraft, as the asset represented by the funds before they are paid into the account is subsumed into the debt owed to the bank, and ceases to exist.

The position is more complex where the traceable proceeds of a breach of trust have become mixed with other assets and a detailed set of equitable rules and presumptions have developed to deal with this situation. These are most helpfully summarised in paragraphs 2–035 to 2–041 of *Goff & Jones: The Law of Restitution* (*Sixth Edition*), and in *Goldspink & Cole on International Commercial Fraud* at paragraphs 2.60 to 2.72.

A recipient of property emanating from the trust who is a bona fide purchaser for value of the legal estate without notice, and who can prove his status as such, has a complete defence against an equitable tracing claim. The onus is on the defendant to prove that he is to be treated as a bona fide purchaser (see, for example, *Boscawen v Bajwa [1996] 1 WLR 328, CA*).

Former trustees

14.15 Trustees are under a duty '*to protect the funds entrusted to their care, and to distribute those funds or hand them over to their successors intact . . . This duty is imposed upon them as long as they remain trustees and must be their guide in every act done by them as trustees. On retiring from the trust and passing on the trust estate to their successors . . . they are acting as trustees, and it is equally incumbent upon them in this ultimate act of office to fulfil the duty imposed on them as at any other time. If therefore they neglect that duty and part with the property without due regard to it, they remain liable . . . for the consequences properly traceable to that neglect*' (*Head v Gould [1898] 2 Ch 250*, per Kekewich J).

If it can be shown that a former trustee retired in circumstances where:

- he knew of, or suspected, an intention on the part of the continuing and/or replacement trustees to commit a breach of trust; or
- there were 'circumstances that warranted any reasonable belief of the insecurity of the trust funds in the hands of those to whom they committed them' (*Head v Gould*),

then the former trustee may remain liable as if he had himself committed the breach of trust of which the beneficiary now complains. Kekewich J believed that the precise breach of trust later committed must have been in contemplation at the time of the former trustee's retirement, but (as discussed in CHAPTER 13), it would appear sufficient if the former trustee has retired, being reckless as to whether a breach would be committed or not, in favour of persons whose probity or ability to execute the trusts the outgoing trustee had reasonable grounds for suspecting. This would, in itself, be a breach entitling the beneficiaries to claim damages for the loss or damage flowing from that breach.

As discussed in paragraph 14.11 above, it may be the case, on the facts, that the retiring trustee can be fixed with liability for having dishonestly assisted in the breach of trust which followed his retirement. A claim involving an allegation of dishonesty is one which, if proved, would never normally entitle the former trustee to be excused or relieved under the express terms of the trust deed, or by the court.

Where former trustees have retired with the benefit of an indemnity from their replacements, the effect of the indemnity is not to relieve the former trustees from liability. Rather, it entitles them to be held harmless by the new or continuing trustees to the extent that the former trustees are made liable. The beneficiaries may thus still claim against the former trustees, who remain personally liable to the beneficiaries, and cannot recoup their liability from the continuing or new trustees to the extent that those indemnitors are impecunious, or to the extent that the liability is not one covered by the indemnity. Liability for dishonesty and for deliberate breaches of trust can never be excluded, and exclusion of gross negligence is increasingly often limited to non-professional or non-remunerated trustees (and in some jurisdictions, this is required by statute, eg Jersey). (See generally CHAPTER 13 on trustees' liability.)

Non-party disclosure

14.16 It may sometimes be the case that beneficiaries believe that information in the hands of a person who is not a party to a claim may be of assistance to them. In such cases, non-party disclosure orders may be made by the court. For example, the settlor or the protector, or even another beneficiary, may have information which would assist the beneficiary. Other third parties may also have information relevant to the issue at hand.

There are three principal methods by which disclosure can be obtained from non-parties:

- the CPR jurisdiction to make disclosure orders;
- the common law jurisdiction (the *Norwich Pharmacal* procedure); and
- the equitable jurisdiction (discussed at paragraph 14.2 above).

CPR disclosure orders

14.17 The procedure for non-party disclosure is set out in CPR Part 31.17. The person seeking information from the non-party must show that:

- the documents sought are likely to assist his own case or adversely affect the case of any other party to the proceedings; and
- disclosure is necessary in order fairly to dispose of the claim, or to save costs.

The person claiming disclosure must specify the documents or classes of documents sought, and the court must (before granting an order) be satisfied that those documents or classes of documents are reasonably likely to exist (*Re Howglen Limited [2001] 1 All ER 376*). The non-party is usually entitled to receive his costs of complying with the order.

Norwich Pharmacal orders

14.18 A non-party may also be ordered to disclose information (not limited, as under CPR 31.17, to documents) if he has become 'mixed up in' a breach of trust (or any other legal wrong), even where that involvement was innocent. The order obtained is called a *Norwich Pharmacal* order after the leading case on this area (*Norwich Pharmacal Co v Customs and Excise [1974] AC 133, HL*).

The applicant must be able to show that there is at least a strong possibility that a wrong has occurred (*P v T Ltd [1997] 1 WLR 1309*) or, if his claim for information is in the context of a tracing claim, that the information he is seeking will assist his tracing claim (*Bankers Trust Co v Shapira [1980] 3 All ER 353, CA*).

The information sought may be able to assist the applicant in determining whether a wrong has in fact occurred; to identify the wrongdoer; or to identify assets in the hands of the wrongdoer to which the applicant may be able to make a proprietary claim.

Chapter 15

Alternative methods of dispute resolution

Introduction

15.1 In CHAPTER 2, the 'overriding objective' under the new Civil Procedure Rules was discussed, which contains fundamental principles such as the saving of costs and the allocation of appropriate court resources to the resolution of disputes.

Consistently with these aims, a central plank of the CPR is the active encouragement to parties to litigation to participate in alternative forms of dispute resolution ('ADR'). Lord Woolf MR, the principal architect of the CPR, has stressed while sitting as a judge what he has called the '*paramount importance of avoiding litigation if possible*' (*Cowl v Plymouth City Council [2002] Fam Law 265)*. Indeed, in most Part 7 claims, specific information needs to be provided during the case management stage of the proceedings as to what attempts (if any) have been made by the parties to resolve or narrow the areas of dispute by means of ADR. The proceedings may be stayed almost as of right for four weeks at any time before trial, at the request of any party, for the purposes of undertaking discussions through ADR.

There are, however, unique difficulties with using ADR for the resolution of trust disputes. It is generally not permitted to purport to oust the jurisdiction of the court to resolve matters relating to trusts. Clauses which purport to give the trustees power to determine any matter (other than matters of fact) are repugnant, as are clauses which forfeit the interest of any beneficiary who issues proceedings relating to the trust, and if a trust instrument contained a clause referring all disputes for resolution by negotiation, or by a specified individual acting as arbitrator, it would certainly be struck out. This is largely because the court's approval is always required where there are minor and unborn beneficiaries, and/or beneficiaries who cannot be ascertained, so as to approve matters on their behalf and to bind them. Other issues also arise which make disputes relating to trusts quite unlike, say, a contractual dispute, or a claim in tort – a claim, for example, that the trustees are not holding the 'trust assets' upon the express trusts, but upon resulting trusts for the victim of a fraud by the settlor, can never be settled by the claimant and the defendant trustees, as the trustees have no capacity to bargain over the beneficial interest in the assets they are holding.

Meaning of ADR

15.2 ADR is 'the collective description of methods of resolving disputes otherwise than through the normal trial process' (CPR Part 1.4.(1)(e)). Its characteristics are as follows:

- it is a multilaterally voluntary process, as no party can be obliged to enter into ADR;
- it is usually a confidential process;
- the parties agree upon the nature of the process to be used;
- the scope of the process may extend to the whole subject matter of the dispute, or limited part(s) of it, such as individual factual issues;
- the question of whether the outcome of the process is binding upon the parties is one on which they can agree, but it is not automatically binding in the absence of agreement; and
- the parties may agree that costs (either of the ADR process, or of the whole dispute) should be dealt with in a particular way, or should be disposed of as part of the ADR process. In default of agreement, the court may determine how the costs are to be dealt with.

Methods of resolving disputes

15.3 The principal means of resolving disputes are (in order of relative formality):

- negotiation between the parties themselves and/or their legal advisers;
- negotiation involving unqualified third parties (such as family members);
- negotiation involving a qualified third party, such as a mediator;
- expert determination;
- arbitration; and
- judicial determination at trial.

There is no bright-line distinction as to exactly which of these (all forms of ADR, other than trial) may be the appropriate means of resolving a dispute, since the essence of ADR is that it is a self-defined process. The first three of these certainly constitute ADR, and have in common the fact that they are entirely autonomous, flexible processes – the parties themselves find the solution to the dispute (with or without the assistance of a third party). These three categories are discussed below in more detail in paragraphs 15.5–15.7 inclusive.

Expert determination may be used as a form of ADR, as it can be of assistance where there is a technical or factual issue upon which the dispute is centred. The finding (by an independent expert agreed upon by the parties) as to the truth of that technical or factual matter may mean that the dispute can be resolved without the court's intervention. For example, if it was alleged by beneficiaries that the trustees had misinterpreted a power of investment, causing loss, the trustees and beneficiaries might agree among themselves to be bound by the expert opinion of Counsel as to the nature of the power in question. An expert finding that the power was insufficient to permit the trustees to act as they did might result in an immediate offer of settlement or might, at least, narrow the issues ultimately to be placed before the court.

Arbitration treads into the more formal arena of judicial determination. In many ways, it is almost akin to trial – whilst the exact arrangements are agreed between the parties, the effect is that a judgment is made by a single arbitrator, or a panel of three arbitrators, which is binding upon the parties and is enforceable (even internationally, if subject to the New York Convention). Formal pleadings and submissions are made, and the decision of the arbitrator(s) (who are usually not lawyers) generally cannot be appealed or varied. The advantage of arbitration for commercial disputes is precisely that it is similar to the trial process, but is confidential, as neither the hearing, nor the award, are public. There is often no substantial saving in costs, however, because of the similarities in process and time between arbitration and trial. Arbitration is unsuitable for trust-related disputes, principally because the legal interests of the beneficiaries who cannot be identified or do not yet exist must be considered, and any settlement (or judgment) must be approved on their behalf so as to bind them. This cannot happen otherwise than in a court application, as noted above.

Trial is the most formal means of determining any dispute. It is the process by which the court, having heard and read the evidence of the parties, and heard legal submissions from their counsel, determines the liability of the defendant(s) in respect of each aspect of the claims made by the claimants. The resultant judgment is imposed on the parties and compliance with it is mandatory. Failure to comply can result in the imposition of interest, fines, or even a prison sentence.

When is ADR appropriate?

15.4 It is said by proponents of ADR that it is always appropriate, and that there is no context in which it cannot be used in an effort to resolve or narrow the issues in dispute. The CPR takes a more moderate approach, noting that, if too little encouragement is given to the parties to use ADR, they may enter into it (if at all) with little commitment; but if too much pressure is placed upon them to use ADR, the essentially voluntary nature of the process is lost. It is therefore apparent that there may be some disputes in which ADR (whilst in theory available) is unlikely to assist the parties.

The parties themselves may sometimes be concerned that an offer to participate in ADR could be perceived by other parties as a sign of weakness. However, in the context of trust-related disputes, it is often appropriate to make a prompt offer to enter into ADR, rather than risking being seen to indulge (at the expense of, or at least inconvenience to the ordinary administration of, the trust) in a game of 'who blinks first'. This applies equally to beneficiaries and to trustees.

Advantages and disadvantages

15.5 The advantages of ADR are clearly considerable:

- as a flexible, non-legal process (although legal advisers may be involved throughout), it concentrates on finding a solution which does not necessarily have as its basis a finding of 'right or wrong';
- it encourages the parties to identify their 'bottom line', the level at which settlement must be achieved for it to be worthwhile (in their own minds) to enter into or continue with the process at all. This may have little (if anything) to do with legal issues;
- since the parties find their own solution, it is often said that, whilst not everyone may be happy with the result, it is at least the case that everyone is equally unhappy; and
- ADR is often quoted as the means by which relationships can be preserved. As an essentially non-adversarial process, it enables parties to emerge with the possibility of future dealings without the animosity which can result from one party being found blameworthy. This is particularly important for family-related disputes.

Its potential disadvantages are, perhaps, as numerous as its advantages, and are equally important to consider:

- frequently, parties to litigation will be heard to say that they 'want their day in court'. It is understandably instinctive, perhaps, for a party to wish not only to be right, but to be found to be right by a person of authority in a public arena. The fact that principles are expensive in human as well as financial terms is not always a deterrent;
- the very fact that parties are encouraged to identify their bottom-line issues can enable the cynical participant to identify areas of weakness in his opponent's case, or commitment to the case;
- the anxiety to reach a deal can encourage the parties (or the mediator) to overlook important legal rights of which the parties present are not competent to agree to dispose (eg where there has been fraud or dishonesty, or undue influence is used in reaching the solution) or which they do not consider (eg where the solution itself has unconsidered tax consequences); and

- a court application for approval of the deal reached is often necessary in any event (particularly in the context of trusts). This means that the matter may not have been disposed of entirely by ADR, leaving open the possibility that some parties may seek to better their position by having a second bite of the cherry when the application is made.

Negotiation between the parties

15.6 The parties to a dispute may, of course, enter into discussions at any stage prior to issue of, or during, proceedings with a view to settling the dispute between them. Frequently, they may simply correspond (either themselves, or through their legal advisers) on a without prejudice basis, seeking to narrow the areas of contention or to settle the dispute. They may, however, agree to meet (with or without legal advisers) to discuss possible settlement of the dispute.

In the context of trusts, it will perhaps rarely be the case that settlement can be reached by the parties alone, without the intervention of the court. If, for example, beneficiaries A, B and C allege that the trustees have committed a breach of trust, the trustees cannot simply resolve the matter as between themselves and A, B and C. Other beneficiaries who are identifiable, over 18 and have capacity must also consent to any settlement, otherwise the trustees remain at risk of future claims, even if they believe the matter to have been disposed of by settling with A, B and C. Further, the court's approval is always required on behalf of minor and unborn beneficiaries, and those who cannot be ascertained, so as to bind them. It is not sufficient, for example, for the parent of a minor beneficiary to agree a solution on his or her behalf (*a fortiori* where the parent is also a beneficiary, the settlor or a trustee).

Negotiation with unqualified third parties

15.7 It is occasionally helpful to involve a third party without formal qualifications in resolving a dispute. For example, where the dispute is (in its true essence) rooted in a disagreement between parent and child (both of them being beneficiaries, or one a beneficiary and one a trustee), a family friend or another relative may be a helpful neutral facilitator in resolving the issues between them, which may in turn make the dispute disappear entirely, or easier to settle. The risk, however, is that the relationship between the intermediary and the parties means that undue influence could be brought to bear (particularly upon the child). A settlement reached on that basis could be set aside at a later date.

The basic principles of such a negotiation, however, remain the same as those set out in paragraph 15.6 above. Depending upon the circumstances, court approval of the settlement is likely still to be required. This might not be necessary where, for example, the allegations of breach or impropriety were made by one beneficiary alone, and were entirely withdrawn (rather than settled), and that beneficiary and his/her legal advisers were able to satisfy themselves that no undue influence had been exerted upon him or her in the negotiation process.

Mediation

Structure of the process

15.8 Mediation is the name given to a structured negotiation in which a qualified, neutral, third party is involved so as to facilitate settlement discussions. The structure of a typical mediation is as follows:

- the parties submit short written summaries of their case in advance;
- the parties begin the mediation itself by making a short presentation to the mediator as to their case (or, in cases of particular hostility, the presentations may be made through their legal representatives, with the protagonists themselves not in the room, or may rest on the written representations alone);
- each party is then placed in a separate room, and the mediator has private, confidential sessions ('caucuses') with them in turn, seeking to encourage them to identify the strengths and weaknesses of their own case, and to understand the viewpoint of each other party;
- in the course of the caucus sessions, the mediator will encourage the parties to identify their 'bottom line' issues, and the areas on which they are prepared to compromise or give way;
- the mediator will seek permission at an appropriate stage to reveal part(s) of each party's discussions to the other party or parties, so as to encourage them to compromise;
- further open sessions may be held, if the mediator feels it is likely to produce or facilitate settlement; and
- ultimately, the parties themselves identify the terms of a settlement which is acceptable to them.

Although mediators are very often lawyers, it is not a legal process, but one aimed at finding a solution to the 'real' issues at stake. Hence, in the context of a dispute relating to a breach of trust, the beneficiaries may have, as part of their 'bottom line', the retirement of the trustees in whom they have lost confidence. They may be prepared to accept the payment to the trust of a figure less than the amount they could secure at trial, provided that the trustees retire.

Features of successful mediation

15.9 It is suggested that the key feature of a successful mediation is, in fact, the agreement to mediate. It should set out the mediator's terms of reference, the way in which the costs will be dealt with, and the agreement of the parties to be bound by the result (subject to the court's approval on behalf of minors, unborns and unascertained beneficiaries). Fundamentally, however, it should set out an agreed, short, time period during which the mediation will take place. Experienced mediators have suggested that this should if possible be no more than one day, as the progress made in discussions during the day can often be negated by the re-gathering of resentment and resumption of positions which can take place overnight if the mediation is to continue on a second day.

A further crucial factor is the capacity and authority of the parties to the mediation to settle. It has been remarked that, despite assurances to the contrary, representatives of corporate defendants have entered into mediation without authority (or later claiming to have no authority) to reach settlement at all. Evidence of corporate authority should, if possible, be provided to the mediator in advance (and perhaps also to the other parties, with any confidential matters, such as the upper level of the authority, redacted). When individual beneficiaries are representatives of a group with similar interests, the written authority of each of them should similarly be provided. It must be recalled, however, that there are matters which no party present is competent to negotiate, including:

- any questions relating to fraud or dishonesty;
- questions relating to the true beneficial ownership of the 'trust assets';
- the interests of minor, unborn or unascertained beneficiaries;
- issues relating to the improper avoidance of payment of tax due to be paid; and
- matters relating to any criminal conduct, including money laundering.

Role of the court

15.10 Trustees have broad powers of settlement, principally those in section 15 of the Trustee Act 1925, where it is provided that the trustees (if more than one, acting unanimously) have power (inter alia) to 'compromise, compound, abandon, submit to arbitration, or otherwise settle any debt, account, claim or thing whatever' relating to the trust, and may enter into agreements, releases and other documents and acts necessary to give effect to such compromise. By virtue of section 40 and paragraph 20 of Part II to Schedule 2 of the Trustee Act 2000, the trustees, in entering into any compromise, must discharge the statutory duty of care set out in section 1(1) of the Trustee Act 2000 (see CHAPTER 6). The case of *Re the Earl of Strafford [1978] 3 All ER 18* is authority for the fact that the trustees also have power to enter into compromises which would affect the beneficial entitlements of the beneficiaries (such as where, for example, a family dispute could only be resolved by division of a discretionary trust fund), but this does not extend to unilateral power to vary the trusts, absent the relevant powers of appointment.

The trustees do, therefore, have power to enter into settlement discussions, including mediation, and to commit to a compromise subject to the court's authorisation. However, as discussed in paragraph 15.1, the authorisation of the court is always required to any proposed settlement where the interests of minor, unborn or unascertained beneficiaries are concerned. It may generally be required in any event, since there may be issues of law to be decided, or one or more of the matters mentioned in paragraph 15.9 above may require the determination of the court. Further, a compromise which results in payment of less than the trustees would otherwise be ordered by the court to return to the trust fund, or any lesser remedy than would otherwise be ordered, is self-dealing (and thus a breach of fiduciary duty) on the part of the trustees and requires the informed consent of all beneficiaries (being competent to do so) or the approval of the court.

Consequently, wherever a settlement has been achieved between the beneficiaries and trustees, it is almost always impliedly (if not expressly) conditional upon the court's approval. The trustees should therefore make an application to the court under CPR Part 8 for the court's directions as to whether they may properly enter into the settlement, and for approval on behalf of any beneficiaries not competent to agree on their own behalves. The court will require an opinion of counsel as to the interests of any such beneficiaries and how those are affected by the terms of the proposed settlement.

Costs considerations

15.11 As noted in CHAPTER 2 AND APPENDIX 4, compliance with any pre-action protocols, and efforts made to settle the dispute, are matters which may be taken into account by the court in determining the appropriate award of costs to be made in any proceedings. It is therefore important that parties should seek actively to pursue any reasonable opportunities for settlement, although, as noted in this chapter, it is sometimes the case that the position a party has taken is so intractable and hostile that there is no realistic prospect of securing an agreement to negotiate, let alone reaching a compromise.

Both trustees and beneficiaries have a duty to the trust fund to minimise the potential costs and disruption to the smooth administration of the trust wherever possible. It is unreasonable to expect that the trust and its beneficial interests (at large) should bear the burden, even indirectly, of protracted proceedings if they can be avoided or brought to an early conclusion. This includes making prompt offers to mediate, wherever possible, and making reasonable attempts throughout the currency of the dispute to narrow the areas of dispute even if they cannot be compromised. Again, the relative compliance of the parties is likely to be taken into account by the court when making any costs order.

Part 36 offers

15.12 It is appropriate, in the context of settlement, to discuss offers to settle. These may be made, under CPR Part 36, by any party (and not only the defendant(s)) at any time prior to the final determination of the proceedings. An offer may be made before proceedings are issued.

The rationale for making an offer under Part 36 is that it affects the parties' liability for costs. If an offer is made by the defendant(s), which the claimant refuses, but cannot better at trial, the costs are usually ordered against the claimant from the closing date of the offer period (but it is within the court's discretion to make other orders if it thinks fit). Conversely, where the claimant has made an offer to the defendant, and the defendant rejects it, if the claimant obtains a more favourable judgment at trial, interest is usually awarded on the judgment sum at 10% above base rate from the closing date of the offer period, and the defendant is additionally ordered to pay the claimant's costs on an indemnity basis, with interest at 10% above base rate from that date. Again, the court has discretion to make other orders if that is appropriate. In determining whether these are the appropriate orders to make, the court will take into account the relative conduct of the parties, the terms and timing of any offers made, and the information available to the parties at the date(s) when the offer(s) were made.

Mandatory terms of a Part 36 offer

15.13 To comply with the requirements of Part 36, an offer to settle must:

- specify that it is an offer to which Part 36 applies;
- state the monetary sum, or other relief, for which the offeror is prepared to settle;
- state that the offer is in settlement of the whole claim, or if not, which part(s);
- identify any counterclaims or other Part 20 claims have been taken into account;
- specify whether interest is included (and if so, at what rate, and over what period);
- be in writing, expressed to be without prejudice save as to costs;
- specify the period for which the offer remains open, which must include the following details:
  - (i) if made before proceedings are issued, the offer period must be not less than 21 days, the claimant must offer to pay the defendant's costs if he accepts within that time, and the offer may not be accepted after proceedings are issued without the leave of the court;
  - (ii) if made not less than 21 days before trial, the specified offer period must be at least 21 days, and after that the offer may be accepted only if the parties reach agreement as to costs, or with the leave of the court; and

(iii) if made less than 21 days before trial, the offer can only be accepted with the leave of the court or if agreement is reached as to costs; and

(iv) where the settlement offer is for a monetary sum (either alone, or as part of a larger settlement including other remedies), and if it is the defendant(s) who make the Part 36 offer, it must be accompanied by a payment into court. The defendant(s) must also file a Part 36 payment notice in such cases. If the offer is made prior to proceedings being issued, payment in cannot be made until after they are issued, but must be made within 14 days thereafter.

Acceptance

15.14 An offer may be accepted without the leave of the court if it is within the specified time limits. The offeree must file a written notice of acceptance, in which the proceedings and the offer are described. If a payment into court has been made, the offeree must apply for payment out, and acceptance of money paid in is deemed to be acceptance of any other non-monetary remedies offered by the offeror.

If the offeree wishes to accept outside the specified time limits, he will require the leave of the court, and should apply under the general procedure for 'other applications' under CPR Part 23.

The claimant is usually entitled to his costs up to the date of acceptance of the offer, even where part of the claim is abandoned as part of the offer and acceptance process. If, however, part only of the claim is settled, with other parts proceeding to trial, the court will determine liability for costs in the usual manner.

A claimant may accept an offer made by one only of several defendants, and proceed with his claim against others against whom he alleges joint and several, or several, liability. This will usually be the case in claims relating to trusts. However, where his claim is one to which joint liability attaches, the consent of all defendants, or the leave of the court, is required to accept an offer from only one defendant and to proceed against the others.

Chapter 16

Disputes with a foreign element

Introduction

16.1 It is often the case that a trust dispute may involve considerations of jurisdiction. There may be several reasons for this:

- as discussed in CHAPTER 1, it has been increasingly popular since the 1960s for offshore trusts to be created by settlors of any domicile (albeit, since changes to UK tax laws in the 1990s, less frequently by settlors who intend to benefit UK-domiciled beneficiaries, or who are themselves UK-domiciled);
- a trust may also hold assets situated in jurisdictions other than the place where it is resident;
- the settlor and/or the beneficiaries may be resident in, or domiciliaries of, states other than the state where the trust is resident; and
- the governing law of the trust may be expressed to be the law of some other state than the jurisdiction in which it is for the time being resident (eg an English law trust with Jersey resident trustees).

The types of jurisdictional issue which may therefore arise relate to the following matters:

- Which law applies to the settlor's capacity to create a trust?
- Which law(s) apply to the devolution of the assets comprised in the trust?
- Which law applies to the interpretation of the trust itself?
- Which law(s) govern the conduct of the trustees?
- Which law governs the dispute (including where there is an exclusive jurisdiction clause)?
- Can the trustees (and other relevant parties) be brought before the relevant court?
- Can the judgment be enforced?

Capacity to create a trust

16.2 States which are parties to the Hague Convention on the Law Applicable to Trusts and on their Recognition (discussed in paragraph 16.4 below) must recognise a trust which has been validly created in accordance with its proper law. However, the Convention does not appear to cover the question of capacity to create a trust. A settlor's capacity to create a trust is governed, as a matter of English law, by the law of his domicile at the time of creation of the trust. Other states may refer to other 'connecting factors' such as habitual residence, citizenship or nationality in order to determine whether the settlor has mental and legal capacity.

Under English law, any person may create a trust, provided that they are over 18 and have the necessary mental capacity to understand the nature and substance of what they are doing. Other states, however, may have laws containing restrictions on the ability of a person to create a trust.

By way of example, if X, a person domiciled (as a matter of English law) in Monaco, purported to create a trust, and the matter was before the English courts (for example, because the trust was governed by English law but a question arose as to his capacity to create a trust at all), the following might be the position:

- English law would look to Monegasque law as to whether X had the legal and mental capacity to create a trust;
- it is understood that the law of Monaco forbids a Monegasque citizen from creating a trust, but in respect of X, although he is regarded by English law as domiciled there, the law of Monaco might not accept the *renvoi* or referral (under its own conflicts of laws rules) and may refer the matter onwards to the state of which the settlor was a citizen at the relevant time;
- the law of X's citizenship (for example, France) might accept the *renvoi* from Monaco. The law of that state might not expressly prevent him from creating a trust (such as to affect his legal capacity), and would determine whether he had mental capacity to create the trust. However (as discussed in CHAPTER 14 and paragraph 16.3 below), many states have laws on community of property and/or forced heirship which would operate so as to put him under a disability in disposing of his assets. It might also have tax laws which charge higher rates of tax on disposals to persons other than immediate family members (including, for these purposes, transfers to trustees who are not family members); but
- if France's own conflicts of laws rules referred the matter to the place where X was habitually resident, then France might not accept the *renvoi* and the matter might once more be referred to Monaco (or, on the facts, to another country entirely).

It can therefore be seen that questions of capacity affecting settlors with a non-UK domicile, citizenship or habitual residence fall to be determined by reference to the laws of more than one state. *Dicey and Morris on the Conflict of Laws* is recommended reading on such complex questions, but it is possible that some trust disputes may result in a finding that the trust may never have been validly created at all.

Devolution of the assets

16.3 The law governing the devolution of the assets the settlor places into a trust differs depending on whether those assets are placed into trust during his lifetime, or by the terms of his will:

- for trusts created by will, or assets transferred into trusts by a person's will, English law looks to the law of the place where the testator was domiciled (other states, as noted, may look to citizenship, nationality or habitual residence as the connecting factor). An important exception is in the case of foreign immovables (such as land). For English law purposes, *lex situs* always governs the testator's ability to deal with immovables (although a few civil law states, notably Spain, have a 'unitarian' regime that looks to the law of the place of which the testator was a citizen, national or habitual resident, for questions relating to all his assets, whether movable or immovable); and
- in contrast, for *inter vivos* trusts, the relevant law governing capacity to transfer assets into trust (for English law purposes) is the law of the state where the assets – whether movable or immovable – are situated at the time of their (purported) transfer into the trust (*Winkworth v Christie Manson & Woods Ltd [1980] Ch 496*).

As discussed in CHAPTER 14, the relevant law governing the transfer of the assets into trust may hamper the transferor's ability to deal with his assets during his lifetime or on death because of community of property and/or forced heirship rules. Such rules may, in effect, mean that:

- for many types of community of property, the transferor owns all his assets as tenant in common with his spouse, such that he is unable to dispose of any assets (or assets other than limited types of which he retains full ownership) without her consent. Alternatively, for states which apply 'deferred community', the transfer may be defeasible by her at the end of their marriage (on death or divorce); and/or
- it is possible, therefore, that, if the transferor lacked competence under the relevant law to dispose of his assets, the trustees may find that some or all of the assets they believed themselves to be holding upon trust could never properly have passed into the trust.

Proper law for interpretation of the trust

16.4 Article 6 of the Hague Convention on the Law Applicable to Trusts and on their Recognition allows the settlor to choose the law which governs the trust, providing that the trust is evidenced in writing. Failing an express choice by the settlor, Article 7 of the Convention applies the law with which the trust has the closest connection. As noted in paragraph 16.2 above, a trust which has been validly created in accordance with the relevant law must be recognised by states which are parties to the Convention.

The Convention has been ratified by a number of states including:

- in Europe – the UK (see The Recognition of Trusts Act 1987), Italy, and the Netherlands;
- Canada (most states except Quebec);
- Australia;
- Hong Kong; and
- of the principal offshore jurisdictions – Bermuda, the British Virgin Islands, the Isle of Man, Jersey, and Gibraltar.

Where a trust has been validly created in accordance with the Convention, therefore, interpretation of the trust instrument will fall to be governed by the chosen (or deemed) governing law.

Where the Convention does not apply, English law would probably give effect to any chosen governing law specified or implied in the trust instrument, although possibly not to the extent that the choice was, on public policy grounds, objectionable. For example, where the effect of applying the chosen law would be to avoid some legal inconvenience which would otherwise arise (such as the English perpetuities rules), or to obtain a legal advantage which would not otherwise be available (such as a broader interpretation of the trustee exculpation clause), under the law with which the trust was most closely connected, English courts might not give effect to it.

Regulation of the trustees

16.5 The conduct of the trustees may be governed by the laws of more than one state:

- the fulfilment of their powers and duties will be assessed by reference to the chosen governing law if the Convention applies (and otherwise, probably also by that chosen law, subject to the comments in the final part of paragraph 16.3 above); and
- they may also be subject to local laws and regulations applying to fiduciary service providers in the trust's 'home jurisdiction' (whatever the trust's specified proper law). These may cover, for example, the corporate governance of a trust company, staff supervision, money-laundering obligations, applicability of exculpation clauses, and other matters.

It seems, therefore, that where an allegation of breach of trust is made by the beneficiaries of (for example) an English law trust with Jersey trustees, English law would apply to the question of whether there has been a breach of trust. Interpretation of the exculpation clause would, however, be subject to Jersey law which (it is understood) forbids professional trustees from purporting to exclude liability for gross negligence. As well as their claim for breach of trust, the beneficiaries might complain to the Fiduciary Services Commission if the conduct of the trustees fell below that expected of a professional, regulated trust company.

Proper law of the dispute

16.6 The proper law to determine a trust-related dispute will depend on the nature of the dispute. Articles 8 and 9 of the Hague Convention on the Law Applicable to Trusts and on their Recognition provides that, if a law is chosen under Article 6, or implied under Article 7, then the relevant law will govern the following matters:

- the interpretation and construction of the trust instrument;
- the appointment, retirement, and removal of trustees, and their capacity to act, as well as other matters relating to the devolution of the trusteeship (eg vesting of assets);
- rights and duties of trustees;
- relationships between the trustees and beneficiaries, including the liability of trustees to their beneficiaries and the duty to account;
- dispositive powers, including powers to acquire new assets and powers relating to distribution of assets;
- administrative powers, including investment powers, powers of delegation and lending and borrowing powers;
- the rules on perpetuities and accumulations; and
- variation and termination of the trust.

If the Convention applies to the trust, then provided that the dispute relates to a matter governed by the Convention, the dispute must be resolved in accordance with the chosen governing law.

If the Convention does not apply at all, the claimants may bring their claim in the place the laws of which were chosen by the trust instrument as the governing law, or where the trustees are resident. In the example of a Bahamian resident trust governed by English law, the beneficiaries might bring their claim for breach of trust in England, or in the Bahamas (where an opinion on English law might be required by the court as to whether there had been a breach of trust).

In other cases, particularly if the dispute is not of a kind governed by the Convention (such as forced heirship disputes, or disputes relating to the transfer of assets into the trust), the claimants may elect to issue proceedings in any jurisdiction the laws of which will deal with the issue at hand. So, for example, they might seek to attack the validity of a trust created by an Italian citizen in England (being the trust's 'home jurisdiction') on forced heirship grounds. Many offshore jurisdictions have laws preventing attacks on the validity of the trust solely on the grounds of foreign forced heirship laws, however. In the case of a Jersey resident trust (Jersey being a Convention jurisdiction, but one which excludes forced heirship claims), it might therefore be preferable to launch proceedings in Italy to attack the transfer of Italian assets into the trust (Italian law being the law of the place where the assets subject to forced heirship rules were subject). If successful, the Jersey trustees could be left trustees of a valid trust, but with few or no assets validly under their control.

English law takes a broad view of trust-related disputes, because of the principle that equity affects the conscience of the trustees in dealing with trust assets. English courts will almost always be prepared to assume jurisdiction over a trust dispute, therefore, irrespective of whether the governing law of the trust is English law or the assets are situated in England and Wales (*Re Ker's Settlement Trusts [1963] Ch 553*). In one case, the court ordered foreign trustees to retire (*Chellaram v Chellaram [1985] Ch 409*), and in another, the court made an order under the Variation of Trusts Act 1958 (*Ker)*. The question of whether the English courts will have jurisdiction is limited only by the ability of the claimants to bring the trustees before the English courts (*Chellaram*), discussed in paragraph 16.7 below.

Bringing the trustees before the relevant court

16.7 Where the proceedings are to be brought in the courts of a jurisdiction in which the trustees (or other defendants) are not resident, a question of central importance will be whether the trustees (or other defendants) can be brought before the court.

Under English law, defendants can be brought before the court if:

- the claim form can be served on each of them in England and Wales. It is sufficient if the trustees are in the jurisdiction even on a temporary visit, so long as they are domiciled here, in the sense of being ordinarily resident here;
- they submit to the jurisdiction;
- proceedings can be served on them outside the jurisdiction without the leave of the court under the rules in CPR Part 6.19. Under this Part, service out of the jurisdiction does not require leave where the dispute is one to which:

  (i) the Civil Jurisdiction and Judgments Act 1982 applies, ie where the defendants are resident in a Brussels Convention (BC) or Lugano

Convention (LC) country. These include Denmark (BC); Iceland (LC); Norway (LC); Poland (LC); and Switzerland (LC); or

(ii) Council Regulation (EC) No 44/2001 applies, ie where the defendants are resident in the remainder of the EU apart from Denmark (namely, Austria, Belgium, Finland, France, Germany, Gibraltar, Greece, Italy, Luxembourg, Netherlands, Portugal, Republic of Ireland, Spain and Sweden, as well as the UK);

(iii) and in either case, it is appropriate not to sue the defendant in his home jurisdiction (as the Regulations and Convention both usually require) because one of the specified exceptions apply. The most relevant exceptions for trust claims include cases where the claim is one relating to real property in England and Wales, or one or more of the defendants are domiciled here, or the dispute relates to a trust whose closest and most real connection is with England;

- the proceedings are of a kind for which the court has power to grant leave to serve the claim form outside the jurisdiction, and does so grant leave (CPR Part 6.20). These include proceedings where (inter alia):

  (i) one of the defendants is domiciled (in the sense of ordinarily resident) within the jurisdiction;

  (ii) the relief sought is an injunction against acts being done within the jurisdiction;

  (iii) the person to be served is a defendant to a Part 20 claim, or is to be joined as a necessary and proper party to extant proceedings where the claim form has already been served, or will be served, on at least one other person against whom there is a 'real issue which it is reasonable for the court to try';

  (iv) the claim is for a non-party costs order under CPR Part 51;

  (v) the claim relates to trusts which ought to be executed according to English law, where the person to be served is a trustee; or

  (vi) the whole subject matter of the claim relates to property located within the jurisdiction.

A party who is served out of the jurisdiction may have a longer period to acknowledge service and enter a defence or admission (see CPR Part 6.22–3). As noted in CHAPTER 2, a defendant in receipt of a claim form who wishes to dispute the jurisdiction of the English court to hear the matter need only acknowledge service, and may within 14 days thereafter enter an application to assert that England is not the appropriate forum for the resolution of the dispute. This may particularly be the case where the trust instrument contains an exclusive jurisdiction clause, although the English courts have discretion to disregard such clauses where the specified exclusive jurisdiction is not that of England and Wales.

Can the judgment be enforced?

16.8 Once judgment has been obtained, the claimants may seek to enforce it against the trustees in their home jurisdiction (if that is not the state where the proceedings have taken place) and/or to enforce the judgment against assets of the trust, or of the trustees, in other jurisdictions. Similarly, the trustees may seek to enforce a costs order against the unsuccessful claimant beneficiaries in their home jurisdictions, or the place(s) where their assets are located.

If a judgment or order is made by the courts of one of the Brussels or Lugano Convention countries, or of an EC state to which the Council Regulation applies, then it is enforceable through the courts of any other convention or regulation jurisdiction without the need for separate proceedings. (There are limited exceptions relating, for example, to public policy matters.) The UK also applies reciprocal enforcement arrangements with a number of other states around the world.

Under CPR Part 74.3–11, a person who has obtained judgment in a foreign court may apply to register and enforce that judgment in England if it is one to which:

- the Administration of Justice Act 1920 applies (governing judgments of the courts of the specified current and former British colonies, dependencies and dominions – see CPR Part 74.11.3 for a list); or
- the Foreign Judgments (Reciprocal Enforcement) Act 1933 applies (governing judgments of any foreign court if that court is in a state which would give similar effect to judgments of the English courts – CPR Part 74.11.5 lists these as currently comprising Israel, Surinam and Tonga, plus the Brussels and Lugano Convention countries, to which those Conventions now apply; and CPR Part 74.11.6 lists the Commonwealth countries which operate reciprocal enforcement of judgments under the 1933 Act);
- CPR Part 74.12 governs the procedure for obtaining a certified copy of a judgment of an English court for the purposes of enforcement abroad. Only judgments for a sum of money can usually be certified under this procedure. Registration and enforcement of the judgment is then governed by the rules of the courts in the state in which the judgment is to be enforced.

Costs considerations

16.9 In principle, there is no reason why the costs of foreign legal advice should not be recoverable in proceedings in the English courts to which those foreign costs relate. It is, however, generally presumed that costs of foreign legal proceedings cannot be recovered through the English courts except in limited circumstances in which the incurring of those costs gives rise to a new cause of action, not repugnant under the principles of *res judicata*, which can be pursued in England (*Union Discount Co Ltd v Robert Zoller [2001] EWCA Civ 1755, [2002] 1 All ER 693*; and see CPR Part 48.14.3).

Foreign courts may, however, apply different rules and caution should therefore be exercised by parties who incur legal costs outside the jurisdiction where the proceedings are issued. For example, it is understood that, under the Cayman court rules, the court has power to make awards of costs only in relation to locally incurred legal fees or the fees of foreign counsel licensed to appear in those proceedings. That is not to say, however, that the trustees cannot agree to pay the costs (wherever incurred) of all parties to non-hostile litigation out of the trust fund. As part of a compromise, the costs (wherever incurred) of all parties to hostile litigation could in principle also be met by the trust fund, provided that all the beneficiaries consented and/or the approval of the court was obtained.

Appendix 1

Sample time-line for the conduct of proceedings under Part 8

A1.1

A. From identification of possible claim to issue

Date	*Claimant action*	*Defendant action*	*Notes*
Up to C-14	C must give notice of intention to issue proceedings – at least 14 days' notice of issue of claim must be given, if a formal letter before action has not been written at earlier stage		Compliance with pre-action protocols and CPR Part 1 is required by all parties throughout pre-action period
Any time before C date	May apply for pre-action disclosure if desirable in order to dispose fairly of prospective proceedings, to assist in settlement, or to save costs (CPR 31.16). May apply for non-party disclosure (ie disclosure by third parties) for the same reasons (CPR 31.17)	May apply for pre-action disclosure (as for C, left)	

A1.1 *Sample time-line for the conduct of proceedings under Part 8*

Date	*Claimant action*	*Defendant action*	*Notes*
Any time before C date	May make offer to settle under Part 36 at any time prior to commencement of proceedings and may be accepted before proceedings are issued (after issue, only with court's consent) (CPR 36.10. Offers to settle are clearly not appropriate where the court's directions are required eg on construction issues. Where minors/unborns are involved, court approval is required.)	May make offer to settle or accept offer (as for C, left)	
C date	Issue of claim form		
C+ before S date	Apply for leave to serve out of the jurisdiction if required (CPR 6.20 to 6.21)		
C to C+ 4 months (or +6 months) ('S date')	Must serve claim form within this time (6 months if serving out of jurisdiction) – evidence to be served at same time		

B. From service to close of pleadings

Date	*Claimant Action*	*Defendant Action*	*Notes*
S to S+14	–	File acknowledgement of service. File & serve evidence (if any) at same time *or* file written agreement of parties for max 14 day extension	
		Apply for court's permission to make Part 20 counterclaim or third party claim (CPR 8.7)	

Date	*Claimant Action*	*Defendant Action*	*Notes*
S+14 to S+28	File & serve evidence in reply to D's evidence (if no extension agreed)	File & serve evidence if 14-day extension agreed	The court may approve further extensions of time for D
S+42	Last day to file & serve evidence in reply if D had extension of time and C does not. *Or* file agreement for max 14-day extension for C		
S+56	Last date for service of evidence in reply if 14-day extensions agreed both for D and for C		The court may approve further extensions of time for C

C. After close of pleadings until trial

Date	*Claimant Action*	*Defendant Action*	*Notes*
Immedi-ate	Case automatically allocated to multi-track (CPR 8.9(c))		
Any time	Case Management Conference or pre-trial review can be held any time, to agree what evidence is needed and set a timetable for the action to continue (see CPR 29 generally for case management of Part 8 claims)		
Any time		May apply for prospective costs order *if* trustees have no power to pay the costs of other parties, *or* have such a power but do not use it (CPR 64PD.6)	
Any time	May apply for disclosure by other parties (at court's discretion) (see generally CPR 31) or for specific disclosure of documents not otherwise disclosed (CPR 31.12)	May apply for disclosure by C or other parties or for specific disclosure (as for C, left)	

A1.1 *Sample time-line for the conduct of proceedings under Part 8*

Date	*Claimant Action*	*Defendant Action*	*Notes*
Any time	May apply for a stay (for Part 8 claims, CPR 26.4 (automatic stay to facilitate settlement) does *not* apply, so an application must be made under the general applications rules in CPR Part 23) or for extension of stay	May apply for a stay (as for C, left) or for extension of stay	
Any time	May apply for other interlocutory orders (CPR Part 23)	May apply for other interlocutory orders (as for C, left)	
Up to T-21	May make Part 36 offer to settle at any time at least 21 days before trial (clearly not appropriate for matters where the court's directions are required eg on matters of interpretation or construction. If minors/unborns are involved, court approval of settlement is needed)	May make Part 36 offer (as for C, left)	Offer may be made less than 21 days before trial only with court's permission (CPR 36.5)
T date	Trial of issues		
T+	Detailed assessment of costs will usually be ordered (CPR 44.8). For trust cases this will often be on the indemnity basis of assessment (this seems implicit in CPR 64PD.6 (prospective costs orders) where there is a presumption in favour of indemnity costs)		

Appendix 2

Sample time-line for the conduct of proceedings under Part 7

A2.1

A. From identification of possible claim to issue

Date	*Claimant action*	*Defendant action*	*Notes*
Up to C-14	C must give notice of intention to issue proceedings – at least 14 days' notice of issue of claim must be given, if a formal letter before action has not been written at earlier stage		Compliance with pre-action protocols and CPR Part 1 is required by all parties throughout pre-action period
Any time before C date	May apply for pre-action disclosure if desirable in order to dispose fairly of prospective proceedings, to assist in settlement, or to save costs (CPR 31.16). May apply for non-party disclosure (ie disclosure by third parties) for the same reasons (CPR 31.17)	May apply for pre-action disclosure (as for C, left)	
Any time before C date	May make offer to settle under Part 36 at any time prior to commencement of proceedings and may be accepted before proceedings are issued (after issue, only with court's consent) (CPR 36.10 – where minors/unborns are involved, court approval is required)	May make offer to settle or accept offer (as for C, left)	

A2.1 *Sample time-line for the conduct of proceedings under Part 7*

Date	*Claimant action*	*Defendant action*	*Notes*
C DATE	ISSUE OF CLAIM FORM		
C+ before S date	Apply for leave to serve out of the jurisdiction if required (CPR 6.20 to 6.21)		
C to C+ 4 months (or +6 months) ('S date')	Serve claim form (within 6 months if serving out of jurisdiction) with forms for acknowledging service, defending and admitting claim. Particulars of claim to be served at same time or within 14 days but only if still within maximum service period		

B. From service to close of pleadings

Date	*Claimant action*	*Defendant action*	*Notes*
S to S+14	Serve Particulars of Claim if not already served	If Particulars of Claim served with claim form: (a) file & serve defence; or (b) if intend to defend, but cannot file defence within 14 days, file acknowledgment of service; or (c) if intend to dispute jurisdiction, file acknowledgment of service; or (d) file & serve admission. May file & serve Part 20 counterclaim against C at same time (otherwise need leave of court, and for claims against third parties need leave)	

Date	*Claimant action*	*Defendant action*	*Notes*
S+14 to S+28		If Particulars served after claim form, file & serve now (as above) *or* file written agreement for extension of time for service of defence (maximum 28 days)	
S+28 to S+42/S+56		File & serve evidence if 28-day extension agreed (by S+42 if Particulars served with claim form, before S+56 if Particulars served after claim form)	The court may approve further extensions of time for D
When defence filed or time expires ('**AQ date**')			Court now serves allocation questionnaire on all parties

C. After close of pleadings until trial

Date	*Claimant action*	*Defendant action*	*Notes*
AQ+14	File allocation questionnaire *and* reply to defence, if any (and, if appropriate, defence to counterclaim)	File allocation questionnaire	(Court may allow longer than 14 days)
After AQ+14			Court allocates case to track (usually multi-track for trusts) and serves all allocation forms with notice of track allocation
Any time	Case Management Conference or pre-trial review can be held, to agree what evidence is needed and set a timetable for the action to continue (see CPR 29 generally for case management of Part 7 claims)		

A2.1 *Sample time-line for the conduct of proceedings under Part 7*

Date	*Claimant action*	*Defendant action*	*Notes*
After AQ	Must comply with timetable for disclosure given by court (see generally CPR 31) and may apply for specific disclosure of documents not otherwise disclosed (CPR 31.12)	Must comply with disclosure timetable and may apply for specific disclosure (as for C, left)	
After AQ	Must comply with timetable for providing witness/expert evidence (see CPR Part 32 generally)	Must comply with timetable for providing witness/expert evidence (as for C, left)	
Any time	May apply for prospective costs order *if* pursuing claim in interests of trust (CPR 64PD.6 – prospective costs orders – does not apply to trusts generally, but only to claims brought under CPR Part 8 (see CPR 64.2 and 64.3). *Re Beddoe [1893] 1 Ch 547* applies to trustees bringing or defending proceedings on behalf of the trust; *Re Biddencare Ltd [1994] 2 BCLC 160* and *Wallersteiner v Moir* (*No* 2) *[1975] QB 373* allow beneficiaries to claim costs pre-emptively out of the trust fund where their action is brought (essentially) on behalf of the trust)	May apply for prospective costs order *if* defending claim or pursuing counterclaim in interests of trust (as for C, left)	
Any time	May apply for a stay of up to 1 month to facilitate settlement (CPR 26.4) or for extension of stay	May apply for a stay (as for C, left) or for extension of stay	(Court will usually grant stay of up to 1 month automatically)

Date	*Claimant action*	*Defendant action*	*Notes*
Any time	May apply for other interlocutory orders (CPR Part 23)	May apply for other interlocutory orders (as for C, left)	
Up to T-21	May make Part 36 offer to settle at any time at least 21 days before trial (If minors/unborns are involved, court approval of settlement is needed)	May make Part 36 offer (as for C, left)	Offer may be made less than 21 days before trial only with court's permission (CPR 36.5)
T DATE	TRIAL OF ISSUES		
T+	Detailed assessment of costs will usually be ordered (CPR 44.8). Trustees cannot claim costs out of the trust fund on any basis greater than the indemnity basis (CPR 48.4)		

Appendix 3

Example Claim Form Under CPR Part 8

A3.1

Claim Form
(CPR Part 8)

In the	**High Court of Justice** **Queen's Bench Division** **Commercial Court** **Royal Courts of Justice**
Claim No.	[Claim Number]

SEAL

Claimant(s)

(1) ADAM JONES
(2) BELINDA JONES

Defendant(s)

(1) JONES TRUST COMPANY LIMITED

(2) CHARLOTTE JONES (a child, by her litigation friend JOHN SMITH)

(3) DAVID JONES (by his litigation friend and receiver, MARY BROWN)

Name and Address of Defendant receiving this claim form

Jones Trust Company Limited
1 High Street
Anytown
Anyshire

	£
Court fee	[Court fee]
Solicitor's costs	[Solicitor's costs]
Issue date	[Issue date]

The court office at the Admiralty & Commercial Registry, Royal Courts of Justice, Strand, London WC2A 2LL is open between 10 am and 4.30 pm Monday to Friday. When corresponding with the court, please address forms or letters to the Court Manager and quote the case number.

N208- Claim form (CPR Part 8) (10.00)

Claim No.	[Claim Number]

Details of claim

The Claimants' claim is against the First Defendant for:

1. An account in common form to be rendered by the First Defendant in respect of a settlement created by a trust deed made between Edmund Jones and Jones Trust Company Limited on 1 January 1985, and known as the Jones Family Trust, of which the Claimants are beneficiaries;

2. Production to them of copies of the trust deed and all supplemental deeds;

3. Costs; and

4. Further or other relief.

Statement of Truth
* The Claimants believe that the facts stated in this claim form are true.
* I am duly authorised by the Claimants to sign this statement

Full name Charles White

Name of claimants' solicitor's firm) White & Co

signed______________ position or office held Partner

*(Claimants' solicitor) (if signing on behalf of firm, company or corporation)

**delete as appropriate*

White & Co
25 Church Road
Anytown
Anyshire
DX 00000
Fax 0000 000 0000
Email: whites@co.uk
Ref: CW

Claimant's or litigation friend's or solicitor's address to which documents or payments should be sent if different from overleaf. If you are prepared to accept service by DX, fax or e-mail, please add details.

Appendix 4

Guidelines for pre-action procedure

A4.1 In CHAPTER 2, note was made of the requirement for parties to disputes to conduct their case reasonably and proportionately, in line with the Woolf Reforms. Consistently with this, the stages before proceedings are issued ought also to be conducted sensibly, and in a manner which can help to avoid the need for proceedings to be commenced, or which means that, if proceedings are issued, the number of issues between the parties is identified and minimised, and costs are kept at a reasonable level. As yet, there is no approved pre-action protocol for trust-related proceedings. It is anticipated that such a pre-action protocol may shortly be approved. A draft unapproved pre-action protocol is available on the website of the Association of Contentious Trust and Probate Specialists at www.actaps.com.

This Appendix contains guidelines for the suggested conduct of the pre-action stages of any trust dispute. These are based on the pre-action protocols for other types of action, and on the general Protocol Practice Direction, all of which are set out in the White Book at Section C.

Aims at pre-action stage

A4.2 The purposes of the protocols which have been approved are set out at Section C1A-001 of the White Book, as follows:

- to focus the attention of litigants on the desirability of resolving disputes without litigation;
- to enable them to obtain information that they reasonably need in order to enter an appropriate settlement;
- to make an appropriate offer under CPR Part 36;
- if pre-action settlement is not achievable, to lay the ground for expeditious conduct of proceedings.

With these aims in mind, the CPR anticipates and requires that:

- litigation is the last resort. Alternatives (including ADR, and CPR Part 36 offers) should always be actively explored (and each party should undertake preliminary examination of his own witnesses to test the strength of his own case);

- parties will adopt a 'cards on the table' approach in setting out their cases in correspondence, exchanging information, identifying relevant documents and evidence, and exchanging key documents;
- the pre-action stages will be pursued proportionately to the value and importance of the case, particularly with regard to costs; and
- the parties must seek to identify and, if possible, narrow the areas of dispute between them.

The court may take pre-action conduct into account when considering costs orders, and at the earliest stages, may dismiss or refuse to allocate proceedings if there appear to be appropriate means of resolving the dispute without litigation.

Guidelines for pre-action conduct

A4.3

(1) The claimant is expected to identify his claim clearly and in reasonable detail to the defendant(s) in a letter. He should enclose copies of any key documents on which he relies. The letter should contain:

(a) details (if relevant, supported by a chronology) of the matters complained of;

(b) an estimate of the value of the claim (if appropriate and possible);

(c) a clear timetable, allowing a reasonable period for the defendant to reply before issuing proceedings – usually not less than 21 days. He must expressly state that he intends to issue proceedings after that date, and ask for a reply or acknowledgment;

(d) details of any documents he wishes the defendant to provide;

(e) an offer of mediation if appropriate at that stage;

(f) a warning to the defendant of the court's powers to impose sanctions for non-compliance with pre-action conduct principles.

(2) The defendant must reply to the letter within the timetable with an explanation of his position (if it is reasonable for him to comply with that timetable), or at least, must reply indicating what steps are being taken to enable him to reply fully, and within what time frame he expects to do so. He should (in his full reply):

(a) identify any matters he agrees or accepts;

(b) enclose any documents the claimant has requested or on which the defendant relies;

(c) ask for any documents he wishes the claimant to produce; and

(d) offer mediation if appropriate.

(3) The claimant is expected to adopt a reasonably flexible attitude to requests for more time by the defendant, and both parties should seek to agree a timetable for future steps.

(4) Both parties must comply with each other's reasonable requests for information or documents. They should also carry out a 'stock-take' so as to identify the documents and other information they have which is likely to be relevant to the case if it proceeds without settlement.

(5) The parties should strive to agree on what witness and/or expert evidence may assist with investigating the claim (and who should instruct and pay for any expert).

(6) The parties should actively seek to explore the possibility of settlement, including making proposals for ADR if appropriate.

(7) The parties must inform each other of any funding arrangements (eg no win, no fee) which he has entered into.

(8) If any pre-action applications to the court are necessary or appropriate (eg pre-action disclosure), they should be made promptly and the parties should co-operate wherever possible so as to reduce the risk of litigation.

(9) In the context of proceedings likely to require the representation of minor, unborn, unascertained and/or mentally incapacitated beneficiaries (or other persons), the parties should co-operate to agree and secure appropriate representation.

Appendix 5

Beneficiary requests information

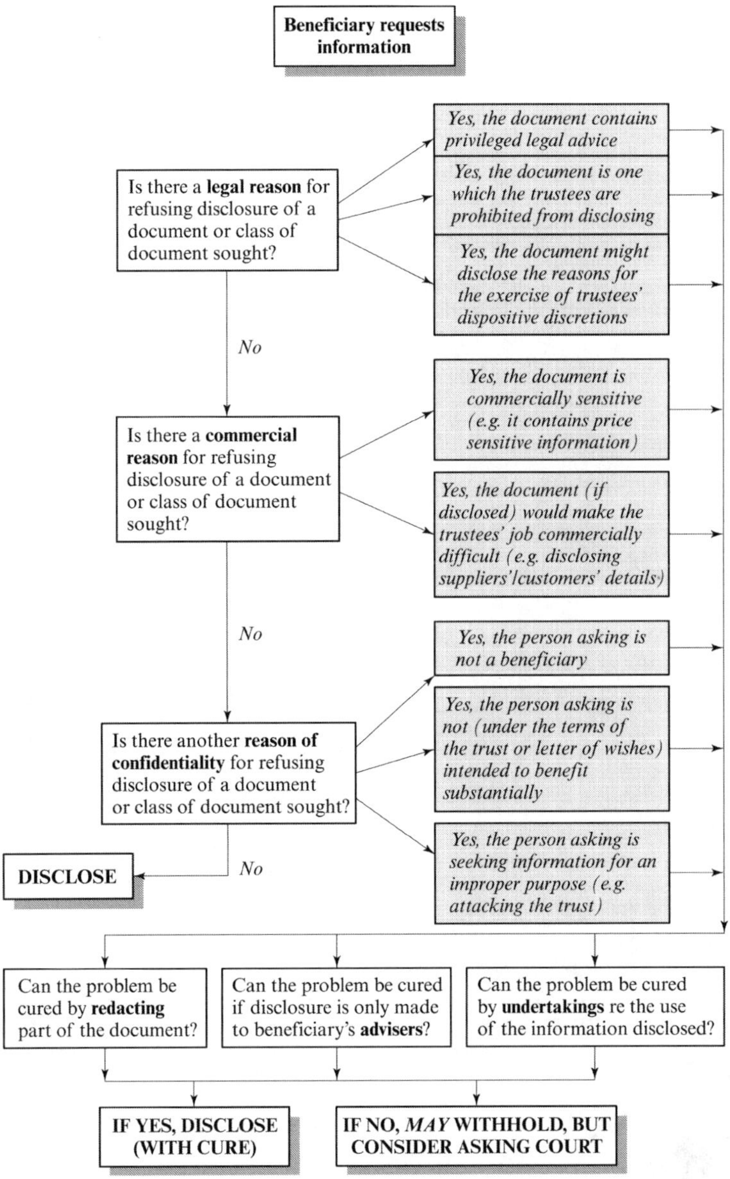

Index